LANGUAGE UNIVERSALS

TYPOLOGICAL STUDIES IN LANGUAGE (TSL)

A companion series to the journal "STUDIES IN LANGUAGE"

Honorary Editor: Joseph H. Greenberg
General Editor: T. Givón

Editorial Board:

Volumes in this series will be functionally and typologically oriented, covering specific topics in language by collecting together data from a wide variety of languages and language typologies. The orientation of the volumes will be substantive rather than formal, with the aim of investigating universals of human language via as broadly defined a data base as possible, leaning toward cross-linguistic, diachronic, developmental and live-discourse data. The series is, in spirit as well as in fact, a continuation of the tradition initiated by C. Li *(Word Order and Word Order Change, Subject and Topic, Mechanisms for Syntactic Change)* and continued by T. Givón *(Discourse and Syntax)* and P. Hopper *(Tense and Aspect: Between Semantics and Pragmatics)*.

Volume 5

W. E. Rutherford (ed.)

*LANGUAGE UNIVERSALS
AND SECOND LANGUAGE ACQUISITION*

LANGUAGE UNIVERSALS

AND

SECOND LANGUAGE ACQUISITION

Containing the Contributions
to a Conference on Language Universals
and Second Language Acquisition
held at the University of Southern California
February, 1982

edited by

WILLIAM E. RUTHERFORD
University of Southern California

JOHN BENJAMINS PUBLISHING COMPANY

Amsterdam/Philadelphia

1984

Library of Congress Cataloging in Publication Data

Language universals and second language acquisition.

(Typological studies in language, ISSN 0167-7373; v. 5)
Includes bibliographies and indexes.
1. Universals (Linguistics) -- Congresses. 2. Language acquisition -- Congresses. 3. Language and languages --Study and teaching -- Congresses. I. Rutherford, William E. II. Series.
P204.L34   1984   410   84-9387
ISBN 0-915027-09-7 (U.S. hb.)
ISBN 0-915027-10-0 (U.S. pb.)
ISBN 90-272-2869-8 (European hb.)
ISBN 90-272-2870-1 (European pb.)

TABLE OF CONTENTS

PREFACE

On February 6 and 7, 1982, the American Language Institute, University of Southern California, hosted a conference on Language Universals and Second Language Acquisition. The conference format called for eleven papers, submitted by invitation, with comments on each paper offered by a designated discussant. It is the majority of those papers, together with their discussant remarks, that comprise the present volume.

Our wish to preserve for this volume as much of the original presenter-discussant symbiosis as possible posed something of a dilemma. The problem was that subsequent post-conference revisions of the papers would incorporate some of the very substance of that symbiotic exchange, thereby vitiating a number of the original discussant comments and criticisms. Our procedure then has been to send the revised papers back to their original discussants for updated commentary and then to allow the authors of the papers one final opportunity to emend if they so wished. This arrangement for rendering a set of conference proceedings of this kind into a published collection is, we think, an effective one.

Of the ten original papers presented at the conference, eight appear in this volume. One of the two papers not available for publication here was given by Paul Hopper (SUNY Binghamton) and Sandra Thompson (UCLA). The second was a paper by Shirley Brice Heath (Stanford) which was given in her absence by Robin Scarcella. One paper, that by Charles Ferguson (Stanford), has been added to this collection since the conference took place.

A note needs to be added here concerning the inception of the conference itself. Credit for this goes exclusively to Robin Scarcella, the co-coordinator. And only the distractions of re-location, completion of a doctorate in linguistics, and motherhood have prevented her from assuming co-editorship of the present volume.

We wish to thank the General Editor, T. Givón, for his enthusiastic support of our efforts. We are also grateful to John and Claire Benjamins for their interest in publishing the proceedings of this important conference.

William E. Rutherford

INTRODUCTION

WILLIAM RUTHERFORD
University of Southern California

Anyone currently engaged in serious language research of whatever kind
will doubtless realize that a book title such as LANGUAGE UNIVERSALS
AND SECOND LANGUAGE ACQUISITION leaves unspecified at least
one piece of important information — namely that concerning the interpretation of the word 'universals' itself. There frequently appear in the literature,
for example, studies of 'acquisitional universals' and 'processing universals',
as well as the universals familiar to those engaged in work on grammatical
theory. All of these (and perhaps others as well) might in some large sense of
the term quite justifiably be considered 'language universals'. In our planning
of the 1982 conference that has resulted in this published collection, however,
we chose to focus upon the theme of language universals in the sense of those
discussed by grammatical theorists. The list of original invitees to our conference indicates, moreover, that by 'language universal' thus defined we were in
fact directing attention more to universals of the sort first articulated by
Greenberg (1963, 1966) twenty years ago and since explored more fully by his
disciples and colleagues. In other words, it was likely that most of the conference participants, given what we believed to be their theoretical stance, would
take the Greenbergian rather than the Chomskyan approach to language universals. This tendency reflected not so much a preference on our part as it did
a recognition of the fact that where universals and L2 acquisition research
were concerned it was largely the Greenbergian framework that prevailed,
whether for L2 researchers resorting to grammatical theory or for the (few)
grammatical theorists interested in the matter of L2 acquisition. Since 1981,
however, when the conference was first conceived, research in L2 acquisition
invoking Extended Standard Theory has been increasing, and we will shortly
consider where the two camps might actually reveal systematic relationships.
The theoretical predilections of our conference invitees notwithstanding,
we chose at least to *suggest* consideration of language universals from several

different perspectives. In our letter of invitation then, we framed a number of questions designed to draw attention to what we thought to be major current issues in L2 acquisition research vis-à-vis language universals. These questions were the following:

1. What, specifically, can a study of language universals contribute to research in L2 acquisition? (To what extent has research in language universals developed such that it can shed light on L2 acquisition?)
2. What can L2 acquisition research contribute to the study of language universals?
3. What role do language universals play in L1 transfer? (To what extent might interlanguage form derive from typological differences between L1 and L2, e.g. differences in branching direction?)
4. What is the relevance of markedness and/or core grammar to L2 acquisition?
5. What might the existence of accessibility hierarchies lead one to look for in the analysis of interlanguages?

It will be apparent to the reader of this collection that it does indeed represent a diversity of perspectives on language universals and the ways in which they may illuminate aspects of second language acquisition. The papers discuss a range of language phenomena that have been identified elsewhere in the literature as parameters[1] of language universals or of language typology. The distinction is one of complementation rather than of contrast, 'since both are concerned with variation across languages, the only difference being that language universals research is concerned primarily with limits on this variation, whereas typological research is concerned more directly with possible variation' (Comrie, 1981:31).

The identifiable parameters that appear in this collection, to a greater or lesser extent and whether implicitly or explicitly, number essentially six, with considerable overlap or interrelatedness among them. We enumerate them here — the ordering is not significant — as 1) core-periphery phenomena, 2) markedness, 3) word order (and, in particular, cross-categorial harmony), 4) branching direction, 5) syntactic-semantic distance, and 6) accessibility hierarchies. The interrelationships become evident when, for example, one associates a markedness differential with core-periphery matter, with degrees of distance between semantic interpretation and syntactic representation, or with location within the noun-phrase accessibility hierarchy. Moreover, difference in branching direction is directly related to canonical word-order; and core-periphery distinctions align to some extent with syntactic-semantic distance. Other associations, of course, are also possible. We will briefly re-examine these parametric relationships in the context of the papers themselves and we will attempt to do this, wherever appropriate, through speculation as to the ways in which the usefulness of these relationships as frameworks for interlanguage research might receive consistent articulation in terms of core grammar itself.

The study of core grammar in theoretical linguistics is represented by a growing list of references, in particular Chomsky 1981a, 1981b. Koster (1978) offers the following very general characterization of core grammar:

> 'Core grammar is the optimally accessible (i.e. learnable), unmarked part of language... Core grammar is also responsible for the most rigid part of language. Its rules and conditions are either invariant across languages, or fall within a very limited range... Beyond this, languages may have rules in different degrees of markedness. On the periphery of language, anything learnable (in whatever way) is possible. Thus, knowledge of language is seen to be organized in different layers from the practically invariant core to the extreme periphery, where languages naturally differ a great deal. Plasticity increases towards the periphery, but at no level is there unlimited choice. For the language learner, core grammar is relatively easy to acquire; it is believed to be deeply entrenched in human biology. Language learning, in this view, is the fixing of the parameters of core grammar, plus the addition of marked rules up to the periphery' (1978:566-67).[2]

Hirschbühler and Rivero (1981) further interpret the nature of core grammar to be of a kind where a 'rule of sentence grammar is an aggregate of dimensions: some belong to the core, and are unmarked; others belong to the periphery, and are marked. The peripheral dimensions impose further restrictions on the core, in the sense that only a subset of what is allowed by the unmarked dimensions should actually be generated by the sentence grammar of the language in question... [Thus] the periphery corrects overgeneration in the core...' (Hirschbühler and Rivero 1981:592).

It is core grammar in this collective sense of the term that would seem to suggest the widest accommodation of the kinds of interlanguage phenomena discussed in these papers.[3]

The application to L2 acquisition research of principles of universal grammar (UG) that derive from Extended Standard Theory (EST) and, in particular, core grammar is not unknown. One of the more interesting of the few such studies so far attempted is White's (1983) speculation as to the ways in which successful language learning will be affected by contrasting parameter settings for L1 and L2, the fact that a marked L2 parameter will require positive evidence for mastery, and a prediction (among others) that the conjunction of L1 marked and L2 *un*marked parameters will manifest in the resulting interlanguage not the unmarked but the marked. Furthermore, 'viewing adult L2 acquisition in the context of a parameter-setting view of acquisition, interacting with a theory of markedness, may go some way towards explaining both the similarities and the differences that have been observed in the second language acquisition of adult learners of different mother tongues learning the same language' (White 1983:17).

A number of contributions to this volume discuss acquisition phenomena that would be of interest to any researcher working within the UG framework. The Zobl paper, for instance, compares the acquisition of English grammaticized subject by French speakers with that by Spanish speakers and explains IL differences between them within a larger framework of 'evolutive change' that has been well attested historically. Two of the differences discussed by Zobl — (a) the absence of non-referential (i.e. dummy) pronoun subjects and (b) subject postposing — are assumed here to be integral parts of the same core grammar 'parameter': PRO-drop; and a 'core grammarian', so to speak, interested in these facts would presumably work from an initial hypothesis that the differential IL data cited by Zobl are the partial result of different settings of the PRO-drop parameter for the learners in question.

The core-periphery principle might serve as another framework for observing the acquisition of relative clauses. The Gass and Ard paper in this volume reviews the L2 acquisition literature concerning relative clauses and the relevance thereto of the Keenan and Comrie (1977) NP accessibility hierarchy. There are several acquisitional facts that one may note in relation to the hierarchy. Gass and Ard have observed (here and elsewhere) that with few exceptions the acquisition of relative clauses proceeds from top to bottom; i.e. beginning with subject relatives. Furthermore, the occurrence of resumptive pronouns (RP), for the production of all relative clauses ranging over the hierarchy during the course of learning and after factoring out native language influence, is distributed in inverse proportion to acquisition; i.e. the lower the position in the hierarchy the more likely the appearance of RP. Finally, for any given position in the hierarchy (and again factoring out native language influence), the frequency of occurrence of RP will be inversely proportionate to language proficiency; i.e. the higher the proficiency the fewer the RP. In terms of core grammar then, one might consider the following possibility:

Under the assumption that RP and preposition stranding represent the unmarked and marked cases, respectively,[4] the onset of RP in the limited (high) positions in the hierarchy during early learning and the vestiges of RP in the (low) positions in the hierarchy during later learning are both instances of overgeneration in the core. Subsequent deletion of RP constitutes the 'correction' at the periphery, where pronoun retention at the lowest point in the hierarchy is the last to be 'corrected'.

It is also not difficult to see a very possible relevance of core-periphery phenomena to the kinds of discourse/syntax relationships discussed in Givón's paper as well as in earlier work of his. 'Pragmatic mode' and 'syntactic mode' have characteristics, for example, that would roughly correlate with 'core' and 'periphery', and fully consistent with this association would also be Givón's observation that it is more at the stages of syntacticization that 'errors' and 'first-language interference' appear. Core and periphery are less and more susceptible, respectively, to extraneous influence, and it is core phenomena that are learned first. Givón's universals of 'discourse-pragmatic or pre-syntactic communication' would thus not be inconsistent with the characteristics of core grammar as outlined by Koster, above.

Bickerton's 'bioprogram' also bears more than a passing resemblance to core grammar. And in his recent book we read that 'in fact, bioprogram theory and Chomskyan formal universals fit rather well together... The bioprogram language would constitute a core structure for human language. Natural languages would be free to vary within the space between the outer limit of the bioprogram and the overall limit imposed by formal universals, which represent neural limits — species specific limits — on human capacity to process language' (Bickerton 1981:297-298).

The Schachter paper takes the Chomskyan concept of UG as a given and then systematically leads the reader to speculate on how the language learner's input can interact with his own rudimentary grammar and thereby contribute 'to the resulting state of mature linguistic knowledge'. Schachter states further that 'knowledge of the properties of the input available to the language learner is crucial, since one's assumptions about this input partially determine one's view of the properties that a model of UG must have' (p.000).

The best known research findings on language universals are probably in the realm of word order and certainly include the insights offered by Greenberg (1963, 1966) nearly two decades ago. Many of the papers in this volume concern themselves — at some point, to varying degrees, explicitly or implicitly — with word order as a language universal parameter and half the papers cite the work of Greenberg as well. Eckman, in speculating upon the importance of IL data, for instance, cites Greenberg's question-word order universal, viz. that if subject-verb inversion occurs in wh-questions then it also occurs in yes-no questions. Although no IL disconfirmation of this universal is attested, it could theoretically come about through language contact and would be more likely in IL than in primary languages (PL) since only with the former is language contact a *necessary* condition. (The IL occurrence of 'schwa paragoge' is cited by Eckman as an instance of IL violation of a PL universal that is explainable in terms of contact.) Eckman argues, however, that of *true* empirical significance would be IL data (a) that violated such a universal and (b) that were *not* attributable to language contact.[5]

Gass and Ard in their paper cite evidence that L2 production does not reveal attempts by the learner to resolve disharmonic word-order relationships in the L2 (even where L1 has the *harmonic*), as one might want to predict. Spanish speakers learning English, for example, do not re-order (disharmonic) English Adj-Noun to Noun-Adj and thereby achieve head-modifier alignment (i.e. harmony) with other orderings in English SVO syntax. Our guess is that facts such as these would constitute counter-evidence to the predictions of core grammar for IL.

The Givón paper examines the interface of discourse and syntax in language ontogeny and arrives at the formulation of a new word-order universal wherein COMMENT *followed* by TOPIC is the unmarked order. For Givón topic-marking can be represented hierarchically such that the least marked would be COMMENT with zero-TOPIC. This would seem to suggest arguments for core-grammar assignment of no markedness to the PRO-drop parameter and would constitute counter-evidence to the claim by White (1983) that PRO-drop is marked, in that positive evidence is presumed to be required for its setting.

Hakuta's paper cites word order as one of six sample variables that describe a language's gross canonical form, the other variables being adposition, branching direction, dummy subject, agreement, and passivization. Word order in turn represents two variables, VO/OV and rigid/free, thus giving Hakuta a list of seven in all. Combinations of these seven variables then serve partially to describe the 'n-dimensional space' of languages, or limits upon the ways in which human languages may vary. Hakuta goes on to explore possible psychological relationships between this n-dimensional space and the learner's 'hypothesis space' about the nature of the language he is learning. Word order is thus but one language-typological dimension among others that

Hakuta proposes statistically to 'collapse' into fewer 'underlying dimensions', which for him constitute 'the essence of human language'.

The Ferguson paper, which closes this volume, discusses the relation to L2 acquisition of a wide range of language universals — viz. of phonology, syntax, and discourse.

We began this Introduction by calling attention to different possible interpretations of the word 'universal' and we have briefly discussed the reasons why insights revealed in these papers would interest a researcher working within Extended Standard Theory. We wish to conclude, however, on a somewhat different note. It is obvious that the conference whose proceedings comprise this volume was convened in order that new light be shed on a research area of growing interest: the role of language universals in second-language acquisition. It is perhaps a little *less* obvious that in convening a conference for such a purpose it was necessary to bring together two groups of researchers — viz. in theoretical linguistics and in second language acquisition — with considerably less than total familiarity with each other's fields, yet who had much to gain from listening to each other's approaches to the topic at hand. Very few theoretical linguists had thus far done serious work in L2 acquisition and very few L2 researchers had thus far woven recent developments in mainstream linguistics into their work. The conference tone was one stemming from the recognition by all participants that much was there to be learned by everyone of whatever theoretical camp or whatever research endeavor. That tone was perhaps best captured in the paper by Comrie that opened the conference, and that opens this volume, wherein he states that 'the literature has pointed to a number of ways in which research on language universals and research on second language acquisition can benefit one another' (p. 11). If this volume is perceived as testimony to that mutual benefit, then it will have served its purpose.

NOTES

1) The term 'parameter' will be used throughout this section in its non-technical sense (i.e. without necessary reference to core grammar and Extended Standard Theory) until otherwise specified.

2) A paper by Hatch and Wagner-Gough (1976) reproduces a 'center-periphery' diagram from Ross (1974) which bears a superficial resemblance to the markedness relations of core vs. periphery in UG. Through a set of concentric circles Ross suggests a close-to-center/farther-from-center relationship for the following pairs:

assertion/presupposition
act/state
sentency/nouny
single clause S/multiple clause S
near to V/far from V
root S/embedded S
true NP/fake NP

It should be noted, however, that Hatch and Wagner-Gough saw Ross's schema as of value to the systematic accounting of the order of acquisition of discrete grammatical forms, whereas the relevance of core grammar to the research discussed in this volume is more in terms of the L2 ontogeny of the forms themselves.

3) The slightly different interpretations of core grammar for Chomsky, Koster, and Hirschbühler and Rivero (as pointed out in H&R 1981:592) will be ignored here since we are more interested at the moment in suggesting future broad avenues of research than in subjecting alternative theories of core grammar to critical scrutiny.

4) The assumption that preposition stranding represents the marked case and the presence of resumptive pronouns represents the unmarked is questioned by White (1983).

5) Schmidt (1978) also found no IL disconfirmation of PL word-order universals.

REFERENCES

Bickerton, D. 1981. *Roots of Language*. Ann Arbor: Karoma Publishers.

Chomsky, N. 1981a. Markedness and core grammar. In A. Belletti, L. Brandi, and L. Rizzi (eds.), *Theory of Markedness in Generative Grammar*. Pisa: Scuola Normale Superiore di Pisa.

Chomsky, N. 1981b. *Lectures on Government and Binding*. Dordrecht: Foris.

Comrie, B. 1981. *Language Universals and Linguistic Typology*. Oxford: Basil Blackwell.

Greenberg, J. 1963 (1966). Some universals of grammar with particular reference to the order of meaningful elements. In J. Greenberg (ed.), *Universals of Language* (Second Edition). Cambridge, Mass.: MIT Press.

Hatch, E., and J. Wagner-Gough. 1976. Explaining sequence and variation in second language acquisition. In H. Brown (ed.), *Papers in Second Language Acquisition*. Special issue no. 4 of *Language Learning*, 39-57.

Hirschbühler, P., and M.-L. Rivero. 1981. Catalan restrictive relatives. *Language 57*:591-625.

Keenan, E., and B. Comrie. 1977. Noun phrase accessibility and universal grammar. *Linguistic Inquiry 8*:63-100.

Koster, J. 1978. Conditions, empty nodes and markedness. *Linguistic Inquiry* 9:551-594.

Ross, J. 1974. The center. Paper presented at Conference on New Ways of Analyzing Variation in English, Georgetown University, Washington, D.C.

Schmidt, M. 1978. Coordinate structures and deletion in learner English. Unpublished masters thesis, University of Washington.

White, L. 1983. Markedness and parameter setting: some implications for a theory of adult second language acquisition. Paper presented at the Twelfth Annual University of Wisconsin-Milwaukee Linguistics Symposium, March.

WHY LINGUISTS NEED LANGUAGE ACQUIRERS

BERNARD COMRIE
University of Southern California

1. *Introduction*

In this paper, I will be giving some of my reactions, as a linguist interested in language universals, to recent work in second language acquisition that impinges upon work on language universals, and also giving some very tentative suggestions on how future cooperation between these two disciplines might develop.[1] I would emphasize that I speak as a 'grammarian' working on language universals and typology: I will not be presenting any empirical work on second language acquisition, nor will I attempt to make any recommendations on how second languages should be taught. I believe, however, that the recent literature has pointed to a number of ways in which research on language universals and research on second language acquisition can benefit one another, and the organization of this conference is evidence that this view is by no means idiosyncratic. More particularly, I will emphasize the gains that theoretical linguists can obtain from acquaintance with work in second language acquisition, but this simply reflects my own standpoint; I hope that the benefit will in fact be mutual.

The approach to language universals that I represent is one that believes that the best way of uncovering and, even more importantly, of validating language universals is by examining comparable phenomena across a wide range of languages.[2] The question of the data base can be put succinctly as follows: in order to be reasonably sure that we are on the right track in investigating language universals, we must test our hypotheses against a representative sample of human language. A number of suggestions have been made in the literature as to how one can avoid undue bias in establishing a representative sample of human languages. The careful reader will, however, have noted the subtle shift in the last two sentences between 'representative sample of human language (singular)' and 'representative sample of human languages (plural)'.

Clearly, our aim in studying language universals is to make claims about universal properties of human language in general, rather than about the set of languages that happens, perhaps accidentally, to be attested. If, as the result of some global catastrophe, all languages other than English were to die out, we would not then want to say that those properties which we know at present to be accidental properties of English have suddenly become, in any interesting sense, language universals. Work on language universals using a wide data base usually makes the assumption, tacit or explicit, that the range of attested languages (i.e. the set of languages spoken in the world today, plus those extinct languages for which we have sufficient documentation) is a representative sample of human language as a whole, whence a representative sample drawn from the set of attested languages is in turn a representative sample of human language as a whole. However, on certain parameters we know that the set of attested languages is skewed: one obvious example is the restriction of click consonants as part of the phonological system to the Khoisan languages of the south-western corner of Africa and adjacent Bantu languages (which have borrowed these sounds from the Khoisan languages). At some stage, then, the linguist interested in language universals must look beyond simply the investigation of attested languages, i.e. of languages as spoken by adult native speakers, to see if other information can be brought to bear on the problem of delimiting the overall human language potential.

The problem for the theoretical linguist is increased if one takes into account the existence not only of absolute universals (i.e. those that have no counterexamples to them) but also of universal tendencies (also, I think misleadingly, called statistical universals). By a universal tendency I mean simply a property that characterizes language with significantly greater than chance frequency. A simple example would be the universal that, in basic word order, subjects always precede direct objects. We now know that there are counterexamples to this universal, since for instance Malagasy has Verb - Object - Subject order (Keenan 1976), and Hixkaryana has Object - Verb - Subject order (Derbyshire 1977); yet still probably over 99% of the attested languages adhere to the universal, while less than 1% go against it. This distribution could scarcely be due to chance. On the one hand, it might reflect a significant property of human language as a whole, as indeed I think it does. However, it might also be the result of extralinguistic factors: one might argue that, for reasons quite unconnected with the structure of language, speakers of Subject - Object languages have tended to be much more dominant socio-politically than speakers of Object - Subject languages, and that therefore languages of the former type have tended to predominate, pushing Object - Subject languages into a few inaccessible parts of the globe. Simply looking at the distribution of these two word orders in the world's languages today will not in itself resolve this controversy.

The process of language acquisition provides us with a potential additional window onto the representativeness of the sample on which language universals studies are based. Here I will concentrate, of course, on second language acquisition, apart from some few remarks in the body of the paper on first language acquisition, although first language acquisition, in principle, can equally provide us with such a potential additional window. In this statement, I would emphasize the word *potential*. One can imagine scenarios where there would be no relationship whatsoever between language universals and, say, second language acquisition, and indeed one such scenario has been elaborated within mainstream transformational-generative grammar: if language universals are innate predispositions that the child brings to the task of acquiring its first language and which are lost quite early in the maturational process, then one might expect that subsequent acquisition of a second language would provide no correlation whatsoever with language universals. One of the main results of recent work linking second language acquisition with language universals, however, has been that there *is* such a correlation. It is hard to imagine that such a correlation could have arisen purely accidentally (i.e. that by chance parameter values relevant in language universals turn out also to be relevant, with the same values, in second language acquisition).

The set of hypotheses relating language universals research to second language acquisition can be made more explicit, following Eckman (1977). In order to do so, it is necessary first to make a distinction between absolute universals, i.e. those which no language can violate, and universal tendencies, i.e. those which the great majority of languages adhere to, but which may be violated exceptionally by a small number of languages. It turns out that the hypotheses relating universal tendencies, rather than absolute universals, to second language acquisition are the more interesting. First, one can formulate the hypothesis that some aspect of a language consistent with a universal should be easier to learn than some aspect that is inconsistent. (Obviously, if a language has some property inconsistent with a universal, then the universal can only be a tendency.) More interestingly, one can formulate two sub-hypotheses: the first, that a property consistent with a universal tendency will be acquired more easily than one that is not, even if the native language is inconsistent with both properties; the second, that a property inconsistent with a universal tendency will be acquired with greater difficulty than one that is consistent, even if the native language is consistent with both properties. Thus the crucial examples are those where difficulty in acquiring a certain property cannot be attributed solely to the fact that native language and second language have different structures (attribution of errors to language contrasts).

The discussion so far has assumed a simple dichotomy with regard to universal tendencies, namely one between consistency (unmarked state of affairs) and inconsistency (marked state of affairs). Some recent work within linguistic theory suggests that the distinction may, in many instances, be more complex than this, with a hierarchy of degrees of markedness rather than simply a binary distinction. One such piece of work would be the Keenan-Comrie Accessibility Hierarchy with regard to relative clause formation (to discussion of which I devote section 2 of this paper). For instance, while it would be misleading to say that relativization on oblique objects is marked in any absolute sense (many languages allow this relativization), one can still say that relativization on oblique objects is marked in comparison to relativization on subjects (and less marked than relativization on genitives). The overall hypothesis is thus that less marked properties will be acquired more easily (more specifically, even where the property in question is found in the second language but not in the first language),[3] and that more marked properties will be acquired less easily (more specifically, even where the property in question is found in both native and second languages); as a special, and particularly strong, case of the second part of this hypothesis, one would predict that properties that are common crosslinguistically (and thus low in markedness) might be acquired easily even where neither native nor second language evinces that property.

In section 2 of this paper, I discuss work in second language acquisition that relates directly to the universals of relative clause formation proposed in connection with the Keenan-Comrie Accessibility Hierarchy; this section is thus largely a reaction on my part to the relevant work within second language acquisition. Section 3 suggests some other areas within recent work on language universals where it might be useful to test out the predictions of the hypothesis outlined above; this section is thus a suggestion for future research, rather than a discussion of validated correlations between language universals and second language acquisition.

2.   *Relative Clause Formation*
The cross-language study of relative clause formation presented in

Keenan and Comrie (1977) has spawned a vast amount of relevant literature in the second language acquisition area, showing how the theoretical conclusions reached by Keenan and Comrie translate fairly directly into valid predictions about the acquisition of relative clauses in a second language, though also noting more specific points where the fit between the two areas is less than perfect. In this section, I wish to react to this second language literature.

Keenan and Comrie's original study is guided by a relatively simple intuition, namely that the Accessibility Hierarchy encodes the degree of difficulty of relativizing on a particular noun phrase. The Accessibility Hierarchy is, from top to bottom: Subject - Direct object - Indirect object - Oblique object - Genitive - Object of comparison. Thus the intuitive claim is that subjects are easier to relativize than direct objects, and so on down the hierarchy. Note that by 'relativize on a given position', we refer to the role of the noun phrase in question within the relative clause, not within the main clause; thus in *I know the man who arrived late*, relativization is on a subject (cf. *the man arrived late*), not on a direct object (cf. *I know the man*); i.e. the relevant fact is that *the man* is subject of the subordinate clause, not that it is direct object of the main clause.

Now there are several conceivable ways in which this intuition might find its realization in actual language. For instance, it might be the case that native speakers of any individual language would feel clearly that relativization on a subject is more acceptable than is relativization on a direct object; in actual fact, however, it is immediately apparent that this is not the case, given the existence of languages like English where both subject and direct object are equally relativizable. The instantiation of the intuition given by Keenan and Comrie is much more specific, and consists of two subparts. First: if a language can relativize on a given position on the Accessibility Hierarchy, then necessarily it can relativize on all positions higher on the Accessibility Hierarchy; note that this captures the intuition, or rather one instantiation of the intuition, that a position lower on the hierarchy cannot be more accessible than one higher on the hierarchy. Second: for each position on the Accessibility Hierarchy, there is some possible human language which can relativize on that position but on no lower position; note that this captures that part of the intuition which claims that each position on the Accessibility Hierarchy is relevant, i.e. that each such position defines a potential cut-off point. We speak of possible human languages rather than actual human languages because, as pointed out at the beginning of this paper, we want the universal still to be valid even if for some reason only one human language were to survive some major catastrophe, i.e. the statement is about human language potential rather than about any accidental set of actual human languages.

The second language literature has worked, for the most part, with the intuition as I have just stated it, and for reasons to be discussed below I believe that the literature was correct in doing so. Essentially, the conclusions reached in this literature are that the behavior of second language learners provides another instantiation of the intuition that the Accessibility Hierarchy corresponds to ease of relativizability: second language learners acquire more readily (use more frequently, make fewer errors in processing and producing) relative clauses where the subject is relativized than where the direct object is relativized, and so on down the hierarchy (though evidence may not be forthcoming for all cut-off points, with mergers between adjacent positions on the hierarchy). If, however, one looks in close detail at the finer points of the discussion by Keenan and Comrie, then one finds that the final statement of the Accessibility Hierarchy universals given by them differs in a rather substantial way from the intuition as stated above.

The main problem that arose in our earlier work is that, within our sample, a relatively small number of languages provide counterexamples to the strict interpretation given above. In particular, a number of Austronesian languages allow relativization on subjects, disallow relativization on direct objects or certain other objects, but then again allow relativization on either certain oblique objects or on genitives. A good example is provided here by Malay (Bahasa Malaysia, Bahasa Indonesia).[4] In Malay, it is possible to relativize on subjects; it is impossible to relativize on direct objects; at least for some speakers, it is possible to relativize on certain indirect and oblique objects (this probably being a single set of nondirect objects in Malay); it is possible to relativize on genitives:

(1)   perempuan yang pergi menyeberang sungai
       woman   that   go   across   river
       'the woman that went across the river'
(2)   *anak yang Ali memukul
       child that Ali hit
       'the child that Ali hit'
(3)   ?perempuan yang kepada-nya Ali mengirim buku
       woman   that   to   her Ali send   book
       'the woman to whom Ali sent a book'
(4)   perempuan yang anak-nya pergi menyeberang sungai
       woman   that   child her go   across   river
       'the woman whose child went across the river'

Thus there is a gap in the range of accessibility to relative clause formation.

Given this observation, there are two ways in which one could proceed. First, one could say that the universal in question is a universal tendency rather than an absolute universal; one could note that the number of exceptional languages is small relative to the overall sample (and probably smaller still in relation to the languages of the world as a whole, since Austronesian languages are rather overrepresented in our sample). Moreover, one could even advance a functional explanation for the gap in the Accessibility Hierarchy: Austronesian languages typically make frequent use of voices other than the active, so that it is readily possible to present an underlying (lexical) direct or other object in derived syntactic structure, whence it can readily be relativized like any other subject:

(2') anak yang di-pukul oleh Ali
      child that be-hit   by   Ali
      'the child that was hit by Ali'

With hindsight, I think that this approach is the correct approach to this set of data, though I will return to this below.

Secondly, one can try and complicate the statement of the universal so that languages like Malay are literally no longer exceptions. This is the tack which we chose in the 1977 article. In the languages in question, the strategies used for forming relative clauses above and below the gap are different, usually in that below the gap a pronoun is retained in the relative clause (i.e. literally 'the woman that *her* child went across the river'), whereas above the gap no pronoun is retained (i.e. literally 'the woman that (*she) went across the river'). If one then builds into the statement of the hierarchy generalizations this distinction in strategy, one can reformulate the universals as follows: (a) any language must be able to relativize on subjects; (b) any given strategy in a given language must cover a continuous segment of the Accessibility Hierarchy. Under this reformulation, the intuition that subjects are more readily relativizable is retained. But otherwise, all that is claimed is that no individual strategy can have a gap in it, although there is no statement corresponding to the initial intuition that, in some sense, direct objects are more relativizable than genitives: note that a number of languages allow relativization on direct objects but not on genitives, whereas there are few languages like Malay with the inverse set of possibilities. Thus the reformulation, despite a closer fit to the range of data, actually loses a crucial part of the original intuition, a part of the intuition that is moreover backed up by the overwhelming majority of the languages of the world, the main exceptions being from a single genetic family and geographical area.

It is currently a question subject to considerable controversy as to whether the linguist working on language universals should aim for a conceptually simple universal, to which individual languages might be exceptions, or whether such a linguist should aim for absolute universals even where these are conceptually more complex. In different individual cases, I think the argument can be made one way or the other, but overall my view is that what the linguist interested in language universals is trying to establish is statistically significant deviations from random distribution. If one compares the distribution of language variation predicted by the intuitive version of the Accessibility Hierarchy generalizations, by the attested distribution of language variation in samples that have been investigated, and by a purely random distribution (i.e. a set where each language is free to choose randomly which of the positions it can relativize), then it is clear that the attested distribution is much closer to that predicted by the intuitive version than to that predicted in terms of random distribution. Thus this conceptually simple account of accessibility to relative clause formation comes remarkably close to the attested variation. Given these observations, what does the work on acquisition of relative clause formation in second languages have to say?

If the reformulation in terms of different strategies were correct, then one might expect to find this reflected in second language acquisition studies, for instance in that speakers of a language allowing relative clause formation on, let us say for the sake of argument, all positions on the Accessibility Hierarchy, would first acquire relativization on subjects in the second language, and then on oblique objects in the second language provided relativization on oblique objects used a different strategy. Since English does indeed use different strategies for relativizing subjects and oblique objects, one might have expected this pattern actually to emerge in studies to date, based largely on the acquisition of English as a second language. Yet I am not aware of any study that has produced a result of this kind, i.e. native mastery of a language with such a gap in accessibility to relativization does not seem to lead to transfer of this pattern to a second language (at least, not where the second language does not in fact have such a gap — presumably, native speakers of Malay might simply retain the gap in acquiring another Austronesian language with essentially the same system).[5] In fact, what we find is precisely what is predicted by the original intuition: ease of acquisition of relative clause formation correlates with position on the Accessibility Hierarchy, and there are no gaps of the Austronesian type. This then strikes me as a clear instance where data from second language acquisition give at least some indication as to which of two competing approaches one should take in the statement of a language universal, in this case that the conceptually simpler tendency has greater validity than the conceptually more complex exceptionless absolute universal. Given that the theoretical linguistic work in question has also been of value to students of second language acquisition, I hope to have shown that this is an area of mutual benefit between the two disciplines.

Before leaving relative clause formation, I would like just to make two further small comments on the acquisition literature, this time involving both first and second language acquisition. In work on acquisition of Japanese as a first language, Hakuta (1981) observes that on a comprehension test, Japanese children demonstrate better comprehension of sentences involving relativization of direct objects than of sentences involving relativization of subjects, as in the following pair (following Hakuta, I use block capital English words rather than actual Japanese lexical items):

(5)   [PATIENT-o KICKED] AGENT-ga CRIED.
      'The agent that kicked the patient cried.'
(6)   [AGENT-ga KICKED] PATIENT-ga CRIED.
      'The patient that the agent kicked cried.'

Note that in Japanese the postposition -ga marks the subject, -o the direct object. Japanese children thus found (6) easier to process than (5). However, there are independent reasons to expect this bias, in particular a clear tendency on the part of Japanese children acquiring their first language to interpret the first noun phrase in the sentence as subject and the second as object, irrespective of the postpositions (i.e. to use word order rather than morphology).[6] This strategy shows up in interpretation of simplex sentences (e.g. misinterpretation of Object - Subject - Verb word order as Subject - Object - Verb word order), and imposition of this strategy on relative clauses can lead to overinterpretation in terms of relativization on direct objects in relation to subjects. The important lesson of this observation is that the claims of a literal psychological interpretation of the Accessibility Hierarchy hold only where other things are equal and does not exclude the possibility that other factors, for instance processing strategies or real world likelihood of interpretations, might at times override the predictions made by the Accessibility Hierarchy on its own. The viability of these claims can, of course, be tested by examining other manifestations of children's acquisition of relative clause formation in Japanese, not confounded by the interference of independently motivated processing strategies.

Similar remarks apply to the observation by Gass (1979a) that her students acquiring English as a second language actually performed better with relativization on genitives than with relativization on direct, indirect, and oblique objects in grammaticality judgement and sentence combining tests. As Gass herself suggests (1979a:339), this may be because the unusual properties of relativization on genitives in English (e.g. use of a special relative pronoun *whose*) give increased prominence to genitive relativization, offsetting the tendency for genitives to be low in accessibility to relativization.

The second point concerns the observation that in instances of first language acquisition, children seem to find easier examples where the role of the noun phrase is the same in both main and subordinate clauses, to the extent of finding easier sentences where that role is direct object in both clauses (e.g. *I know the man that you saw*) over those where the role is subject of the subordinate clause but direct object of the main clause (e.g. *I know the man that arrived late*); i.e. with this configuration it is actually easier to relativize on a direct object than on a subject (Sheldon 1974). As far as I am aware, this pattern has not been reported for second language acquirers, and it may therefore reflect a real difference between the characteristics of first language acquisition and the characteristics of both the languages spoken by adults and language acquisition by adults. (I return to this general possibility in section 3.) The conclusion remains speculative, but I would note that certain languages (as spoken by adults) do contain traces of a system like that reported for children acquiring their first language. This is the relative clause strategy called the Equi strategy by Givón (1975) and involves omission of the overt marking of the role of the noun phrase in question in the subordinate clause if this role is the same as that in the main clause, i.e. as if one were to be able to say in English: *Harry left with the girl that Sam arrived* meaning 'Harry left with the girl with whom Sam arrived', given that *the girl* is a comitative in both clauses. This strategy is found, for instance, in Israeli Hebrew (for all prepositional phrases), at least for some speakers:

(7) Natati sefer le oto yeled [še Miriam natna (lo)   sefer].
     I-gave book to same boy that Mary   gave to-him book.
     'I gave a book to the same boy that Mary gave a book to.'

Thus it may be that adult languages contain certain traces of this property of children's languages, though without their being so salient in the former to justify their being considered in any nontrivial sense as universals.

3. Ergative and Accusative Patterns

In this section, I want to look at some more recent work in language universals and typology and suggest ways in which this work may, in turn, feed into the investigation of second language acquisition, to the ultimate benefit of both disciplines. The theoretical work to which I will be referring is some of that on ergativity, in particular ergativity as a syntactic (rather than a morphological) phenomenon. For expository purposes, I will restrict myself to a very brief account of the general phenomenon, in order to concentrate in greater depth on the particular aspects of ergativity that are of interest here.[7]

The essence of syntactic ergativity is whether the subject of an intransitive clause is treated syntactically in the same way as the agent of a transitive clause (accusative, or more fully: nominative-accusative syntax) or whether it is treated in the same way as the patient of a transitive clause (ergative, or more fully: ergative-absolutive syntax). In English, most syntactic processes that are sensitive to this distinction operate on an accusative basis, as can be illustrated by examples of conjunction reduction as in (8):

(8) The man hit the woman and ran away.
(9) The man hit the woman.
(10) The man ran away.
(11) The woman ran away.

In English, sentence (8) is interpreted to mean 'the man hit the woman and the man ran away', even though the second, intransitive, clause has no overt subject. The rule in English is that, for purposes of conjunction reduction, intransitive subjects and transitive agents are treated alike, while transitive patients are treated differently: sentence (8) is interpreted as the conjunction of (9) (*man* as agent) and (10) (*man* as intransitive subject), not as the conjunction of (9) (*woman* as patient) and (11) (*woman* as intransitive subject). In the Australian language Dyirbal, however, we get precisely the converse interpretation:[8]

(12) Jugumbil   yara-nggu   balgan, baninyu.
     woman-ABSOLUTIVE man-ERGATIVE hit   came-here
     'The man hit the woman, and she came here.'
(13) Jugumbil   yara-nggu   balgan.
     woman-ABSOLUTIVE man-ERGATIVE hit
     'The man hit the woman.'

(14) Yara   baninyu.
      man-ABSOLUTIVE came-here
      'The man came here.'

(15) Jugumbil   baninyu.
      woman-ABSOLUTIVE came-here
      'The woman came here.'

In Dyirbal, the only permitted interpretation of (12) is that that the woman came here, i.e. (12) is interpreted as the conjunction of (13) (*woman* as patient) and (15) (*woman* as intransitive subject), not as the conjunction of (13) (*man* as agent) and (14) (*man* as intransitive subject).

In some instances, as with conjunction reduction, the difference between accusative and ergative syntax seems to be a purely formal difference between languages. In other instances, however, recent work, including my own ongoing research work, suggests strongly that the incidence of accusative or ergative syntax has a functional basis. Part of the evidence in favor of this hypothesis is that different languages, irrespective of whether their syntax is otherwise largely accusative or ergative, show a strong preference for accusative syntax in certain constructions identifiable cross-linguistically, and for ergative syntax in other constructions identifiable cross-linguistically.

For instance, in constructions where the verb of a subordinate clause (typically in infinitive form) lacks a subject of its own under coreference with some noun phrase in the main clause, we can ask which noun phrase in the main clause controls this omission of a noun phrase in the subordinate clause. Relevant English examples are (16) and (17) below:

(16) I want to leave now.

(17) Harry told me to leave now.

In (16), the omitted subject of the subordinate clause is in fact interpreted as coreferential with the intransitive subject of *want*, i.e. the infinitive construction refers to my going; this is the usual pattern with intransitive verbs in the main clause (i.e. verbs which take no object other than the infinitive construction). In (17), on the other hand, the omitted subject of the subordinate clause is interpreted as coreferential with the patient of the main clause verb *told*, i.e. the infinitive construction is about my going, not about Harry's going, even though here two noun phrases, *me* and *Harry* are potentially available as controllers. The pattern evinced by *tell* is that usually found with transitive main clause verbs, though there are some exceptions, as noted below.

Technically, this is an instance of syntactic ergativity in English, since intransitive subjects and transitive patients, but not transitive agents, are the usual controllers for the omission of infinitive subjects. But unlike the case of conjunction reduction mentioned above, this is not a purely formal property of English, but has rather a functional (semantic-pragmatic) basis. With verbs of ordering and requesting, it is normally assumed, for the order or request to be felicitous, that the recipient of the order or request is also the person who is to carry out that order or request. Most of the transitive verbs permitted in constructions like (17) belong to the semantic field of directives (orders and requests), and encode the recipient of the directive as their patient; moreover, the person carrying out the directive would normally appear as subject of the infinitive. Thus the most natural state of affairs is for main clause patient and subordinate clause subject to be coreferential. All English syntax does is to allow omission of the coreferential infinitive subject when this state of affairs holds.

The validity of this functional account can be tested by looking at the few transitive verbs occurring in sentences like (17) but belonging to semantic fields radically different from directives, for instance verbs referring to various kinds of promises, such as *promise* itself:

(18)   Harry promised me to leave now.

In (18), despite the apparent superficial similarity to (17), the interpretation is that the omitted subject of the infinitive is *Harry*, i.e. reference is to Harry's going, not to my going (cf. the paraphrase: *Harry promised me that he would leave now*). For a felicitous promise, the person making the promise must have control over the event that he is promising to bring about, such events being typically (in some languages, apparently, always) encoded as a clause with the promiser as subject. With verbs of the *promise* class, then, our expectation is that the main clause agent and the subject of the subordinate clause should be coreferential, and indeed English syntax allows omission of the infinitive subject with *promise* if and only if it is coreferential with the main clause agent. Thus the formal syntactic difference in behavior between *tell* and *promise* can be correlated with the semantic-pragmatic properties of the different classes of lexical item.

Turning now to language acquisition, these observations lead to some interesting hypotheses for testing. In purely formal terms, it would be simpler if, in English, all transitive main clause verbs behaved like *tell*, given that *tell* represents the majority class. In semantic-pragmatic terms, however, the attested distribution is simpler, since it involves omission of the infinitive subject under coreference with that noun phrase with which coreference would be expected, given the nature of the main clause verb. Descriptively, we have evidence for the predominance of a functional principle over a formal principle. How, then, will language acquirers proceed: will they operate initially in terms of the functional principle, or will they rather go by the formal principle.

With this particular example, we have evidence from first language acquisition suggesting that up to a certain age, children learning English go by the formal principle, thereby consistently misinterpreting sentences like (18), to mean something like 'Harry promised me that I would leave now' (Chomsky 1969:32-41). Later on, they give the correct interpretations to sentences of both types (17) and (18). To supplement Chomsky's observations of children, it should be noted that many adult speakers of English have apparently still not made the leap from formal to functional interpretation of sentences like (18), with *promise*, either judging such sentences as ungrammatical or giving them the interpretation (often only under pressure) 'Harry promised me that I would leave now'. However, there is a clear statistical difference between children acquiring English as a first language and adult native speakers: the vast majority of the latter have the functional principal operative, whereas children go through a stage of operating primarily in terms of the formal principle.

If this is indeed a difference between children and adults, then investigation of the acquisition of the *promise* construction by adult second language learners should be able to demonstrate it (or, conversely, to disprove the difference if in fact it does not exist). Adult speakers of a language with the same distribution as in English, and who acquire the English distribution correctly, would obviously not provide a crucial text, since they might simply be transferring from their native language to English. What would be interesting would be to take native speakers of languages lacking the English distribution (e.g. by not allowing subjectless subordinate constructions after 'promise') and to see whether, in acquiring the English use of the infinitive after *promise*, they give preference to the formal or the functional principle in interpreting and constructing English sentences with *promise* and a following infinitive. Of course, if native speakers of languages with the English system, where moreover those adult native speakers use the English system in their native language, were to acquire English as a second language relying on the formal rather than the functional principle, then this would tend to call the functional principle into question as a psychologically real principle. But even this result would provide an interesting basis for further investigation of the problem, since it would point out an interesting contrast between a psychologically based principle (the formal principle, in this case) and a principle based on properties of social interaction (promises commit the person making the promise, not the recipient of the promise).

So far, we have considered the syntax of the main clause in English infinitive constructions. It is now time to turn to the subordinate clause, in order to find an example where the semantic-pragmatic expectation is for accusative rather than ergative syntax. For ease of exposition, the main clause verb will be kept constant as *tell*. A directive is addressed to an entity who must, for the directive to be felicitous, be assumed to have control over the event referred to by the subordinate clause. The entity most likely to have control over the event referred to in the subordinate clause is the agent of that clause, and indeed directives are typically felicitous where it is the agent of the subordinate clause that is coreferential with the recipient of the directive:

(19)   Harry told the doctor to examine Mary.

In (19), the doctor is both recipient of Harry's instruction and agent of the examination. With intransitive infinitives, the directive is felicitous if the intransitive subject has control over the event referred to:

(20)   Harry told the doctor to leave.

Thus, from the semantics-pragmatics of directives, our expectation is that it is intransitive subject or transitive agent that will be coreferential with the recipient of the directive, and therefore deletable. Note that, although it is possible in English to put an underlying transitive patient into this position by application of passive, the resulting sentence must be given an interpretation where the patient has control over whether he is subjected to the event in question:

(21)   Harry told Mary to be examined by the doctor.

I am aware of one language where, despite the semantics-pragmatics of directives, the omission of the embedded subject operates not on an accusative basis (as in English) but on an ergative basis. That language is Dyirbal. Where the omitted noun phrase in the subordinate clause is an intransitive subject (with control over the event), we have sentences like (22) below:

(22)   Ngana   yabu   gigan banagaygu.
       we-NOMINATIVE mother-ABSOLUTIVE told   to-return
       'We told mother to return.'

Where the recipient of the directive is coreferential with the patient of the subordinate clause, again Dyirbal constructs the sentence with no complication, in particular using the unmarked voice of the subordinate verb (contrast the passive in English sentence (21)):

(23) Ngana   yabu   gigan
      we-NOMINATIVE   mother-ABSOLUTIVE told
      gubi-nggu   mawali.
      doctor-ERGATIVE   to-examine

While the best translation for (23) is 'we told mother to be examined by the doctor', a more accurate gloss would be something like 'we told mother for the doctor to examine (sc. her)', making it clear that *gubinggu* is a regular transitive agent and that the patient is omitted under coreference with the noun phrase *yabu* in the main clause.

In Dyirbal, if the agent of the subordinate clause is coreferential with the appropriate main clause noun phrase, then the so-called antipassive voice must be used in the subordinate clause, in order to make the agent syntactically into an intransitive subject:

(24) Ngana   yabu   gigan
      we-NOMINATIVE   mother-ABSOLUTIVE told
      nguma-gu   buralngaygu
      father-DATIVE   to-watch-ANTIPASSIVE
      'We told mother to watch father.'

A more accurate gloss to the Dyirbal sentence might be 'we told mother to look at father', with the intransitive verb *look (at)*, mirroring the intransitive nature of the Dyirbal antipassive. Note that as a result of these various facts, Dyirbal actually requires more complex syntax (as in (24) versus (23)) to express the pragmatically more natural situation, where the recipient of a directive is also agent of the event which the directive is to bring about.

The predictions for second language acquisition, if this functional principle accounting for accusative syntax in the subordinate clause of directives is correct, is that it should be easier to acquire a system like that of English, which is in accord with the functional principle, than to acquire one like Dyirbal, which goes against the principle. On the one hand, one could investigate speakers of languages with the English system or with a neutral system (e.g. one where there is no omission of a noun phrase in the subordinate clause) who are acquiring languages with the Dyirbal system. This may not be a very practical proposal, given that I can point only to Dyirbal as an instance of the Dyirbal system, and I am not aware of any relevant instances of non-native speakers acquiring Dyirbal.[9] However, the inverse experiment ought to be possible. In particular, one could compare acquisition of the syntax of directives (in accord with the functional principle) and acquisition of conjunction reduction (where the accusative syntax seems to be an arbitrary formal property) in English, by native speakers of languages with neutral syntax in both instances (e.g. no omission of noun phrases, or in the case of coordination reduction omission of any noun phrase provided the sense is not distorted) or by native speakers of languages with the Dyirbal system. Since speakers of Dyirbal do acquire English as a second language, this last suggestion may be more than just a thought experiment. It would be interesting to know whether Dyirbal speakers find it easier to acquire the accusative syntax of English in directives, where it has a functional basis, than in conjunction reduction, where we simply have an arbitrary formal difference between English and Dyirbal.

4. *Conclusions*

Recent work in language universals has uncovered a number of areas where one property can be described as more marked than some other property. In terms of cross-language distribution, this can be realized as a significant skewing away from random distribution of the parameter involved, as with the occurrence of accusative syntax in omission of a noun phrase in the subordinate clause of a directive. In other terms, this can often be expressed as an implicational universal: for instance, if a language has accusative syntax anywhere, then it is likely to have it in the omission of a noun phrase in directives. The Accessibility Hierarchy as applied to relative clause formation is a clear illustration of a chain of implicational universals: if a language can relativize on position n, then necessarily it can also relativize on position $n - 1$, where n is any position on the Hierarchy and a lower number corresponds to a higher rank on the Hierarchy. Language universals of this kind lend themselves to ready transposition into predictions about ease of acquisition, and the large number of such universals that have been proposed in recent theoretical work should provide a fruitful field for interaction between language universals research and second language acquisition research.

NOTES

1) This paper is a revised version of a paper presented at the Conference on Second Language Acquisition and Language Universals, University of Southern California, Los Angeles, in February, 1982. I am grateful to my official discussant, Josh Ard, and to many other conference participants for comments on the conference paper.

2) For a fuller exposition of this approach to language universals, reference may be made to Comrie (1981).

3) This property has been demonstrated for acquisition of the lexicon by Jordens and Kellerman (1978), in which study Dutch learners of English were slower in acquiring idiomatic uses of *break* (e.g. *break a promise*) even though literal translations are possible in Dutch.

4) For discussion of relative clause formation in Malay, I am grateful to C.K. Yeoh (Universiti Sains, Malaysia). The discussion in the text follows his native-speaker judgements, which do not always agree with those given in Keenan and Comrie (1977).

5) Gass (1979a; 1979b) notes that for the students she investigated, frequency of use of relativization on different positions on the Hierarchy correlated directly with position on the Hierarchy, with more frequent relativization on the higher positions; lower positions were used even less frequently than by native speakers. However, in tests involving grammaticality judgements and sentence combining, students performed better with genitives than with any grammatical relation other than subjects. Gass (1979a:339-340) suggests that there may be independent factors giving rise to the apparent discrepancy (see further below). Gass's findings overall, however, show a strong correlation between hierarchy position and successful formation/interpretation/use by students, irrespective of the student's native language.

6) Compare the claim by Zobl (this volume) that learners pass through a stage where subjects are analyzed as the first syntactic constituent in surface structure, and the claim by Bickerton (this volume) that first language learners pass through a stage of interpreting N - V - N sequences as actor - action - patient.

7) For a fuller exposition of my approach to ergativity, reference may be made to Comrie (1978). In the discussion given in the text here, a number of simplifications are introduced (e.g. identification of A with Agent, P with Patient), though these do not affect the issues involved.

8) Except where otherwise stated, all Dyirbal examples are taken or adapted from Dixon (1972).

9) The linguist R.M.W. Dixon has, of course, acquired Dyirbal as a second language, but acquisition by a linguist who is simultaneously working on the analysis of the language being acquired is probably not to be treated as a typical case of second language acquisition. For what the information is worth, however, Dixon informs me (personal communication) that the grammaticality judgement on the crucial sentence (23) is one of the last points he has acquired in Dyirbal.

REFERENCES

Chomsky, Carol. 1969. *The acquisition of syntax in children from 5 to 10.* Cambridge, Mass.: MIT Press.

Comrie, Bernard. 1978. Ergativity. In W.P. Lehmann (ed.), *Syntactic typology: studies in the phenomenology of language*:329-394. Austin: University of Texas Press.

Comrie, Bernard. 1981. *Language universals and linguistic typology: syntax and morphology*. Chicago: University of Chicago Press.

Derbyshire, D.C. 1977. Word order universals and the existence of OVS languages. *Linguistic Inquiry 8*:590-599.

Dixon, R.M.W. 1972. *The Dyirbal language of north Queensland*. Cambridge: Cambridge University Press.

Eckman, Fred R. 1977. Markedness and the contrastive analysis hypothesis. *Language Learning 27*:315-330.

Gass, Susan. 1979a. Language transfer and universal grammatical relations. *Language Larning 29*:327-344.

Gass, Susan. 1979b. Second language acquisition and language universals. Paper presented to the 1979 Delaware Symposium on Language Studies.

Givón, T. 1975. Promotion, accessibility and case-marking: toward understanding grammars. *Working Papers on Language Universals 19*:55-125. Stanford, Calif.: Linguistics Department, Stanford University.

Hakuta, Kenji. 1981. Grammatical description *versus* configurational arrangement in language acquisition: the case of relative clauses in Japanese. *Cognition 9*:197-236.

Jordens, P. and E. Kellerman. 1978. Investigation into the strategy of transfer in second language learning. Paper presented at the Fifth AILA Congress, Montreal.

Keenan, Edward L. 1976. Remarkable subjects in Malagasy. In Charles N. Li (ed.), *Subject and topic*, 247-301. New York: Academic Press.

Keenan, Edward L. and Bernard Comrie. 1977. Noun phrase accessibility and universal grammar. *Linguistic Inquiry 8*:63-99.

Sheldon, Amy. 1974. The acquisition of relative clauses in English. Bloomington, Ind.: Indiana University Linguistics Club.

COMMENTS ON THE PAPER BY COMRIE

JOSH ARD
The University of Michigan

Comrie's paper is excellent for a collection such as this, emphasizing, as it does, important contributions that can come from both second language research and language universals research. The comments here are intended to augment certain ideas that Prof. Comrie's contribution brings to mind and are presented from the perspectives of theoretical work both in language universals and in second language acquisition.

1. *Interaction*

In his presentation Prof. Comrie has argued that linguistics needs to consider the interaction of different factors in predicting results. The particular cases he mentioned, of course, concerned the Accessibility Hierarchy. How often have we seen statements to the effect that some slight deviation from what the Accessibility Hierarchy alone predicts necessarily 'disproves the universal nature of the hierarchy'. We need to be more subtle than this. There is simply no reason to believe, as is so often assumed in linguistics, that every phenomenon must have a single triggering factor. I am gratified that Prof. Comrie has taken steps in this direction.

I can only hope that others will take up this approach. The Accessibility Hierarchy is not an isolated case in this regard. We need to realize that multiple factors are often at work. Just to take one example important to many participants in this conference, language transfer should not be viewed as an all-or-nothing affair. There is no reason why native language factors, target language factors, and language universal factors could not all be interacting in the derivation of a single structure.

2. *The importance of a wide data base*

Prof. Comrie stresses the need for research on language universals to be founded on a wide data base, including as many languages of as many types as possible. I agree strongly. Moreover, I submit that this same goal holds true for second language acquisition research: to be more certain of our claims, we need to consider as many combinations of native languages and target languages as possible. Unfortunately, most theoretical discussions about second language acquisition, at least those conducted in the United States, have been based almost exclusively on the acquisition of English, with some sporadic consideration of French and German. Furthermore, the native languages involved in such research are generally restricted to a dozen or so, and the research also largely concerns only acquisition in institutional settings. This is not a wide data base from which to make generalizations. Certainly there are many other types of second language acquisition going on. Millions of people are learning Russian, Arabic, Indonesian, Chinese, Hindi, Swahili, and so forth, as second languages. It is important to learn what paths second language acquisition takes in those cases. For example, there are several fascinating structures in these languages, unlike any found in English, which may place special demands on learners. Obviously, some of these data are hard to obtain, but much can be learned from perusing the vast amounts of material in Russian and other languages that are purchased by American academic libraries.

3. *Ergativity*
    Ergativity is a fascinating area of universals research. Unfortunately, there is very little literature readily accessible on the acquisition either of ergative second languages or of other languages by speakers of ergative languages. However, with regard to the latter, there are several ergative languages spoken in the Soviet Union. Therefore, there should be Soviet material available at least on acquisition *by* speakers of ergative languages.

    There are intriguing questions to consider, as suggested by Prof. Comrie. I would like to add one more. Itel'men, also known as Kamchadal, another language of the Soviet Far East, has amazingly parallel passive and anti-passive structures. In fact, both can be derived via a single general demotion rule. Now, would speakers of ergative languages find the anti-passive easier? Would speakers of accusative languages find the passive easier? The Itel'men community is so small that perhaps no one is learning it as a first language, much less a second language. That's a pity.

    Nevertheless, there are relevant points to ponder closer to home. English does have some ergative-like patterns. Consider a verb like *compare*. We can say

> Nancy compared John with Henry.

or

> John compares favorably with Henry.

From my personal experience in teaching foreign students they always seem surprised to find that a certain verb follows this pattern. I haven't yet devised any rigorous experients, but this could certainly be done. I agree that work on exotic second language acquisition sites is very interesting, but there is much of interest left to be done in the situations that are most readily available around us.

In conclusion, I would like to reiterate my praise of Prof. Comrie's contribution to this conference.

SECOND LANGUAGE ACQUISITION
AND THE ONTOLOGY OF LANGUAGE UNIVERSALS*

SUSAN GASS AND JOSH ARD
The University of Michigan

1. *Introduction*

In recent years researchers have begun to pay serious attention to the relationship between language universals[1] and adult second language acquisition (Adjémian 1976; Eckman 1977; Flynn 1981; Frawley 1981; Gass 1983; Gass and Ard 1980; Rutherford 1983; Schachter and Rutherford 1979; Sharwood Smith 1980; Schmidt 1980; Gundel and Tarone 1983). In this paper we continue this line of inquiry by looking at different types of universals and the potential impact they have on the adult second language acquisition process. We ask the following question: what can we expect the influence of language universals to be on the acquisition process and how might this influence be manifest depending on the type of universal it is based on?

2. *An overview of the nature of language universals and their potential influence on adult second language acquisition*

Before turning to an analysis of actual cases in second language acquisition, we first attempt to establish a framework in which one can explore the effects of language universals on the second language acquisition process. In Table 1 potential relationships between language universals and adult second language acquisition are synopsized. Several different types and sources of language universals have been suggested. Similarly, there have been different views of the acquisition process, particularly with regard to the critical age hypothesis (the hypothesis that language-acquiring ability atrophies before adulthood). Given different assumptions about these factors, we claim that different predictions will obtain concerning the potential influence of universals on second language acquisition. Under some assumptions a strong role of

TABLE 1: Nature of Language Universals and their Potential Influence on Adult Second Language Acquisition

Statistical or Absolute	Source of Language Universal	Validity of Critical Age Hypothesis	Probability of Influence	Remarks on the Locus of Influence
statistical	physical basis	valid	moderate	
statistical	physical basis	invalid	moderate	
absolute	physical basis	valid	high	
absolute	physical basis	invalid	high	
statistical	perceptual/cognitive	valid	moderate	
statistical	perceptual/cognitive	invalid	moderate	
absolute	perceptual/cognitive	valid	high	
absolute	perceptual/cognitive	invalid	high	
statistical	lang. acq. device	valid	very low	just on static competence
statistical	lang. acq. device	invalid	moderate	just on static competence
absolute	lang. acq. device	valid	very low	just on static competence
absolute	lang. acq. device	invalid	high	just on static competence
statistical	neuro. basis of lg. use	valid	low	
statistical	neuro. basis of lg. use	invalid	moderate	
absolute	neuro. basis of lg. use	valid	low	
absolute	neuro. basis of lg. use	invalid	high	
statistical	diachronic basis	valid	very low	
statistical	diachronic basis	invalid	very low	
absolute	diachronic basis	valid	very low	
absolute	diachronic basis	invalid	very low	
statistical	interactional basis	valid	moderate	
statistical	interactional basis	invalid	moderate	
absolute	interactional basis	valid	high	

language universals would be expected. Under other assumptions a minimal role or no role at all is more probable. Furthermore, there are different expectations about the nature of potential influences. Some assumptions yield predictions about a learner's use and competence, while other assumptions yield predictions only about a learner's static competence.

2.1.   Referring to Table 1, the first column indicates the predictive power of universals over the class of human languages. Some proposed universals, like those in Greenberg's (1963) article, are statistical or, as Comrie (this volume) says, represent tendencies. This amounts to a claim that most, but not necessarily all, languages will display the putative universal. In general, one would expect that absolute universals will have an equal or greater effect on the second language acquisition process than statistical universals or universal tendencies.[2]

2.2.   The second column includes six potential sources for language universals. These potential sources include most of the commonly suggested ones. However, we do not intend this list to be exhaustive. Moreover, it is not necessary that each language universal have a single origin. For example, what is subsumed under the traditional label of a 'functional' or 'pragmatic' basis (see Comrie 1981) might be the result of a combined influence of both perceptual/cognitive and interactional bases.

Finally, there is often a great deal of controversy with regard to the assignment of an origin to a particular language universal. For instance, some scholars proclaim that *all* language universals result from the nature of a language acquisition device, while others deny the very existence of such an entity. The purpose of this chart, therefore, is not to provide the final answers to questions of the origin of language universals. Its purpose, rather, is to provide a framework in which questions concerning the origin or source of language universals and their relationship to adult second language acquisition can meaningfully be discussed.

2.2.1.   The first type of potential source, physical basis, refers to influences due to a physical fact, perhaps dependent on the way the world is or, on a more local level, on the way the human body, especially the vocal and aural apparatus, is structured. As will be discussed in more detail below, a physical explanation may be particularly appropriate in the case of certain phonetic universals.

2.2.2.   The second type refers to influences of factors in the human perceptual and cognitive apparatus and processing capabilities which affect more than language related phenomena. This type of source has frequently been offered by scholars opposed to narrowly innatist views of language acquisition (Slobin 1973; Sinclair-de Zwart 1973).

2.2.3.   The third and fourth sources, a language acquisition device and a neurophysiological basis for language use, are usually not divided. We have bifurcated what is normally called a language acquisition device into two entities: 1) one called a language acquisition device that only contributes to the acquisition of competence proper, and 2) one called the neurophysiological basis for language use that also contributes to more general factors of use and performance. Our reason for this distinction is simply that one would predict that the second type of entity would have broader effects than the former on language use during the second language acquisition process.

It is important to note that these sources are essentially 'default' explanations. That is, these last two sources can be invoked as explanations for universals only when there are no physical, perceptual, cognitive or interactional facts, either singly or in combination, that can account for the universal. At the present stage of research, it is impossible to provide direct evidence for these language-particular sources. Rather, their existence is inferred, because some mechanism is required to account for language competence and language universals.

2.2.4.   The fifth potential source of language universals, historical change, is perhaps the most difficult to accept and understand. Nonetheless, there are reasonable grounds for supposing that language change plays a major role in creating and shaping universals.

This is easier to motivate for statistical universals than for absolute ones. When something changes into something else, it still retains many of its former characteristics, at least for a while. For example, most auxiliaries develop from main verbs, so it is not surprising that auxiliaries possess several characteristics of main verbs. Anttila (1972:356) suggests that complementizers frequently develop from heralding objects, as in (1):

(1)   I know that; you will come ›
       I know that you will come.

If this is the case, one could predict from this alone that complementizers will frequently be clause initial, particularly in VO languages.

Absolute universals that cannot be accounted for by means of cognitive/perceptual, interactional, or physical bases have generally been accounted for through constraints on language acquisition rather than constraints on language change. The argument, essentially, is that patterns are missing from all languages because they cannot be acquired. The converse is unquestionably true: if something cannot be acquired, it cannot persist in a human language. However, we are unaware of any direct experimental evidence for the hypothesis itself.

It is certainly possible that patterns are missing from all languages because they cannot diachronically arise from the types of language extant. Diachronic investigations have not yet progressed to the point where this can be stringently tested. Nevertheless, there is good reason to believe that there are limits on possible changes. It is well established that constraints on phonological changes are (often) more strict than constraints on synchronic phonological rules, i.e. many phonological rules could not result from a single change, but 'telescope' many changes together. For example, k never changes to s in one step; several intermediate stages are required. Ard (1979b) presented evidence for a similar state of affairs in syntax. If one wishes to demonstrate that some particular structure cannot arise historically and is thereby universally ruled out, it is not enough to show that no single change can create that structure from extant language structures. Rather, one must show that no series of changes could lead to that structure. Yet, if this could be demonstrated, then a very plausible explanation for the universal absence of the structure in question would be an historical constraint.

2.2.5.   The sixth and final source consists of factors due to the nature of human social interaction. This area is important for linguistics, because notions such as speech acts and much of pragmatics, including Grice's maxims, presuppose models of social action and interaction and role behaviour.

Interesting suggestions about universals of social interaction and role behaviour have been offered by the philosopher and sociologist Habermas, who asserts that the development of communicative competence presupposes the development of interactive competence (McCarthy 1981:386).

> I would like to provide a systematically warranted division into cognitive, linguistic, and interactive development; corresponding to these dimensions I shall distinguish cognitive, linguistic and *interactive competences*. This proposal signifies that for each of these dimensions, and indeed only for these dimensions, a specific developmental-logically ordered *universal sequence* of structures can be given. (1974:10; translated in McCarthy 1981:338) (emphases added)

> Sociological action theory ‹should be developed› as a theory that attempts to reconstruct the *universal components of the relevant pre-theoretical knowledge of sociological laymen*... Only competence-theoretic approaches in lin-

guistics and developmental psychology have created a paradigm that con-
nects the formal analysis of known structures with the causal analysis of observable processes. The expression 'interactive competence' stands for the
assumption that *the abilities of socially acting subjects can be investigated from
the perspective of a universal — i.e. independent of particular cultures — competence*, just as are language and cognition (1977:27, translated in McCarthy
1981:335-336) (emphases added)

As Habermas admits, the development of a theory of interactive competence
is still in the programmatic stage. Nevertheless, results in this area are interesting for linguistics in general and pragmatics in particular. Universals of
interactive competence could certainly play a strong role in shaping the universal nature of language.

2.3.   The third column lists the assumed validity of the critical age
hypothesis. For most of the potential sources of language universals, the correctness of this hypothesis is unimportant. For example, universals due to
physical factors should not be affected by whether or not language-acquiring
mechanisms atrophy before adulthood. For other potential sources, especially those due to a language-acquisition device, the validity of this
hypothesis is crucial in predicting the effects of the relevant universals.

2.4.   In the fourth column is recorded the probability that universals
arising under the conditions recorded in the first three columns will affect the
second language acquisition process for adults. The possibilities listed in the
column 'probability of influence' are to be read in a statistical sense. That is,
'moderate' means that given, let's say, 20 examples of a particular type of universal and its relation to L2 acquisition, we would expect that it would affect
the acquisition process perhaps 10-15 of those times, whereas if the universal
is predicted to have a 'high' influence, we would expect the influence to be
manifest 15-20 times. We would like to emphasize that the numbers cited here
are intended to serve as examples, not as absolutes. What we have not claimed
is perhaps as important as what we have claimed. There are no implications
about how strongly the universal will be manifested. The implications refer
only to the likelihood of its being felt at all. In sum, our claim is that certain
universals are much more likely to affect the second language acquisition process than others.

2.5.   The fifth column includes some remarks on the locus of influence
on the acquisition process. There are several different ways in which a universal can have an effect. For example, a universal could merely shape the final
nature of a learner's competence. Several progressively stronger effects are

also plausible: universals could shape each developmental stage of a learner's acquisition; universals could absolutely constrain each developmental stage; universals could also have several other effects, e.g. they could motivate fewer errors for some features, they could affect relative surety of grammaticality judgments, etc. In the chart most entries are blanks, because there is as yet little basis for predicting just what types of effects a universal will have.

3. *Test cases*

In what follows we will present examples from second language acquisition to better illustrate the predictions our framework makes. We first give four brief examples from the areas of phonology, word order, and syntax and then go into more detail about data on the acquisition of tense/aspect systems.

3.1. Our first case is the acquisition of final voiced obstruents in English. Many of the world's languages have no word final voiced obstruents. It has long been noted (cf. Passy 1891) that languages tend to have only final voiceless consonants. Ohala (1972) has suggested a physical phonetic explanation for final devoicing.

If we accept the probable physical basis, our model predicts a strong effect on second language learners. In fact, Eckman (1981) found that both Chinese and Spanish learners of English failed to produce final voiced obstruents. Spanish speakers devoiced English final obstruents, while Chinese speakers added a final schwa-like vowel. Eckman argued that the solutions chosen could be predicted from the overall patterns of Spanish and Chinese, but could not be described as the transfer of a standard phonological rule from the native language. It is our claim that because this is a universal tendency, based on the physical nature of the human articulatory apparatus, it is not surprising to find a deviance from both native and target language phonological systems. This type of universal does have a strong effect on L2 learners and can in fact override facts of native and/or target languages. This is further supported by recent research by Eckman (this volume) where he claims that there will be no deviations from both the native language *and* the target language unless the deviation can be accounted for on the basis of universal principles.

Another example of the effects of physically based universals involve the pronunciation of palatalized consonants in Russian by speakers of languages without distinctive palatalization. Often the degree of palatalization is affected by the surrounding environment, i.e. the consonants assimilate to nearby sounds, which is motivated by a physical factor. For example, native

Lak speakers are more likely to produce fully palatalized consonants in Russian only after front vowels (Šurpaeva 1979), a pattern found neither in Lak nor in Russian.

3.2.   We turn next to the class of universals that is probably most responsible for the upsurge of interest in universals over the past two decades: that of word order. This of course goes back to Greenberg's classic article (1963). Subsequently, several articles have appeared concerning universals of word order — in diachrony, synchrony, and acquisition. The universals that have attracted the most attention have been those concerned with predictions that can be made based on the relative order of verbs and direct objects. For example, the relative orderings of nouns and adjectives, nouns and genitives, auxiliary verbs and 'lexical head' verbs, and the presence of prepositions or postpositions can be predicted (at least in the sense of statistical universals or universal tendencies) on the basis of whether the language is a VO or an OV language.

Vennemann (1975) and Lehman (1974) have argued that there is a psychological basis for the predominant orderings, but to our knowledge no direct evidence has been offered in support of this thesis. Moreover, there is counter-evidence. Several languages violate the predominant orderings and there is little evidence that such systems are unstable. There are even languages that change from orderings relatively consistent with their putative normative orderings into less preferred orderings (e.g. several Slavic languages have changed from NA to AN order, see Ard 1975). Nevertheless, it appears that the best explanation of the ordering relationships is a diachronic one. As Givón (1971) and Jeffers and Lehiste (1979) suggest, items that violate the preferred orderings are *replaced* by items that do not. In other words the mechanisms through which these universals arise is the creation of new items and structures.

If these relationships are indeed motivated by diachronic factors, then it is quite reasonable to expect that universals will have little or no effect on the second language acquisition process. We will now present some evidence in support of this.

One of the strongest of these word order universals is that languages with basic verb-final order exhibit the order *lexical verb + auxiliary* rather than the reverse. In dependent clauses German is verb final and the auxiliary is placed after the lexical verb as can be seen in (2):

(2) a. Er sagte dass sie das Buch gelesen hat.
he said that she the book read has
'He said that she read the book."
b. Er sagte dass sie gestern das Buch gelesen hat
he said that she yesterday the book read has
"He said that she read the book yesterday"
c. Er sagte dass sie das Buch liest.
he said that she the book reads
"He said that she is reading the book."

In main clauses German places the verb in second position as is seen in (3):

(3) a. Sie hat das Buch gelesen.
she has the book read
"She read the book."
b. Gestern hat sie das Buch gelesen.
yesterday has she the book read
"Yesterday she read the book."
c. Sie liest das Buch.
she reads the book
"She is reading the book."

English learners of German at times place the verb phrase in the reversed order at the end of the clause — that is, Auxiliary + Lexical Verb (Large, personal communication). Examples of these error types are given in (4) below:

(4) a. *Er sagte dass sie das Buch hat gelesen
he said that she the book has read
b. *Er sagte dass der Mann das Kind wollte sehen
he said that the man the child wanted to see

Several grounds can be offered as explanations for these errors, among which is language transfer. However, the precise cause is not important for the present purposes. What is important to note is that in the domain of word order, other influences can overrule a language universal. In fact, it is plausible that universals of relative order have very little effect on the second language learner. This is not to say that learners will be expected to generate patterns that differ widely from those found in natural languages. The input they receive from the target language will guard against this. The German example is particularly interesting in that the error pattern that arises is 'sufficiently close' to what really occurs in German. In fact, this reversed order (i.e. Auxiliary + lexical verb at the end of a dependent clause) is possible in Dutch, a language closely related to German.

A second example of word order universals having little effect on L2 learners' production can be seen in the area of noun + adjective sequences. In languages with verb + object order, the typical order of adjectives and nouns is noun + adjective. English, of course, violates this tendency. If the universal had a strong effect, we would expect that a learner of a language with consistent order (such as Spanish) would have difficulty in sorting out the correct English order since it violates both the native language and universal norms. On the other hand, native English speakers learning Spanish should not have difficulty with the Spanish ordering since it is consistent with universal principles. However, we find that this prediction does not hold. First, Spanish speakers learning English make few errors in adjective-noun word orders. To verify this, we examined 29 compositions of Spanish speakers learning English at the English Language Institute, University of Michigan, and ranging in proficiency from beginning to high intermediate. In the 29 compositions there were 141 examples of adjective-noun sequences and only one example of a noun-adjective sequence. At the same time, within the sequence of adjective-noun there were numerous examples of agreement errors (e.g. *differents cities*). On the other hand, English speakers learning Spanish make errors in the adjective/noun sequence initially, although the problem is straightened out early in the learning process (Dvorak, personal communication). Again, as with Spanish learners of English, agreement remains an area in which a considerable number of errors surface. This suggests that the universal tendency has little effect on the learning of an L2.

A third example from the realm of word order universals has to do with the placement of genitives in SOV languages. Neither Greenberg (1963), in his original study, nor Hawkins (1979) found any examples of SOV languages with Adj + N order in which the genitive follows the noun. Yet English speakers learning Sanskrit and other Indian languages (which are SOV with Adj + N order) produce both orders Gen + N and N + Gen, possibly in direct translation of English constructions (e.g. the *father's* book; the top *of the house*) (Deshpande, personal communication). What is important to note is that the universal tendency of possible word orders does not affect behaviour in an L2.

3.3.   Now let us consider the acquisition of English relative clauses by second language learners. There are universals of relative clause formation which most probably have perceptual/cognitive bases.

Keenan and Comrie (1977) and Comrie and Keenan (1979) investigated relative clause structures in approximately 50 languages, finding that there exists universally an implicational hierarchy (the Accessibility Hierarchy) based on positions which can be relativized. This hierarchy is presented in (5).

(5)   SU > DO > IO > OPREP > GEN > OCOMP
      > = more accessible than
      SU = subject
      DO = direct object
      IO = indirect object
      OPREP = object of preposition
      GEN = genitive
      OCOMP = object of comparative

If a language can relativize on any of the positions on that hierarchy, then it can also relativize on any position to the left of it, that is, higher on the hierarchy. The reverse implication is not true. One cannot determine *a priori* where a language will stop on the hierarchy. A second part of this universal concerns pronominal reflexes within the relative clause. They are more likely in lower positions on the hierarchy than in higher ones.

While this hierarchy was established on the basis of cross-linguistic data, Keenan (1975) suggested that there is intra-linguistic validity to it as well. He presented data from native texts showing that the positions which were higher on the hierarchy were used more frequently than those lower on the hierarchy. In fact, there was a monotonic progression from high to low. Furthermore, writers who were independently judged 'good' used more relative clauses at the lower end of the hierarchy than did writers independently judged less good.

Keenan and Bimson (1975) and Givón (1975) have suggested different explanations for this universal, but both are in the class of perceptual, cognitive explanations. From this we predict that there is a strong likelihood of influence on many different aspects of language use during the second language acquisition process.

We would like to illustrate this by presenting relevant data from second language learners. Gass (1979, 1980, 1983) has shown that the acquisition of relative clauses by adult L2 learners was primarily governed by universal phenomena. Learners of all languages tested followed the constraints of the Accessibility Hierarchy in their English regardless of the positions on which their own languages were able to relativize. Seventeen adult L2 learners were

TABLE 2: Relevant Relative Clause Data from the Languages Represented in the Present Study

Positions Relativizable and Pronoun Retention[1] / Languages	SU	DO	IO	OPREP	GEN	OCOMP
English	x	x	x	x	x	x
French	x	x	x	x	x	
Portuguese	x	x	x	x	x	
Italian	x	x	x	x	x	
Arabic	x	Ⓧ[2]	Ⓧ	Ⓧ	Ⓧ	Ⓧ
Persian	x	Ⓧ[2]	Ⓧ	Ⓧ	Ⓧ	
Thai	x	x	x			
Chinese	x	x	Ⓧ	Ⓧ	Ⓧ	
Korean	x	x	x	x	Ⓧ[2]	
Japanese	x	x	x	x	Ⓧ[2]	

[1] x indicates the presence of a relativization feature, and (circled) Ⓧ indicates pronominal retention in that relativized position as well.
[2] Pronominal retention is optional in this position.

tested on their knowledge of English relative clauses. Three tests were given six times over a period of four months although only 2 will be discussed in this paper. The native languages of the subjects are given in Table 2 as well as some basics of those languages with regard to relative clauses. As can be seen, the subjects were from a wide variety of native languages whose relative clause types were diversified with regard to the variables under consideration.

On the first task subjects were asked to combine two sentences which had one NP in common to form one English sentence containing a relative clause. The sentences were such that the first sentence (the one the subjects were instructed to begin with, i.e. the matrix sentence) had the head NP as either a subject or an object of its own sentence while in the second sentence the NP in common occurred in one of the six positions on the Accessibility Hierarchy. All possible combinations were represented resulting in 12 sentences.

The second task was a free composition task. Subjects wrote compositions with no controls for topic or length (other than a time limit imposed).

3.3.1.   Turning to the results of these tasks, let us look first at the written compositions. These results are given in Figure 1. In terms of frequency, not all positions were relativized, but more importantly, the hierarchical orderings were followed. This is consistent with the results of Keenan's (1975) study. While the results for this and the following figures are based on grouped data, it is important to note the results for individual languages follow the same pattern. They are presented and discussed in greater detail in Gass (1983).

FIGURE 1
Percentage of Total Relative Clauses in Free Compositions

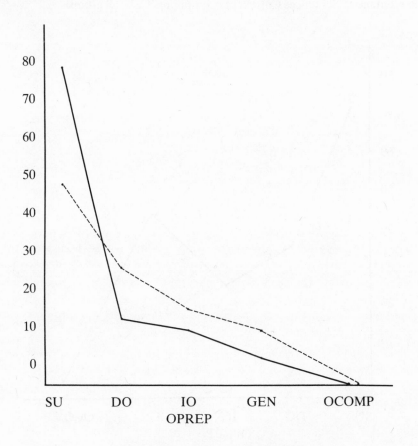

broken line represents Keenan's (1975) data

Turning to the sentence combining task, there is again evidence to put forth suggesting the positive shaping force of the Accessibility Hierarchy with regard to second language learners. First, in looking at sentences correct we find that with one exception the hierarchical orderings were followed. This is seen in Figure 2. Speakers of all languages, regardless of the positions which their own languages relativized, had more correct responses to subject relatives than to direct object relatives and so forth. There were no differences found between sentences in which the head was a subject versus those in which the head was a direct object of its own clause. Thus, the syntactic function of relativized head nouns within the matrix does not seem to have an effect.

FIGURE 2

Percentage of Sentences Correct on Combining Task (all group)

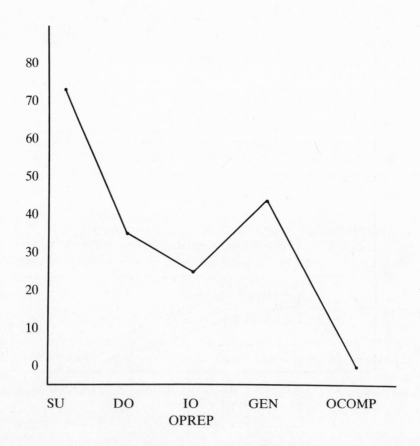

Additional evidence for the 'use' of the hierarchy comes from looking at those sentences in which the intended relative clause type was not produced. Recall that subjects were instructed to combine the sentences in the order given. This particular task had been designed so as to produce a particular type of relative clause. In some cases they failed to follow these instructions, performing some other manipulation instead. There were essentially four ways of deviating from the intended structure: 1) substitution of one lexical item for another, 2) switching the order of the two sentences so as to embed the sentence which was intended as the matrix, 3) changing the NP which was to be relativized, and 4) changing the syntactic structure of the second sentence (see Gass 1980 for further details). In all instances but one the resulting sentence was a relative clause formed on a higher position on the hierarchy than the intended one.

What was found was that avoidance[3] of the intended structure was predictable on the basis of universal principles independent of language background. Specifically, there were more examples of this type of avoidance on the lower end of the hierarchy than on the higher end. In fact, with one exception (as was also seen with the number of sentences correct) the reverse hierarchical ordering is witnessed. These results are given in Figure 3. These data then suggest greater difficulty, or at least greater confusion at the lower end of the hierarchy.

It would, however, clearly be inaccurate to claim that universal factors are the only relevant ones involved in relative clause acquisition. Even though we have presented many examples of the positive influence of a language universal, there are examples of influence from both the native and the target languages. That is, there are language specific facts which seem to counterbalance the influence of this language universal.

We will briefly present two examples from the same relative clause study to illustrate this. First we will discuss specifics relating to the native language and then specifics relating to the target language — in this case, English.

The examples come from instances of pronominal reflexes in the relative clause; that is, sentences like (6):

(6)   *The man that I saw *him* is a professor at the university.

Keenan and Comrie found that the likelihood of languages having pronominal copies in the relative clause is inversely related to the hierarchy. That is, it is most likely in OCOMP relatives and least likely in subject relatives. This was found to be true for all speakers in this study regardless of whether or not their languages had pronominal reflexes. However, perhaps, even more interesting is the pattern of pronoun retention in these data which reflects language transfer and that which reflects universal strategies. In Gass 1979 it was found that there were significant differences between speakers of languages with and speakers of languages without pronominal reflexes in relative clauses only on the higher positions of the hierarchy, suggesting the use of one's native language. On the other hand, no such differences between language groups were found on the lower end of the hierarchy, suggesting universal difficulty with the processing and production of these complex structures.

FIGURE 3

Percentage of Sentences Avoided on Combining Task (all group)

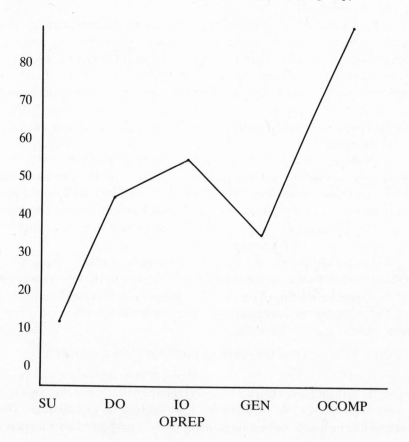

Turning finally to the targer language, we found that in all measures discussed so far — frequency of use, accuracy, and avoidance — the hierarchical orderings were not strictly followed. Possessive relatives were more accurately produced and less frequently avoided than would have been predicted by a consideration of the accessibility hierarchy alone. It seems that there is something about the English genitive relative which makes it particularly unusual and hence more salient. One possible explanation for this increased prominence is the unique coding of the relative marker *whose*. The use of *whose* is restricted to genitives. Furthermore, genitives allow no other marker. Another possible explanation suggested by Jessica Wirth is that the relative ease of the genitive has to do with its position in the sentence. For example, in (7) below,

(7)   The man *whose daughter* John loves....

it is possible that the phrase *whose daughter* was viewed as a unit and interpreted as a direct object of the verb *loves*. In the corpus of this study all examples would have been interpreted as either subjects or direct objects, thus accounting for the relatively high number of correct responses. It may be that each of these explanations is appropriate to account for the deviance in both the productive and receptive tasks these data were based on.

Thus, while the accessibility hierarchy is an important guiding force in second language acquisition, intralingual factors can and do play a role.

Summarizing the relative clause data, these results indicate that 1) universal principles are necessary to the understanding and interpretation of second language data, 2) native language and target language factors can play a counterbalancing role, and 3) universals can affect many aspects of performance by second language learners, including errors produced, frequency of production of some language items as opposed to others, and avoidance.

A second example of universals based on hierarchical data comes from a recent study by Frawley (1981). Frawley based his L2 study on work by Dryer (1980) in which Dryer suggests a universal hierarchy of complement structures. According to this hierarchy, given in (8),

(8)   Complement hierarchy (Dryer 1980)
       clause-final > clause-initial > clause internal

it is most likely for complements to be in clause-final position and least likely in clause-internal position. Dryer presents arguments for this hierarchy suggesting that the most appropriate explanation is in terms of cognitive principles or the function of language. In a sentence construction task, Frawley found that L2 learners followed the hierarchical orderings regardless of the positions complements occupied in the subjects' native languages.

3.4. The next and final area of language universals we will consider from the second language acquisition perspective concerns the semantics of tense/aspect systems.

In analyzing the semantics of tense/aspect systems, linguists have typically investigated the entire meaning range of an element in the system and given a single, all-embracing description to account for this entire range. For example, one could provide a single characterization of *all* uses of the form (am/is/are + VERB-ing) in English. This often leads to insightful results within a language system, but obscures relationships between the tense/aspect systems of different languages.

In what follows we investigate the influence on second language acquisition of the following proposed universals (based on Kurylowicz (1964) and extended by Ard (1979a, 1981b)):

a.   There is a central meaning range, called the core, for each element of the tense/aspect system of a language.

b.   The core can be described in terms of 'distance' from a 'distinguished point of meaning' called a focus.

c.   There is a universal set of available foci from which every language may 'choose'.

d.   The semantic range of a tense/aspect element in a language is determined exclusively by the foci and pseudometric.[4]

In the study we report on in this paper, the foci for certain English tense/aspect elements were investigated, in particular those corresponding to the forms given in (9):

(9)   a. that coded by the marker is/am/are + VERB + ing
            (often called the present progressive)
        b. that coded by the marker VERB + Ø or VERB-s
            (often called simple present, generic or habitual)
        c. that coded by the marker will + VERB
            (generally called future)

The foci corresponding to each of the forms of (9) are given in (10):

(10)   a. ongoing, witnessed activity which persists for an extended period of time.

  b. law-like regular state or expectable events characteristic of their subject at the present time.

  c. states or events expected in forseeable future.

For ease of explication, these foci are described in terms of a list, as Coleman and Kay (1981) propose in their prototype semantics. However, we believe that a more adequate characterization is in terms of basic events and situations. In other words, we propose that certain events are basic, prototypical, and stereotypical and that the events are the reference points around which tense/aspect systems characterize other verbal phenomena. Importantly, it is most likely that perceptual/cognitive factors are crucial in determining which events are basic.

As stated above, these foci are universal. The primary evidence for what we have investigated until this point has come from typology and diachrony. It is beyond the scope of this paper to give detailed arguments for this claim. In brief, consider the following comparison of English and Hopi. Both languages have forms with the focus being ongoing, witnessed action which persists. In English the pseudometric that measures distance from this focus gives most weight to presentness and persistence of the action, while in Hopi the pseudometric gives most weight to the fact that the action was witnessed. In diachrony, new tense/aspect elements that arise are centered around one of the existing foci in highly constrained manners. Other dynamic aspects of tense/aspect systems are similarly constrained by the presence of foci, aspects such as the spread of meaning of certain elements, the loss of elements, etc.

Before proceeding with the discussion, we would like to compare this model to more common accounts of tense/aspect systems. Essentially, this model can be seen as a generalization and refinement of more traditional models. What is traditionally described as progressive would be reformulated as follows: the focus includes on-going action and the pseudo-metric gives highest weight to this one parameter. That is, other things being equal, something with on-going action would be closer to this focus than something without. What is traditionally called a distinctive feature could be modeled by assigning total weighting to the parameter corresponding to the distinctive feature and no weight at all to any redundant feature.

Past typologies of tense/aspect systems have described pseudometrics, as they have discussed the features, the measures of distance important for tense/aspect elements. Thus, Comrie (1976) discusses progressives, perfectives etc. cross-linguistically. In addition to Comrie, important typological results are found in Bull (1963), El'čeva (1978) and Traugott (1976), a work which is important for its consideration of first and second language acquisition.

Since these accounts can be viewed as particular instances of this more general model, nothing is lost in considering data from this more comprehensive format. In this paper we concentrate on the most universal part of this model, the foci.

The particular universal facet of tense/aspect systems we will consider is the following: there is a basic sense of tense/aspect elements in all languages. Furthermore, when different languages are compared, there is a germ of similarity in that elements can be grouped so that the same basic situation is highlighted as prototypical for all these languages. In short, Spanish, English and Japanese, for example, differ in the *ranges* of tense/aspect elements, but in the core meaning of these languages there is fundamental similarity.

3.5. To demonstrate the importance of this fundamental similarity in core meaning, we present a subset of data gathered from 139[5] L2 learners studying at the English Language Institute of the University of Michigan. The native language backgrounds of the subjects tested were of a wide variety; however, for statistical purposes we will only present the data from the Japanese and Spanish speakers for they were the only two language groups with large enough numbers of speakers to allow statistical analyses. The subjects represent a range of proficiency levels from the first to the sixth of a six-level intensive course program, with the lowest level group consisting of speakers with minimal proficiency and the highest group consisting of pre-academic students.

There were four tasks given to the subjects, all dealing with the three tense/aspect elements discussed above: 1) a single sentence intuition task; 2) a contextualized intuition task; 3) a grouped intuition task; and 4) a guided sentence writing task.

The first task consisted of 29 randomized sentences all containing an underlined tense/aspect element in which subjects were asked to give grammaticality judgments, concentrating on underlined elements of the sentences. They were to respond to one of four categories — definitely correct, possibly correct, possibly incorrect or definitely incorrect. The second task was similar to the first. However, the sentences on this task were contextualized in short conversations as opposed to being in isolation. On the third task, the sentences were displayed on the page in groups of five with the only changes in the groups being changes in the verb forms. Examples of these 3 tasks are given in (11):

(11) Tasks

(Task 1) John *is travelling* to New York tomorrow.

(Task 2) Mary: I need to send a package to my mother in a hurry. Do you think the post office will get it there in two days?

Jane: Where does she live?

Mary: In New York.

Jane: Oh, in that case John can take it. John *is travelling* to New York tomorrow.

(Task 3) The ship *sailed* to Miami tomorrow.
The ship *is sailing* to Miami tomorrow.
The ship *will sail* to Miami tomorrow.
The ship *sails* to Miami tomorrow.
The ship *has sailed* to Miami tomorrow.

The fourth task was one in which subjects were given a verb form and told to write as long a sentence as possible including that form.

All subjects did task 1 and either 2 or 3. Only a subset of subjects did the writing task. Decisions concerning who would be assigned which task were made with an effort to balance different tasks among subjects of different native languages and proficiency levels.

With regard to our model, we predict that subjects will respond more positively to sentences which refer to situations closer to the universal focus than to sentences which do not.

3.5.1. Semantics is particularly difficult to study directly in second language acquisition because one cannot determine *exactly* or, at times, even approximately what a learner intended by an utterance or what was interpreted from a sentence produced by another. For this reason we have concentrated on sentences with gross differences in canonical interpretations rather than fine ones. We are concerned with how differences in canonical interpretations affect learner performance, not with how learners actually process sentences.

We turn first to the category typically glossed as the progressive or, for the sake of convenience, the expanded form. Subjects were given sentences with this form describing a wide range of situations. We found that judgments of correctness of these sentences depended on the closeness of the canonical

TABLE 3
Results from Verb + ing Tasks

	Japanese (n=37)	Spanish (n=52)	
	% definitely correct		
Task 1			
Sentence			
1	76	88	John is smoking American cigarettes now.
2	32	8	John is travelling to New York tomorrow.
3	19	81	Dan is seeing better now.
4	24	46	The new bridge is connecting Detroit and Windsor.
5	5	8	Mary is being in Chicago now.
Task 2			
Sentence	(n=22)	(n=32)	
6	68	75	Mike: What kind of drink is that?
			Walter: Oh, that man is drinking apple cider.
7	36	26	Mary: I need to send a package to my mother in a hurry. Do you think the post office will get it there in two days?
			Jane: Where doe she live?
			Mary: In New York.
			Jane: Oh, in that case John can take it. John is travelling to New York tomorrow.
8	14	59	Bill: Did you hear about Dan's operation in the hospital?
			David: No, what happened?
			Bill: They operated on his eyes. He says he is seeing better now.
Task 3 (sentences in groups)			
Sentence	(n=15)	(n=19)	
9	87	94	Sam is wearing a tie now.
10	33	18	The ship is sailing to New York tomorrow.
11	13	29	The new law is prohibiting driving without seat belts.
12	53	0	Your car is being ready now.

Distinctness Matrices[1]

| Japanese | | | | | | Spanish | | | |

Sentences	1	2	3	4	5		1	2	3	4	5
1	-					1	-				
2	dist.	-				2	dist.	-			
3	dist.	non-dist.	-			3	non-dist.	dist.	-		
4	dist.	non-dist.	dist.	-		4	dist.	dist.	dist.	-	
5	dist.	non-dist.	non-dist.	non-dist.	-	5	dist.	non-dist.	dist.	dist.	-

Sentences	6	7	8		6	7	8
6	-			6	-		
7	non-dist.	-		7	dist.	-	
8	dist.	non-dist.	-	8	non-dist.	non-dist.	-

Sentences	9	10	11	12		9	10	11	12
9	-				9	-			
10	non-dist.[2]	-			10	dist.	-		
11	non-dist.	non-dist.	-		11	dist.	non-dist.	-	
12	non-dist.	non-dist.	non-dist.	-	12	dist.	non-dist.	non-dist.	-

[1] Distinctness indicates that the response patterns for the sentences in question is significant at at least the .01 level on two measures: the Wilcoxen signed sum of ranks test for contingency table data and median test.

[2] Distinct on one of the measures only.

TABLE 4
Guided writing task (VERB + ing data)

% core-like[1]		% non-core-like	
Japanese	Spanish	Japanese	Spanish
82 (14)	81 (30)	18 (3)	19 (7)

[1] Raw data in ( )

interpretation of the given sentence to the focus. That is, the results basically correspond with what would be predicted on the basis of universal principles. The results for both Spanish and Japanese learners are given in Tables 3 and 4, along with statistics (viz. the median test and the Wilcoxen signed sum of ranks test for contingency table data) performed on within-language comparisons which measured differences in the patterns of *all* responses and not only the correct responses.

We can see that the most acceptable sentence in both groups was that sentence with canonical interpretation closest to the focus, with the Japanese accepting it 76% of the time and Spanish 88% of the time. With some exceptions, the less focus-like, the less it is viewed as acceptable (cf. also Kellerman 1977, 1979, 1983). There are some interesting language specific exceptions which will be discussed later.

Looking at the results across tasks (displayed vertically), we see that the same ordering obtains, albeit with different percentages.

A further indication that there is a recognizable distinction between sentences describing situations close to the focus and those further away comes from the writing task. This is seen in Table 4. Recall that subjects were given verb forms and told to write sentences using those forms. In an attempt to guarantee that the subjects made their meanings clear and unambiguous, they were instructed to make their sentences as long as possible. An example is in order: if they were given the word *running* and then wrote 'He is running', it would be impossible to correctly interpret the intent of the sentence with regard to the time frame of the act. Of the sentences which could be unambiguously assigned to focus-like or non-focus-like categories, the Spanish speakers wrote 30 which could be called focus-like and 7 which were not, while for Japanese speakers the results were in the same direction, 14 focus-like and 3 not.

In Tables 5-8 we present similar results for the other two verbal forms, again finding a similar directionality of results.

4. *Discussion*

What we have presented here are data from adult L2 learners of English concerning their performance on tasks dealing with the English tense/aspect system. The tasks were designed to elicit information about universal principles, principles which have to do with the way one views the world (cognitive/perceptual in our framwork), and hence, according to our framework, have a moderate to high likelihood of having an influence on L2 acquisition. We found a verification of our original hypothesis that subjects will respond more positively to sentences which refer to situations closer to the universal focus than to sentences which do not. In the data for expanded forms on Table 3 there were more correct responses to the sentences referring to situations describing an on-going action than to sentences describing events which will take place in the future or which describe states with limited duration. (Again, exceptions will be dealt with later.)

As we stated above, the focus for simple forms (VERB + Ø or VERB + s) is:

> a law-like regular state or repeatable event characteristic of its subject at a given time

As expected, subjects responded most positively to two sentence types — 1) those with the verb *to be* describing a present state, and 2) those expressing a habitual or generic event — and least positively to those which involve future actions.

The results for the *will* form are similar, with the most correct responses given for those sentences which refer to situations describing an action which will take place in the future and least positively to those forms referring to a present possible situation, in a probabilistic sense.

In these data we have seen that the orderings are universal but the distance between elements is language-specific. Therefore, we would not expect there to be comparability across languages with regard to the specific percentages of acceptability, only with the relative ordering.

In general, we found that the Japanese followed these universal principles more closely than did the Spanish speakers. Additional factors are important for the Spanish speakers, but not for the Japanese speakers. The responses to the two sentences in (12) below are particularly interesting.

(12) a. Dan is seeing better now.
      b. John is travelling to New York tomorrow.

Results on chi-square showed a significant difference between Spanish and Japanese speaker performance on these two sentences ($x^2 = 12.23$, df=3, $p < .01$, for sentence 12a; $x^2 = 34.55$, df=3, $p < .01$, for sentence 12b). Spanish speakers are more likely to judge 12a as grammatical while Japanese speakers are more likely than Spanish speakers to judge 12b as grammatical. Literal translations of both sentences into Spanish yield grammatical sentences with roughly the same senses as those in English. Therefore, an explanation based solely on transfer would not account for the differential results for these two sentences.

TABLE 5
Results from Verb + Ø/VERB-s data

	Japanese (n=37)	Spanish (n=52)	
	% definitely correct		
Task 1			
Sentence			
1	92	88	Mary is in Chicago now.
2	73	79	The new bridge connects Detroit and Windsor.
3	43	65	Dan sees better now.
4	51	56	Fred smokes American cigarettes now.
5	19	8	John travels to New York tomorrow.
Task 2			
Sentence	(n=22)	(n=32)	
6	86	72	Salesclerk: Anything else? How about some cigarettes? Bob: I don't like cigarettes. I smoke cigars.
7	32	28	Tom: I need to get to London as soon as possible. Travel Agent: Let me see. There are no flights leaving today, but Pan Am flies to London tomorrow.
Task 3	(n=15)	(n=19)	
8	80	100	Your car is ready now.
9	73	78	The new law prohibits driving without seat belts.
10	80	72	Sam wears ties now.
11	13	17	The ship sails to Miami tomorrow.

Distinctness Matrices[1]

Japanese						Spanish				
Sentences	1	2	3	4	5	1	2	3	4	5
1	-					1 -				
2	non-dist.	-				2 non-dist.	-			
3	dist.	dist.	-			3 dist.	dist.	-		
4	dist.	dist.	non-dist.	-		4 dist.	dist.	non-dist.	-	
5	dist.	dist.	dist.	dist.	-	5 dist.	dist.	dist.	dist.	-

Sentences	6	7		6	7
6	-		6	-	
7	dist.	-	7	dist.	-

Sentences	8	9	10	11	8	9	10	11
8	-				8 -			
9	non-dist.	-			9 non-dist.	-		
10	non-dist.	non-dist.	-		10 non-dist.	non-dist.	-	
11	dist.	dist.	dist.	-	11 dist.	dist.	dist.	-

[1] Distinctness indicates that the response patterns for the sentences in question is significant at at least the .01 level on two measures: the Wilcoxen signed sum of ranks test for contingency table data and median test.

TABLE 6
Guided writing task (VERB + Ø/VERB-s data)

% core-like[1]		% non-core-like	
Japanese	Spanish	Japanese	Spanish
100 (20)	100 (45)	0 (0)	0 (0)

[1] Raw data in ( )

TABLE 7
Results from *will* + VERB data

	Japanese (n=37)	Spanish (n=52)	
	% definitely correct		
Task 1			
Sentence			
1	81	86	John will travel to N.Y. tomorrow.
2	87	67	The new bridge will connect Detroit and Windsor.
3	14	10	Mary will be in Chicago now.
4	3	10	John will smoke American cigarettes now.
Task 2			
Sentence	(n=22)	(n=32)	
5	91	84	Laura: I need to return these books to the library.
			Jason: If they are not due today, I can return them. I will go to the library tomorrow.
6	32	29	Carl: Could I speak to Jack please?
			Betty: I'm sorry. He has already left on his trip to Hawaii: He left a few hours ago, so he will be in Chicago now.
7	0	10	Miriam: Have you finished your homework yet?
			Sandra: I will do it last night.
Task 3			
Sentence	(n=15)	(n=19)	
8	100	95	The ship will sail to Miami tomorrow.
9	67	47	The new law will prohibit driving without seat belts.
10	7	26	Your car will be ready now.
11	0	11	Sam will wear ties now.

Distinctness Matrices[1]

Japanese					Spanish			
Sentences	1	2	3	4	1	2	3	4
1	-				1 -			
2	non-dist. -				2 non-dist. -			
3	dist.	dist.	-		3 dist.	dist.	-	
4	dist.	dist.	non-dist. -		4 dist.	dist.	non-dist. -	

Sentences	5	6	7	5	6	7
5	-			5 -		
6	dist.	-		6 dist.	-	
7	dist.	dist.	-	7 dist.	non-dist.	-

Sentences	8	9	10	11	8	9	10	11
8	-				8 -			
9	non-dist. -				9 non-dist. -			
10	dist.	dist.	-		11 dist.	non-dist. -		
11	dist.	dist.	non-dist. -		11 dist.	dist.	non-dist. -	

[1] Distinctness indicates that the response patterns for the sentences in question is significant at at least the .01 level on two measures: the Wilcoxen signed sum of ranks test for contingency table data and median test.

TABLE 8
Guided writing task (*will* + VERB data)

	% core-like[1]		% non-core-like	
	Japanese	Spanish	Japanese	Spanish
	100 (18)	100 (49)	0 (0)	0 (0)

[1] Raw data in ( )

Two hypotheses developed by Kellerman (1977, 1979, 1983) are helpful in accounting for these results. First, the likelihood that one facet of a learner's NL will affect L2 usage depends on what Kellerman calls the learner's 'psychotypology'. Part of the learner's psychotypology involves the learner's perceived 'distance' between the native language and target language, at least for a particular local domain, e.g. syntax, etc. This perceived distance often changes as proficiency changes. The origins of a learner's psychotypology are many, including experience with the target language, actual linguistic typology, a learner's own psychological organization of the native language, and other languages the learner is familiar with. The more closely related the NL and TL are in the learner's psychotypology, the more likely the NL is to affect target language use.

Second, Kellerman sets up a continuum of language specific to language neutral phenomena. The more language specific a phenomenon is perceived to be, the less likely the learner is to transfer that phenomenon. For example, idioms are often considered language specific and relatively unavailable for transfer. Kellerman has presented experimental evidence showing that learners do differentiate between more basic core meanings of lexical items (which in his framework are language neutral) and more peripheral non-core meanings (language specific) of these items in their native language. He has further demonstrated that they are more likely to believe that translation equivalents in a psychotypologically close second language share the core meanings rather than the non-core meanings. Core meanings are more often transferred than non-core meanings.

There is good reason to believe that English is psychotypologically closer even in verbal semantics for Spanish learners than for Japanese learners. In general, due to areal and genetic factors, Spanish resembles English much more closely than Japanese does. Ard (1982) has shown that this holds true for lexical semantics as well. Moreover, the descriptions for the semantic functions of verbal paradigms found in grammar books (Lehmann 1951, Bull 1961) are more divergent for Japanese and English than for Spanish and English. Thus, based on Kellerman's hypothesis, we would expect that the semantics of tense/aspect elements in Spanish would affect the English language performance of Spanish learners more than would facts of Japanese affect Japanese learners.

This prediction is borne out in these data. The judgments of Japanese speakers correspond to what would be predicted on a universal basis. The facts of Japanese apparently made little difference in these judgments. That is, transfer is of little significance.

As Kellerman stated, the greater distance a meaning is from the core meaning range, the less likely that meaning is assumed to be conveyed by a translation equivalent. In Spanish as in English the future sense involved in (12b) is further away from the core of tense/aspect elements centered around ongoing, witnessed activity than is the 'state with limited duration' involved in (12a). The latter situation is perhaps difficult to imagine, but not as far from the universal focus.[6] Based on Kellerman's hypothesis, we would predict that Spanish speakers, compared with speakers of more 'distant' languages, would respond more affirmatively to sentences such as (12a) than sentences such as (12b). With the b sentence we have an example of what could be called 'anti-transfer'. Spanish speakers tend to reject b *because* it is found in Spanish and because it is far from the core meaning. This is an especially strong counterexample to the predictions made by the contrastive analysis hypothesis. Here, we have an example of an interaction between universal principles and native language facts which makes it *less* likely that a pattern will be accepted in the target language.

We might further speculate that anti-transfer may also be involved in the high acceptance of sentence (12a) by Spanish speakers. In Spanish, as in English, the verb *see* does not commonly occur in the progressive, even when describing present situations. Possibly Spanish speakers consider this an idiosyncratic fact about Spanish and therefore assume that this lexical restriction does not hold in English. Hence, *is seeing* would be the normal form for describing present situations in English.

5. Conclusion

In this paper then we have established a framework in which one can meaningfully investigate the influences of language universals on the adult second language acquisition process. This assertion is an empirical one which can be tested. If it could be shown that the predictions we have made are incorrect, then the framework would have to be modified or rejected. For example, we have claimed that universals with a physical basis are highly likely to have an influence on the adult second language acquisition process. If it were the case that after examining many test cases of universals of this type, no influence could be found, our hypothesis would then require modification or rejection. However, it is just this type of test case which must be examined before more precise prediction values can be established. It is important to keep in mind that what we are proposing is a probabilistic model, not an absolute one.

The framework we have offered is still in a programmatical stage. Nevertheless, much has already been learned about the influences of language universals on the adult second language acquisition process. At present, the research has been primarily in one direction: discovering how language universals can be used to better explain details of adult second language acquisition. As this framework becomes more highly articulated and refined, explanations in the opposite direction will be more plausible. Once it is established that universals of a particular type will have a particular effect on the adult second language acquisitions process, then data from adult second language acquisition will be available for testing a claim that a phenomenon is a language universal of a certain type.

Language universals are just one facet of linguistic theory. As research progresses, we hope there will be increased cross-fertilization between theoretical and so-called applied linguistics. In the future adult second language acquisition may prove just as normal a data source for linguistic description and theory as are native speaker intuitional judgments.

NOTES

*) We are grateful to Bill Rutherford and Robin Scarcella for comments on an earlier draft. We also appreciate the statistical assistance which David Smith of the University of Michigan provided. An earlier version of this paper was presented at the University of Michigan Linguistics Colloquium. We are grateful to our colleagues for helpful comments.

1) Precision with regard to defining characteristics of a universal is beyond the scope of this paper. However, minimally we consider a universal to be an essential property of the class of human languages, actual and potential. Thus a universal holds true for all or almost all (in the case of statistical universals) languages. Furthermore, we agree with Chomsky and Halle (1968) that true universals should not be due to an accidental showing of the set of observed languages compared to the larger class of possible languages, although it is not clear how one could determine such an accidental skewing.

2) Note that statistical universals and universal tendencies are not two different notions but merely two different names for the same notion (cf. Comrie's paper in this volume).

3) The term 'avoidance' has been discussed in recent literature on second language acquisition, most notably by Schachter (1974) and Kleinmann (1977). Avoidance implies some intentionality on the part of the learner not to do something. We feel that the data discussed in this paper fit this concept of avoidance. However, it should be noted that the data are not similar to those discussed by Schachter which come simply from learners' lack of use of particular structures.

4) A pseudometric is simply a mathematically formalized generalization of distance. As with other measures of distance, 1) the distance between any two objects is always equal to or greater than zero, 2) any object is zero distance away from itself, and 3) the distance between any two objects is always based on the shortest path between them. What is more general about a pseudomet-

ric is that two objects may be zero distance apart without being equal. An everyday example of a pseudometric is difference in time. Any two cities in the same time zone (such as Los Angeles and Seattle) would be zero distance apart, while the distance between Los Angeles and Chicago would be two hours.

5) The data presented in this paper represent the results from levels two through six only. Level one was given a subset of the items given to the other levels in an effort to make the task shorter given their very limited abilities in English. The tasks given to the other levels consisted of the items relevant to this study as well as items with other verbal forms. These latter were eliminated for the lowest level. The results for the lowest level were consistent with the other results, with the most correct responses given to the core items and the least to the non-core items.

6) The distinction we are making between focus and core is a subtle one. Core is determined on a language particular basis. It corresponds to the basic meaning of a lexeme or a grammatical morpheme. Focus, on the other hand, is determined on a language independent, and hence universal, basis, which can be specified via the characteristics of certain basic situations. The theoretical claim being brought forward is that cores (which are language particular) can be accounted for in terms of foci (which are universal).

REFERENCES

Adjémian, C. 1976. On the nature of interlanguage systems. *Language Learning 26*:297-320.

Anttila, R. 1972. *An Introduction to Historical and Comparative Linguistics*. New York: Macmillan.

Ard, J. 1975. *Raising and Word Order in Diachronic Syntax*. Doctoral Dissertation, University of California, Los Angeles.

Ard, J. 1979a. A comparative and historical study of locative-based periphrastic verbal forms in Fula dialects. *Studies in African Linguistics 10*:119-158.

Ard, J. 1979b. A diachronic explanation for constraints on transformations. Paper presented at the IVth International Conference on Historical Linguistics. Stanford, California.

Ard, J. 1981. Acquisition of the semantics of the English verbal system. Paper presented at the TESOL Conference, Detroit, Michigan.

Ard, J. 1982. The use of bilingual dictionaries by ESL students while writing. *I.T.L. Review of Applied Linguistics 58*: 1-27.

Ard, J. 1983. Qualitative differential models of the semantics of tense/aspect systems. Unpublished ms.

Bull, W. 1963. *Time, Tense and the Verb: a study in theoretical and applied linguistics, with particular attention to Spanish*. University of California Publications in Linguistics 19.

Chomsky, N., and M. Halle. 1968. *The Sound Pattern of English*. New York: Harper and Row.

Coleman, L., and P. Kay. 1981. Prototype semantics: the English word *lie*. *Language 57*:26-44.

Comrie, B. 1976. *Aspect*. Cambridge: Cambridge University Press.

Comrie, B. 1981. *Language Universals and Linguistic Typology*. Chicago: University of Chicago Press.

Comrie, B., and E. Keenan. 1979. Noun phrase accessibility revisited. *Language 55*:649-664.

Eckman, F. 1981. On the naturalness of interlanguage phonological rules. *Language Learning 31*:195-216.

El'čeva, A. (ed.). 1978. *Voprosy sopostavitel'noj aspektologii. Problemy sovremennogo teoretičeskogo i sinxronno-opisatel'nogo jazykoznanija*. Vypusk I. Leningrad: Izd. Leningradskogo universiteta.

Flynn, S. 1981. Effects of the reversal of principal branching direction (from L1 to L2) in L2 acquisition. *Cornell Working Papers* Vol. 2.

Frawley, W. 1981. The complement hierarchy: evidence for language universals from L2. Paper presented at the Winter LSA meeting, New York.

Gass, S. 1979. Language transfer and universal grammatical relations. *Language Learning 29*:327-344.

Gass, S. 1980. An investigation of syntactic transfer in adult L2 learners. In Scarcella and Krashen (eds.), *Research in Second Language Acquisition*. Rowley, Mass.: Newbury House.

Gass, S. 1983. Second language acquisition and language universals. In Di Pietro, Frawley, and Wedel (eds.), *First Delaware Symposium on Language Studies*. Newark, Delaware: University of Delaware Press.

Gass, S., and J. Ard. 1980. L2 data: their relevance for language universals. *TESOL Quarterly 14*:443-452.

Givón, T. 1971. Historical Syntax and Synchronic Morphology: An Archaeologist's Field Trip. *Papers from the Seventh Regional Meeting, Chicago Linguistics Society*.

Givón, T. 1975. Promotion, NP accessibility and case marking: toward understanding grammars. *Working Papers in Language Universals 19*:55-125.

Greenberg, J. 1963. Some universals of grammar with particular reference to the order of meaningful elements. In Greenberg (ed.), *Universals of Language*. Cambridge: MIT Press.

Gundel, J., and E. Tarone. 1983. Language transfer and the acquisition of pronominal anaphora. In Gass and Selinker (eds.), *Language Transfer in Language Learning*. Rowley, Mass.: Newbury House.

Habermas, J. 1974. Zur Entwickling der Interaktionskompetenz. ms.
Habermas, J. 1977. Zur Einführung *Die Entwicklung des Ichs.*, R. Dölbert, J. Habermas and C. Nunner-Winkler (eds.). Köln.
Hawkins, J. 1979. Implicational universals as predictors of word order change. *Language 55*:619-648.
Jeffers, J., and I. Lehiste. 1979. *Principles and Methods for Historical Linguistics.* Cambridge: MIT Press.
Keenan, E. 1975. Variation in universal grammar. In Fasold and Shuy (eds.), *Analyzing Variation in Language.* Washington, D.C.: Georgetwon University Press.
Keenan, E., and K. Bimson. 1975. Perceptual complexity and the cross-language distribution of relative clauses and NP-question types. *Papers from the Parasession on Functionalism*: 253-259. Chicago: Chicago Linguistic Society.
Keenan, E., and B. Comrie. 1977. Noun phrase accessibility and universal grammar. *Linguistic Inquiry 8*:63-99.
Kellerman, E. 1977. Towards a characterization of transfer in second language learning. *Interlanguage Studies Bulletin 2*:58-146.
Kellerman, E. 1979. Transfer and non-transfer: where we are now. *Studies in Second Language Acquisition 2*:37-57.
Kellerman, E. 1983. Now you see it, now you don't. In Gass and Selinker (eds.), *Language Transfer in Language Learning.* Rowley, Mass.: Newbury House.
Kleinman, H. 1977. Avoidance behavior in adult second language acquisition. *Language Learning 27*:93-107.
Kurylowicz, J. 1964. On the methods of internal reconstruction. In Lunt (ed.), *Proceedings of the Ninth International Congress of Linguistics.* The Hague: Mouton.
Lehmann, W., and L. Faust. 1951. *A Grammar of Formal Written Japanese.* Harvard-Yenching Institute Studies, Volume V. Cambridge: Harvard University Press.
Lehmann, W. 1974. *Proto-Indo European Syntax.* Austin: University of Texas Press.
McCarthy, T. 1981. *The Critical Theory of Jürgen Habermas.* Cambridge: MIT Press.
Ohala, J. 1972. How to represent natural sound patterns. *Project on Linguistic Analysis, No. 16*:40-57.
Passy, P. 1891. *Étude sur les changements phonétiques et leur caractères généraux.* Paris.

Rutherford, W. 1983. Language typology and language transfer. In Gass and Selinker (eds.), *Language Transfer in Language Learning*. Rowley, Mass.: Newbury House.

Schachter, J. 1974. An error in error analysis. *Language Learning 24*:205-214.

Schachter, J., and W. Rutherford. 1979. Discourse function and language transfer. *Working Papers in Bilingualism 19*:1-12.

Schmidt, M. 1980. Coordinate structures and language universals in interlanguage. *Language Learning 30*:397-416.

Sharwood Smith, M. 1980. Contrastive studies and acquisition theory. Paper presented at the Conference on Contrastive Projects. Charkowy, Poland.

Sinclair-de Zwaart, H. 1973. Language acquisition and cognitive development. In Moore (ed.), *Cognitive Development and the Acquisition of Language*. New York: Academic Press.

Slobin, D. 1973. Cognitive prerequisites for the development of grammar. In Ferguson and Slobin (eds.), *Studies in Child Language Development*. New York: Holt, Rinehart and Winston.

Šurpaeva, M.I. 1979. Fonetiko-fonologičeskie javlenija interferencii v uslovijax laksko-russkogo dvujazyčija. In N.A. Baskakov (ed.), *Puti razvitija nacional no-russkogo dvujazyčija v nerusskix školax RCFCR*. Moskva: Nauka.

Traugott, E.C. 1976. Natural semantax: its role in the study of second language acquisition. *Actes du 5ème Colloque de linguistique appliquée de Neuchâtel. The Notions of Simplification, Interlanguages and Pidgins and their Relation to Second Language Pedagogy*. Corder and Roulet (eds.).

Vennemann, T. 1975. Topics, subjects and word order: from SXV to SVX via TVX. In Anderson and Jones (eds.), *Historical Linguistics*. Amsterdam: North-Holland Publishing Co.

Whorf, B. 1956. *Language, Thought and Reality*. Carroll (ed.). Cambridge: MIT Press.

COMMENTS ON THE PAPER BY GASS AND ARD

LORRAINE KUMPF
University of California, Los Angeles

My comments on this provocative paper by Sue and Josh will come in two parts: the first concerning the framework presented, and the second concerning the supporting studies.

The paper claims that predictions can be made about the influence of a universal on the process of acquisition and, depending on the type and source of universal, that these influences will be manifest in various ways. On the basis of the source, and on other factors such as the validity of the critical age hypothesis and societal versus individual orientation, the probability of influence was predicted in terms of low, medium or high influence.

In general, I am in accord with this research: it makes good sense to claim that certain characteristics of the universal (e.g. status as absolute or statistical) will lead us to assumptions about the importance of its role in acquisition. A good example is provided by the authors: the acquisition of voiced final obstruents (the Eckman study). Recall that the rules used by the learners of English in this case are characteristic of neither the native languages (Chinese and Spanish) nor the target. Here, a universal tendency to devoice, probably based on the physical structure of human articulation seems to have overcome the influence of transfer or input. Because devoicing under these conditions is a physical universal, of 'high' influence on acquisition, the authors claim that the learners' behavior can be explained. Furthermore, similar behavior can be predicted: for example, German speakers, with final devoicing in the native language, will find it difficult to voice final obstruents in English, a language which goes against the tendency; however, English speakers learning German will not find it hard to devoice them. In the former case, where the learners have invented rules, the explanation based on the universal seems appropriate. In the latter, however, how do we separate the influence of transfer from that of the effect of the universal? English speakers can transfer a category 'final devoiced obstruent' when learning German, but German speakers cannot transfer a category 'final voiced obstruent' when learning English. Although it is obvious that transfer and universals have simultaneous effects, how can we distinguish one from the other?

The conspiring influence of transfer and universals is a problem in explaining learner behavior about which the framework can make a claim. But other problems can be seen with the construction of the framework itself, problems which leave its validity in doubt. In order to use the framework, one must type a particular universal in several ways, and I find the categorizations precarious — particularly the ones that name the 'source' of the universal. One category, the physical source, is perhaps the most clear-cut in terms of the human articulatory apparatus (and such universals help in explaining acquisition phenomena such as the one mentioned above). Yet if the universal is defined in this way, it limits the range of phenomena to which it can be applied. If the word 'physical' is extended to 'the way the world is,' as suggested by the authors, how is it to be distinguished from perception, neurological factors, or interaction? Another category, the LAD, is an abstraction which seems to have little value when discussing *process*. Furthermore, in order to use the framework, one must oppose to one another, not only these 'source' categories but also the 'valid' to the 'invalid' critical age hypothesis and the individual to his society. Of course, none of these categories is discrete, but in order to use the model for prediction, they must be perceived as discrete.

The categorization by source, type, and so on are no more than different ways in which linguists have looked at universals and acquisition. The categories are artifacts of viewpoints. The source categories, for example, may be seen as different ways of viewing the same universal. In such a view, the categories may be valid ways of looking, but the framework in its predictive sense is not. Predictions will conflict for a given universal.

It is certain that we need a language for discussing the influence of universals in acquisition, but the framework as presented does too much more than that. Obviously, factors of acquisition and characteristics of universals must be separated out in the process of analysis, but it is premature to establish those categories as the basis for prediction. At this point what is needed is more careful studies of particular acquisition situations where universals may be shown to operate, for example where the learner's language resembles neither the native nor the target languages.

Turning to the two studies presented, I have questions in the area of data collection which relate to a broader question: how can we call the results of a given task an effect of a universal, rather than an effect of something else?

Here, two intervening factors may act to shape the data: first, the effects of the subjects' language instruction, and second, the effects of the type of task used to elicit data.

Regarding the instructional effects, both the relative clause study and the tense-aspect study use as sources of data students in a particular kind of instructional environment — the English Language Institute of the University of Michigan. In the tense-aspect study I see this effect as potentially very strong. The tense-aspect system is the focal point of rule learning in the instructional setting, regardless of how broadly one wishes to define rule learning. I am not being unrealistic about the amount of conscious rule learning that goes on in the classroom; however, response to instructional method is a perfectly legitimate way to interpret the results of the tense-aspect judgements and production of these students. Whether the student succeeds in remembering the rule is beside the point — his language is affected.

The instructional environment is obviously reflected in the responses to that part of the task which tests the WILL + Verb structure. Almost all of the students judged the WILL + Verb structure to mean 'future action' and therefore unacceptable in conjunction with adverbs such as NOW. In the free-writing task, 100% of the students created WILL + Verb sentences with future interpretations. This tells me that prescriptive rule application was playing a part. When observing the spontaneously-produced data of untutored learners of English, one finds that the future is rarely expressed with WILL + Verb. It is often carried by lexicon, and when future morphology is seen at all, it is usually some form of '(be) goin to'. If the future reference is PROMISORY, as in *I'll be there* or *We'll help you*, either the base form or the contracted *'ll* (+) appears. So when the students produced WILL + Verb at 100% in the free writing task, they were tapping their inventories of prescriptive rules — the usual approach, perhaps, to any writing task.

To the authors' purpose, this might make no difference at all. The fact is that learners are relating the form to the focus 'future'. In order to validate their hypothesis about the influence of the universal, it may not matter which form appears as long as it designates the focus. But the question of how the form got there remains. In this case I am convinced that the rule learning process is operating at a different level, and overriding the effect of the universal. One may ask how the WILL + Verb form is representative of the competence of these students. Would the student, on leaving the elicitation environment, use this form to refer to the future? If so, what kind of competence does he have? If not, what was the study measuring?

In the Accessibility Hierarchy study, a further effect of instruction is seen. The genitive construction was relativized more accurately than would be predicted on the basis of the hierarchy. This looks to be the effect of the particular emphasis that the WHOSE form is given in the instructional setting. WHOSE is an emphasized form, and at that point in the hierarchy, instruction in relative clause formation usually ceases. If a comparable task were given to untutored learners of English, I think that the hierarchy would be even better supported. The WHOSE form would be rare in the input of these learners, and they would produce it less accurately or consistently.

The second intervening effect is intimately related to the effect of instruction. The influence of the task on the learner is likely to shape the kind of language he produces. In the first study, one task is the discrimination of grammaticality, a difficult task which is compounded by factors such as this: when you put a piece of paper in front of a student of a language and ask him to make grammaticality judgements, you are maximizing the probability that he will focus attention on the prescriptive rules he has learned. Such a task brings out the 'this is a test' mentality, where the desire to produce one correct answer may be translated into the strategy of applying one 'correct' rule. Of course, the attempt may not work, but the task is apt to affect the response. Similarly, the task of producing long sentences which contain prescribed verbal morphology is apt to elicit prescribed forms. How can we separate this influence from the tendency that students may have to draw on their more basic knowledge of a universal category such as 'future' or 'state'?

The influences on acquisition are complex in any setting, and the factors mentioned above should be controlled for when possible, and addressed in any case. One way in which the instructional effects and the effects of task can be controlled for is to balance the research which is undertaken in the instructional environment with research using data from untutored learners, and from learners interacting in free communication. From my own research I see that untutored learners often come up with systematic relations between form and meaning or function which are unlike those of the native language or the target; universals may help to explain such relations. As for data from 'natural discourse', its gathering and use is inconvenient for many reasons — particularly because the structures desired for analysis may not arise in the discourse. However, using natural discourse may be the only way to see the systematic nature of the learner's interlanguage, and this approach is therefore vital. What we need is, of course, everything — from experimental studies which look at a minimal process through tightly controlled input conditions to analyses of vast amounts of free-form discourse.

REPLY TO KUMPF'S COMMENTS

SUSAN GASS AND JOSH ARD

In responding to Kumpf's remarks we will limit our comments to five central issues, which for ease of explication we discuss in the order in which they are presented in her remarks: 1) nosography, 2) category selection, 3) status of universals, 4) data collection and instructional environment, and 5) object of inquiry.

1. *Nosography*

Kumpf questions the etiologies we propose in our discussion of word-final devoicing as it relates to English speakers learning German and German speakers learning English. She rightly notes that we cannot really distinguish in many cases between the influence of language transfer and language universals. Many researchers have discussed the problem of assigning an error to a single category (Jain 1974; Dulay and Burt 1972). Zobl (1980b) has in fact shown that transfer may be prolonged in cases where there is multiple causation. A recurrent problem in L2 acquisition research is the search for 'single' etiologies in dealing with errors. The notion of multiple causation has been implicitly and explicitly dealt with in recent years (Gass 1979b, 1982a, 1982b; Zobl 1980a, 1980b; Sharwood Smith 1982). We further point out that multiple causation is also witnessed in other types of dynamic language situations, e.g. in historical change. (For an explicit discussion see Steinke 1968.)

The example cited in our paper suggests that transfer is not always a bidirectional process, unlike claims made by proponents of a strict contrastive analysis approach. In the absence of influence by other variables, we would expect an identical relationship between speakers of language A learning language B and speakers of B learning A. Differences/similarities should be the same regardless of the direction of the learning. However, recent work on language transfer which places language transfer within a cognitive framework (Kellerman 1979, 1983; Gass 1979a,1979b; Zobl 1980a,1980b; Sharwood Smith

1979) suggests that learners do make 'decisions' at some level about what forms to transfer. If it is the case that there is selectivity on the part of the learner (Zobl 1980a), then it stands to reason that the same linguistic structure may be treated differentially by speakers of language A learning language B and speakers of B learning A. If elements are transferred in one direction and not in another, this is evidence that language transfer is not purely a matter of an automatic transference of overt form as was previously thought. It is precisely with data of the sort cited in our paper that we can gain greater insight into what factors other than purely structural ones (in our case language universals) must be taken into account in understanding the second language acquisition process. We claim that the influence of native language (English) on the L2 (German) learner's grammar is not a sufficient explanation for the ease of production of final devoiced obstruents in L2 German, for such an explanation does *not* account for the difficulty involved in the case of English speakers learning German.

2.   *Category selection*

When we used the word 'physical' we did not wish to transcend to metaphysical questions such as whether the mind is a physical entity. These questions are important but beyond the scope of applied and theoretical linguistics. Perhaps all mental facts and even societal ones can ultimately be reduced to a physical basis. Whether or not this is true, our only proper choice at present is to treat these domains as separate. Under physical facts we included primarily non-linguistic and non-neurological phenomena which could impinge on language and language use. Physical constraints of the human body are easy to see: there are no linguo-nasal trills, for example. Other physical constraints are more difficult to recognize because it is difficult to recognize alternative universes. For example, the humorous word meanings discussed by philosophers — e.g. grue: head-and-tail-and-legs-of-a-cow-but-not-the-torso — are presumably ruled out by the way the world is, not by the way language is. We stated that the categories we have suggested are not discrete and that furthermore the list is not exhaustive (see section 2.2).

We would like to restate that the intent of our paper was to set up a *framework* within which the investigation of universals and second language acquisition could meaningfully take place. The categories we selected are those most frequently suggested as the source of universals. It may be that further investigations into the source of specific universals will render them all obsolete. Precisely which categories are used is of little relevance to our major hypothesis. What *is* important is that universals and their effect on second language acquisition not be considered a monolithic phenomenon.

3. *The status of universals*

Kumpf suggests that one needs to have more studies showing where universals operate in addition to factors from native and target languages. While we are in complete agreement with the need for more studies of this sort, we would like to reiterate points made in reference to both the relative clause and the tense/aspect studies. In both cases we presented examples of learner data which resemble neither the native nor the target language. As an example of the former, resumptive pronouns were evidenced in the object of comparative position by speakers whose languages did not have resumptive pronouns. For the latter, there were judgments of 'ungrammatical' on sentences such as *I am flying to New York tomorrow* from Spanish speakers. This sentence-type is grammatical in English and in Spanish. Hence, neither set of data could be explained on the basis of L1 and/or L2 facts, while the results are in the direction consistent with independently established universals.

4. *Data collection and instructional environment*

Before dealing with Kumpf's comments on the two studies in question, we would like to clarify one point — the relative clause data were not collected at the ELI of the University of Michigan. Rather, they were collected at Indiana University from students in a non-intensive English language training program (cf. Gass 1979a).

The issue of data collection is an important one — one which cannot be underestimated. Kumpf rightly concludes that different sorts of data are required in order to get a total picture of the learner (Gass 1980). Yet it is also the case that certain questions can only be meaningfully answered using particular methodologies. Hence, it is not so much the data collection methods which must be broad in L2 acquisition research. Rather, the types of questions we ask serve as the fundamental means of gaining appropriate information about second language acquisition.

It is not our intent to deny the effect of conscious-rule learning. Rather, we wish to show that universals of particular sorts do have an effect on the learner's evolving grammar with or without instruction. We point out that with the tense/aspect data there were subjects who were essentially untutored learners. Of the 139 subjects tested for the T/A study, 13 were in the ELI's lowest level. These students had had little or no English language instruction prior to coming to the ELI. Furthermore, testing on these students was carried out during the first week of class prior to which there had been no explicit instruction on the English verbal system. Importantly, their results followed the same pattern as that of the other groups, albeit with different percentages. That is, they had more 'incorrect' responses, but the relative orderings were the same.

Kumpf claims that the 'instructional environment is obviously reflected in the responses to that part of the task which tests the WILL + Verb structure.' However, the argumentation which follows does not explain why the instructional environment should be felt differentially — why it is witnessed in some areas but not in others. She also claims to be 'convinced that the rule learning process' is 'overriding the effect of the universal', whereas the evidence presented shows only that the two would predict the same general results. Learning a second language is a complex process involving a multitude of factors. It may be that no one of the factors overrides any of the others for all times for all learners (cf. Long 1980 for a similar point of view). Furthermore, one cannot attribute motivating force to one variable in one case without simultaneously accounting for why that same variable does not operate in the other cases.

5. *Object of inquiry*

The final point we would like to address concerns the use of the WILL + Verb and the GOING TO + Verb constructions. As Kumpf points out, it is not of particular importance to us which is used more frequently in discourse. Clearly, if that were a criterion about what is relevant or interesting as an object of inquiry, the field would not have progressed as far as it has. A major reason for selecting Will + Verb over other semantically similar constructions is that other constructions are more likely to bear special nuances and are hence more likely to have been taught as having special meanings. For example, BE GOING TO + Verb is often taught to Russian native speakers as meaning INTEND TO + Verb. Such complications are less likely to occur for WILL + Verb.

REFERENCES

Dulay, H., and M. Burt. 1972. Goofing: an indicator of children's second language learning strategies. *Language Learning* 22:235-252.

Gass, S. 1979a. *An Investigation of Syntactic Transfer in Adult Second Language Acquisition*. Ph.D. Dissertation. Indiana University.

Gass, S. 1979b. Language transfer and universal grammatical relations. *Language Learning* 29:327-344.

Gass, S. 1980. Variability in L2 experimental data. *Indian Journal of Applied Linguistics* 6:60-74.

Gass, S. 1982a. Second language acquisition and language universals. First Delaware Symposium on Language Studies. Di Pietro, Frawley and Wedel (eds.). Newark: University of Delaware Press.

Gass, S. 1982b. Language transfer and language universals. Paper presented at RELC workshop, Singapore.

Jain, M. 1974. Error analysis: source, cause and significance. In J. Richards (ed.), *Error Analysis: Perspectives on Second Language Acquisition*. London: Longman.

Kellerman, E. 1979. Transfer and non-transfer: where we are now. *Studies in Second Language Acquisition* 2:37-57.

Kellerman, E. 1983. Now you see it, now you don't. In Gass and Selinker (eds.), *Language Transfer in Language Learning*. Rowley, Mass.: Newbury House.

Long, M. 1980. Inside the "Black Box": methodological issues in classroom research on language learning. *Language Learning* 30:1-42.

Sharwood Smith, M. 1979. Strategies, language transfer and the simulation of the second language learner's mental operation. *Language Learning* 29:345-362.

Sharwood Smith, M. 1982. Transfer in competence and performance. Paper presented at RELC workshop, Singapore.

Steinke, K. 1968. *Studien uber den Verfall der Bulgarischen Deklination*. Munich: Verlag Otto Sagner.

Zobl, H. 1980a. The formal and developmental selectivity of L1 influence on L2 acquisition. *Language Learning* 30:43-58.

Zobl, H. 1980b. Developmental and transfer errors: their common bases and (possibly) differential effects on subsequent learning. *TESOL Quarterly* 14:469-479.

UNIVERSALS, TYPOLOGIES AND INTERLANGUAGE*

FRED R. ECKMAN
University of Wisconsin-Milwaukee

1. Introduction and purpose

It is generally agreed that the central goal of descriptive linguistics is to characterize the notion *human language*. One of the ways in which linguists have tried to reach this goal is through the formulation and testing of universal statements. The logical form of these universals is shown, respectively, in (1a) and (1b), where X and Y are assertions about structural properties of language.

(1)   a. In all languages, Y
        b. In all languages, if X then Y

Examples of these types of statements are shown in (2).

(2)   a. *Non-implicational universal*
           In all languages, there are at least two color terms.
        b. *Implicational universal*
           In all languages, if there are passive sentences with expressed agents, there are also passives without expressed agents.

Both types of universals contribute to characterizing what can and cannot be a human language. Non-implicational universals define what are assumed to be the essential properties of language; implicational universals help to delimit the range of possible variation among languages. According to (2a), a communication system that did not have at least two color terms would not be a human language. Likewise, languages may not differ from one another such that one language has only agentless passives whereas another has only agentive passives. Thus, it is claimed that a system with only agentive passives cannot be a human language.

Almost without exception, universal statements such as the above have been formulated on the basis of data from primary languages (PL) (in the sense of Lamendella 1977). This is most likely due to the well-known fact that primary languages are describable in terms of a system of rules and are therefore amenable to this type of study. Within the last decade, however, research on secondary language acquisition (SLA) has determined that a learner internalizes a set of rules termed an interlanguage (IL) (Selinker 1972), which may be independent of both the native language (NL) and the target language (TL).

Within this context, we wish to raise two questions: 1) Is it possible to characterize the notion *human interlanguage* in terms of implicational and non-implicational universals? And 2) if so, what is the relationship between these universals and those formulated for primary languages? Given these questions, the purpose of this paper is as follows: (a) to investigate some of the methodological considerations involved in attempting to characterize the notion *human interlanguage* in terms of universals, (b) to consider the implications of the language-contact situation in attempting to define interlanguages in these terms, and (c) to provide examples of logically-possible, but empirically-unsubstantiated, types of interlanguages which we will attempt to explain within our framework.

2. *The hypothesis*

2.1. *A priori*, a reasonable way to attempt to characterize IL's with respect to PL's would be to formulate a set, U_{il}, of interlanguage universals and to compare it with the set, U_{pl}, of primary language universals. If such a comparison could be made, we would have one of the relationships shown in (3).[1]

(3) a. U_{il} and U_{pl} are identical
     b. U_{il} and U_{pl} are disjoint
     c. U_{il} and U_{pl} intersect
     d. U_{il} is a subset of U_{pl}
     e. U_{pl} is a subset of U_{il}

If (3a) turned out to be true, then, of course, IL's and PL's would be structurally the same, if (3b) were true, on the other hand, then there would be no universal statements which are true of Pl's which are also true of IL's and vice versa. In this case, PL's and IL's would be structurally distinct. If (3c) were the case, then there would be some universal statements which are shared by primary languages and interlanguages, but there would also be universals which are true for primary languages which are not true for interlanguages, and vice versa. If either (3d) or (3e) were true, then one type of language would be a subtype of the other, where they shared a number of universal statements, but some universals were true of one type of language but not true for the other.

From a practical point of view, however, this way of proceedings is precluded by the fact that we do not as yet have a set of IL universals in which we would have sufficient confidence to warrant a comparison with U_{pl}. On the other hand, we do have a reasonably sizable stock of PL universals which we could test against IL's. Given this situation, it seems that the strongest hypothesis that we can test at present is that stated below.[2]

(4)   Given the set U_{pl} of absolute and typological universals formulated on the basis of primary languages, there will be no interlanguage which violates any statements in U_{pl}.

Thus, the present state of the art in SLA allows us to test whether any PL universals are violated by IL's; it does not allow us to test (1) whether U_{pl} and U_{il} are identical; or (2) whether there are any universals which are particular to interlanguages.

This being the case, the hypothesis in (4) allows us to test some of the potential relationships between IL's and PL's stated in (3), but it does not permit us to test all of them. If (4) turns out to be true, then any one of the statements (3a, d, or e) could still be true. It would remain an open question whether universals of interlanguages and primary languages were identical, or in a subset relationship. Alternatively, if (4) turns out to be false, then it remains to be seen whether the two sets of universal statements are completely different or are overlapping.

One further point needs to be made about the hypothesis in (4). The purpose in proposing such a hypothesis is not only to know *whether* it is true or false, but also to determine *why* this is so. Therefore, in considering various IL's with respect to (4), we want to know whether it is possible to offer an explanation for any given IL adhering to or deviating from any statements in U_{pl}. A reasonable domain in which to look for such an explanation is the structure of the respective NL and TL. This is not to say that no other factors could be involved, or that there are no other explanations outside of the structural aspects of the NL and TL. Rather, it just seems likely at this stage of our knowledge that structural properties of IL's will be explainable only if they can be related to structural properties of the NL, TL or language in general. We shall return to this point below.

In what follows we will attempt to test our hypothesis against some IL data. However, before we proceed with this test, there are two considerations which must be discussed: (1) the originality of the proposed hypothesis; and (2) the relationship of the NL and TL in testing our hypothesis.

2.2. First of all, if the hypothesis in (4) can be maintained, then interlanguages and primary languages are clearly similar types of language systems. As stated above, it would still remain to be seen whether they are in fact structurally identical, or whether one is a subtype of the other. However, the point to be made here is that the proposition that PL's and IL's are similar types of languages is not new. In fact, much of the research on SLA during the last ten years has been devoted to arguing for the truth of this hypothesis. Thus, for example Richards (1971), Dulay and Burt (1973, 1974a, 1974b), Bailey, Madden, and Krashen (1974), and Schumann (1978) have claimed that secondary and primary language acquisition are fundamentally the same process, and that any deviations in the outcome can be systematically explained in terms of psychological and/or sociological variables. Similarly, Andersen (1979) has argued that secondary and primary language acquisition are similar in that they both involve progression toward an internal and an external norm in their early and late stages, respectively. Tarone (1979) and Beebe (1980) have shown that IL's function similarly to PL's in that they both exhibit systematic variation according to the speech-situation and interlocutor relationship. And finally, Adjémian (1976) has claimed that IL's and PL's are alike on the basis of how they develop, function, and are transmitted to other learners.

The primary assumption underlying the above-mentioned work and the hypothesis in (4) is that there will be some significant similarities between IL's and PL's. The major distinction between the above works and our hypothesis is that the latter attempts to make a testable claim about what can and what cannot be a viable interlanguage. That is, the hypothesis in question attempts to exclude certain systems from the class of human IL's and in so doing makes a prediction about what kinds of IL's are possible. On the other hand, statements concerning the form, acquisition, function, and variation exhibited by IL's approach the question of the nature of interlanguages from a different side. Such statements do not have the effect of making a prediction about what types of IL's can occur and what types cannot. Consequently, the present paper differs from the works cited above in that it attempts to test certain structural aspects of IL's against universal properties of PL's, with a view toward empirically determining whether IL's and PL's are identical or distinct on structural grounds.

The second consideration which must be made clear concerns the treatment of evidence for our hypothesis. It seems plausible that a first guess as to whether PL universals will be true for interlanguages is that some will and some will not. That is, pre-theoretically we see that IL's are similar to PL's in some ways and different from PL's in other ways. More specifically, IL's and PL's are alike in that they both function as verbal communications systems; however, IL's are different from PL's in that IL's are learned by adults and always involve at least two languages coming into contact, whereas PL's are learned by children and do not necessarily involve language contact. Thus, it seems at least reasonable that there could be certain structural similarities between the two language types, as well as certain structural differences. Given this situation, it seems that it is incumbent upon us to say something about the universals which hold for IL's as well as those that do not hold. A reasonable way to proceed along these lines would be to investigate whether IL's which adhere to or deviate from statements in U_{pl} can be explained on the basis of the structural characteristics of the NL and TL.

This approach accomplishes two things: (1) it attempts to offer an explanation for at least some of the structural similarities or differences that may exist between IL's and PL's; and (2) it recognizes a fundamental difference between IL's and PL's; namely, that IL's always entail contact between at least two other languages, whereas PL's do not. We will refer to the hypothesis in (4) and our assumptions about explaining properties of IL's in terms of the NL, TL, and/or principles of language as our general framework.

Now given these asssumptions, we have two parameters along which we may consider interlanguages with respect to our hypothesis: (1) whether the IL conforms to the statements in U_{pl}, and (2) whether any conformity/violation with respect to U_{pl} can be explained in terms of the structure of the NL and TL. Thus, within this framework, we have the logically-possible situations depicted in (5).

(5) Type of IL   Violates U_{pl}?   Explainable in terms
                                                 of NL/TL contact?

(A)	No	Yes
(B)	Yes	Yes
(C)	No	No
(D)	Yes	No

The type A interlanguage clearly poses no problems for our general framework because, on the one hand, it does not violate any statements in U_{pl}

and, on the other hand, its structural properties are explainable in terms of the contact situation. Type B interlanguages violate at least one statement in U_{pl}, but such violations can be explained in terms of the NL and TL. Therefore, type B IL's do not pose any significant problems in attempting to explain why IL's are the way they are. Similarly, type C IL's do not present serious difficulty, because they do not violate any statements in U_{pl}. The fact that some of their structural properties are not derivable from the contact between the NL and TL suggests that the present state of our knowledge does not permit us to say why they share certain structural properties with PL's. Type D interlanguages, however, do present a problem in that they exhibit violations of U_{pl} without it being possible to explain these violations in terms of the NL and/or TL structures. Should such IL's exist, they would pose a serious threat to the idea that IL's and PL's are fundamentally similar.

We shall give examples of each of the IL types in (6) below. Before we do so, however, let us consider one further aspect of the role that the NL and TL play in the nature of IL's.

2.3.   In attempting to test the hypothesis in (4), it is necessary to bear in mind that at least some of the structure of any IL may be attributable to transfer from the native language. This fact has a bearing on what we would consider to be an interesting test of our hypothesis. In this section we will consider the types of IL's that will provide an interesting confirmation of our hypothesis as well as those IL's that will falsify it.

Ostensibly, it appears that for any given non-implicational universal in U_{pl}, we have a case supporting the hypothesis in (4) if what the universal asserts about primary language is also true of the interlanguage in question. Conversely, it would seem that the hypothesis is false if what the universal claims to be true for primary languages is not true for IL's. However, because at least some of the IL system may be attributable to NL transfer we do not have both of the above-mentioned situations as an interesting test of the hypothesis. More specifically, those non-implicational universals which are true for interlanguages provide only trivial support for the above hypothesis. This is because any such universal will be true for every NL, making it possible for an IL to conform to the universal in question via transfer. On the other hand, if the non-implicational universal being tested is violated by the IL, then we have falsified our hypothesis, because there is at least one statement in U_{pl} which is not true for at least one IL. We would then attempt to explain this violation in terms of the language-contact situation.

We have a different situation when we test our hypothesis with respect to implicational universals. Consider, for example, the language-contact situation shown schematically in (6).

(6) a. In all languages, if X then Y
         X = implicans
         Y = implicatum

    b.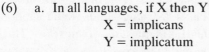

    c. Resultant IL's

         i. | IL | IL contains neither   ii. | IL | IL contains only
                                                    | Y | implicatum

        iii. | IL | IL contains both   *iv. | IL | IL contains only
             | X, Y | | X | implicans

We are attempting to test the typological statement in (6a), where X is the implicans and Y is the implicatum. Our hypothesis is supported if the resultant interlanguage in question contains 1) neither the implicans nor the implicatum; or 2) only the implicatum; or 3) both the implicans and the implicatum. The hypothesis is falsified if the IL has only the implicans.

To take a concrete example, consider the typological statement in (7a):

(7) a. In all languages, if there are voiced, aspirated (i.e. murmured) stop phonemes, there are also voiced unaspirated stop phonemes.

    b. NL   TL
       Korean   Hindi

    c. i. | IL |
           | /ptk/ |

       ii. | IL |
           | /ptk/ |
           | /bdg/ |

      iii. | IL |
           | /ptk/ |
           | /bdg/ |
           | /b^h d^h g^h/ |

      *iv. | IL |
           | /ptk/ |
           | /b^h d^h g^h/ |

The NL, Korean, has no voiced stop phonemes; the TL, Hindi, has both aspirated and unaspirated voiced stop phonemes. The IL's shown in (7c i-iii) which resulted from a Korean speaker learning Hindi would support the hypothesis in (4) because none of the IL's in question violates (7a). The IL in (7c iv), however, violates (7a) and would therefore falsify the hypothesis.

In general, we can obtain an interesting test of our hypothesis with respect to any given implicational universal if we make two assumptions about the NL and TL. The first is that the NL must contain neither the implicans nor the implicatum, and the second is that the TL must contain both the implicans and the implicatum. The first assumption, that the NL contain neither, is necessary to prevent the universal from being satisfied by means of NL transfer. Consider, for example, a situation where the TL has both the implicans and the implicatum and the NL has neither. Our hypothesis is falsified if the interlanguage, at some stage, contains the implicans but not the implicatum. However, if we test the hypothesis in a situation where the NL has only the implicatum, we have not provided an unambiguous test of our hypothesis. This is because the IL may contain the implictum not because of the presence of the implicans, but because of NL transfer.

The second assumption, that the TL contain both the implicans and the implicatum, is necessary to ensure a reasonable chance that both can occur in the IL. If the implicans is absent in the TL, it is unlikely that a learner will acquire it as part of the IL.

To recapitulate briefly, we have, up to this point, argued for the following four propositions: (a) that the hypothesis in (4) makes empirically testable claims about possible interlanguages by making predictions about what can and cannot occur in IL; (b) that, in testing (4), IL structures should be considered in light of the structural properties of the respective NL and TL; (c) that only implicational universals provide a reasonable and interesting confirmation of the hypothesis; and (d) that such tests should consider only certain NL-TL combinations where both the implicans and implicatum are part of the TL and neither is part of the NL.

Having made these proposals, let us now consider some typological universals and attempt to test our hypothesis against some interlanguage data.

3. *The Test*
3.1. *Typologies*
We shall test our hypothesis with respect to the four typologies shown in (8).

(8)   a. In all languages,
    1. If there are voiced obstruents word-finally, there are voice-
    less obstruents word-finally;

    2. If there are voiceless obstruents word-finally, there are sono-
    rant consonants word-finally.

   b. In all languages,
    If there are word-initial or word-final consonant sequences
    of length n, there is also at least one continuous subsequence
    of length n-1 (where n>1) in that same position (Greenberg
    1966).

   c. In all languages,
    If a language can relativize an NP out of a given position on
    the Accessibility Hierarchy (AH) (Keenan and Comrie,
    1977), it can, using the same relative clause formation
    strategy, relativize an NP from all highter positions on the
    AH, but not necessarily all lower positions, where the AH is

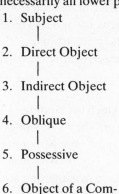

    1. Subject
       |
    2. Direct Object
       |
    3. Indirect Object
       |
    4. Oblique
       |
    5. Possessive
       |
    6. Object of a Com-
       parative Particle

   d. In all languages, inversions of statement order in questions so
    that the verb precedes the subject occurs only in languages
    where the question word is normally sentence-initial.
    If this inversion occurs in interrogative-word questions, it
    also occurs in yes-no questions (Greenberg 1978).

Given these universals, and given further our assumptions concerning
the language-contact situation, it is possible to test the statements in (8) with
speakers of the language shown, respectively, in (9).

(9)   *NL*   *TL*
    a. Japanese, Mandarin   English
    b. Japanese, Korean, Spanish   English
    c. Arabic, Persian   English, Swedish
    d. Japanese, Korean   English

Thus, for example, Japanese and Mandarin speakers learning English provide an adequate test of (8a1) because English has the implicans — viz. voiced obstruents finally — and Japanese and Mandarin have neither the implicans nor the implicatum, because they have only sonorant consonants and vowels word-finally. Likewise, since Japanese, Korean, and Spanish disallow initial obstruent clusters, speakers of these languages learning English provide an interesting test of the hypothesis with respect to (8b). Arabic and Persian relative clauses provide an interesting test of (4) relative to (8c) because both either allow or require resumptive pronouns in positions 2-6 on the AH in relative clauses, whereas English does not. Since these positions can be implicationally arranged as in (8c), the relative clauses of the TL and NL differ in a number of respects which can be used to test (4). Finally, English has sentence-initial interrogative words and also requires subject-auxiliary inversion in both yes-no and interrogative-word questions, whereas Japanese and Korean do not have initial interrogative-words and do not require inversion in any questions.

3.2. *Data*

The IL data against which the typologies in (8) were tested were gathered from several sources and are shown in Tables 1-4.

The data in Table 1 and 2 were gathered from students in the ESL Intensive Program at the University of Wisconsin-Milwaukee between 1978 and 1980. The methodology used to gather the data consisted of a set of elicitation techniques, as well as free conversations, which were used in several hour-long interviews. During the sessions, the subject's speech was recorded and then transcribed by the investigator and independently by an assistant for reliability (see Eckman 1981 for details).

The data summarized in Table 3 were taken from Gass (1979) and Hyltenstam (1981). Gass' data were obtained by having the subjects perform two tasks: one required subjects to combine two sentences into one sentence containing a relative clause; and the other required subjects to make grammaticality judgements to determine the acceptability of a set of sentences containing relative clauses, where some sentences in the set were well-formed and

TABLE 1

	IL Form	Gloss		IL Form	Gloss
A.			**B.**		
Japanese	lʌv~lʌvə	love	Mandarin	tægə~tæg	tag
Subj N.M.	dʌn	done		rab	rob
	bev~bevə	bathe		bigɔr	bigger
	tʊk	took		ɔθər	author
	bæd~bædə	bad		sɪt	sit
	lɛt	let		zon	zone
	pɪg~pɪgə	pig		sop	soap
	tun	tune		ɔf	off
	tus	tooth		si	see
	rud~rudə	rude		fayf	five
	tæv~tævə	tab		bæd	bad
	lidə	leader		tel	tail
	kul	cool		lɛt	let
				gʌn	gun
				pig	pig
				jabə~ǰab	job
				rɛdə~rɛd	red
C.			**D.**		
Spanish	tæk	tag	Farsi	bɪk	big
Subj P.C.	bɪk	big	Subj A.B.	bɪgəst	biggest
	bigər	bigger		bap	Bob
	rap	rob		babi	Bobby
	rabər	robber		bet	bathe
	ɔtər	author		beðɪ	bathing
	sɪt	sit		sæt	sad
	pækɪŋ	packing		sædər	sadder
	son	zone		pik	pig
	sop	soap		piki	piggy
	tæpɪŋ	tapping		nit	need
	pæs	pass		nidɪŋ	needing
	dek	deck		pɪkɪŋ	picking
	lesi	lazy		næpɪŋ	napping
	fayf	five			
	bot	vote			
	dʌn	done			
	ovər	over			
	kil	kill			
	gʌn	gun			
	isi	easy			

others were ill-formed. The data from Hyltenstam were obtained through an elicitation exercise whereby the subjects were shown a set of pictures about which they were asked questions. In answering the questions, the subjects were to produce relative clauses.

Table 4 shows data which were elicited from a Japanese student, during the fall of 1981. This subject is a twenty-nine-year-old female who had studied English in Japan for four years before coming to the U.S. to study English in January of 1980. The data were gathered using pictures about which the subject was directed to ask questions. The subject's speech was recorded and then transcribed using standard orthography.

3.3. Results

The data in Table 1 were taken from native speakers of Japanese, Mandarin, Spanish and Farsi. Whereas Farsi does exhibit a voice contrast in word-final position, none of the other three languages does. Japanese and Mandarin allow no obstruents word-finally; Spanish does allow word-final [ð] and [s], but does not exhibit a voice contrast.

When we consider the data in Table 1, we see that they are in conformity with the typological statement in (8a). Specifically, the data in A and B taken from, respectively, native speakers of Japanese and Mandarin, exhibit voiced and voiceless obstruents, sonorant consonants, and vowels word-finally; the data in C and D, on the other hand, exhibit only voiceless obstruents, sonorants, and vowels word-finally. Thus all the data in Table 1 are in line with the implicational universal in (8a1). The fact that these data conform to this statement in (8a) is particularly interesting since there is no obvious way to account for these data by means of language transfer. As pointed out above, Japanese and Mandarin allow no final obstruents. Consequently the presence of these obstruents in the IL's in A and B of Table 1 cannot be explained by transfer. Nor can we appeal to the NL, Spanish, to explain the final voiceless obstruents shown in C of Table 1. And finally, whereas the NL, Farsi, *does* have a final voice contrast, the IL in question lacks such contrast. Thus, there appears to be no way of accounting for the data in Table 1 on the basis of NL transfer alone.

The situation is similar when we consider the data in Table 2 with respect to the typological statement in (8b). Either the IL's of the Japanese and Spanish subjects manifest tri-literal and bi-literal consonant clusters, or they exhibit just bi-literal clusters. Thus, if a subject can produce a tri-literal cluster he/she can also produce the bi-literal subsequences of such a cluster. For example, subject CA produced initial *str* in *stringy* and also initial *st* in *stop*.

TABLE 2 IL data pertaining to typology (7b).

IL Form		Gloss
Japanese		
Subj Y.Y.	stərit	street
	skul	school
	skərim	scream
	skəræp	scrap
	tray	try
	kray	cry
	spil	spill
	spəlɛd	spread
	spəlin	spleen
	spɛl	spell
	spəray	spry
	spay	spy
	ple	play
	klos	close
	kəlæs	class
	təřet	treat
Spanish		
Subj A.M.	ɛsplæš	splash
	ste	stay
	slip	sleep
	ɛstartəd	started
	ɛstim	steam
	stim	steam
	ɛstrit	street
	ples	place
	spIl	spill
	tray	try
Spanish		
Subj C.A.	ɛstrɔŋ	strong
	strŋgəst	strongest
	stəp	stop
	spɛl	spell
	skul	school
	spɛs	space
	sket	skate
	striŋgi	stringy
	skrim	scream
	splæš	splash

On the other hand, Y.Y. and A.M. produced initial bi-literal obstruent clusters like *sp*, *st* and *sk*, without producing any initial tri-literal clusters. Therefore the data in Table 2 are in conformity with the statement in (8b). The fact that these data support the typology in (8b) confirms the hypothesis in (4). Again, what is interesting, is that the forms in Table 2 cannot be accounted for by transfer since Japanese and Spanish do not allow any word-initial obstruent sequences.

TABLE 3
Data from Gass (1979)

Percentage of sentences correct by language groups

S	DO	IO OPREP	GEN	OCOMP	
48	28	27	47	10	(Arabic)
90	30	25	30	13	(Thai)
68	28	17	33	0	(Romance)
70	20	18	38	4	(Persian)
78	60	28	88	0	(Chinese, Japanese, Korean)

Data from Hyltenstam (1981)

Implicational scales showing pronominal retention for learners of Swedish with different NL's.

(+ = retention of pronoun; − = non-retention of pronoun; 0 = retention of nominal; circle = deviation from implicational pattern [Cf. Hyltenstam, p. 16]).

NL = Persian; Scalability = 93.1

Subj nr	SU	DO	IO	OBL	GEN	OCOMP
21	−	−	−	−	−	−
32	−	−	−	−	+	+
17	−	⊕	⊕	−	+	⊖
18	−	⊕	⊕	−	+	+
7	−	−	+	+	+	+
16	−	−	+	+	+	+
6	−	−	+	+	+	+
34	−	+	+	+	+	+
30	−	+	+	+	+	+
28	−	+	+	+	+	+
29	−	+	+	+	+	+
15	−	+	+	+	+	+

NL = Finnish; Scalability = 85.2 (if 0 = +) or 92.6 (if 0 = −)

Subj nr	SU	DO	IO	OBL	GEN	OCOMP
48	−	−	−	−	0	−
52	−	−	−	−	0	−
44	−	−	−	−	⊕	−
47	−	−	−	−	⊕	−
51	−	−	−	−	⊕	−
45	−	−	−	0	⊕	−
50	−	−	−	−	0	+
46	−	−	−	−	+	+
49	−	−	−	−	+	+

NL = Greek; Scalability = 97.1 (if 0 = −) or 98.7 (if 0 = +)

Subj nr	SU	DO	IO	OBL	GEN	OCOMP
20	−	−	−	−	−	−
41	−	−	−	−	+	⊖
14	−	−	−	−	+	0
43	−	−	−	−	+	+
12	−	−	−	−	+	+
13	−	−	+	+	+	+
40	−	−	+	+	+	+
27	−	+	+	+	+	+
42	−	+	+	+	+	+
22	−	+	+	+	+	+
11	−	+	+	+	+	+
10	−	+	+	+	+	+

NL = Spanish; Scalability = 90.3

Subj nr	SU	DO	IO	OBL	GEN	OCOMP
2	−	−	−	−	−	−
31	−	−	−	−	⊕	−
37	−	−	−	−	⊕	−
33	−	−	−	−	⊕	−
3	−	−	−	−	−	+
8	−	−	−	−	+	+
5	−	−	⊕	−	+	⊖
4	−	−	⊕	−	+	+
9	−	−	⊕	−	+	+
19	−	−	+	+	+	+
24	−	+	+	+	+	+
35	−	+	+	+	+	+

When we consider the data in Table 3, we see that the AH in (8c) is, in general, borne out. The data from Gass (1979) show that the percentage of correct sentences across the various grammatical functions corresponds to the AH, with the exception of the genitive. Gass offers two possible explanations for why her subjects performed better on the GEN position than the DO and IO-OPREP positions: (1) the genitive position is uniquely coded in that it has only a single relative marker, *whose*, as opposed to *that/which* and is therefore more salient; or (2) the subjects may have treated the *whose* + NP as a unit, which was then used as one of the grammatical functions such as subject, direct object etc. Since all of Gass' sentences with respect to the genitive position involved a combination of *whose* + a subject NP or *whose* + an object NP, this may account for the relative degree of success which her subjects found in relativizing this position. Whatever explanation turns out to be defensible, it seems clear that the typology in (8c) is, in general, supported by Gass' data.

The data from Hyltenstam (1981) are also, in general, supportive of the AH. As can be seen from Table 3, the pronoun retention pattern exhibited by learners from various NL's acquiring Swedish parallels the AH with high scalability.

Thus, while the data relevant to (8c) are not in perfect agreement with the AH, they do generally support the typological statement in question. To the extent that the data are supportive, the hypothesis in (4) receives confirmation.

Finally, the data in Table 4 support the typological statement in (8d) with respect to the hypothesis in (4). Specifically, the subject is a native speaker of the NL, Japanese, which does not have sentence-initial interrogative words, nor does it have inversion in either yes-no or interrogative-word questions. The data show that although the subject does produce some interrogative-word questions which are deviant (viz. 3, 5, 10, 12, 15, and 21), all such questions have initial interrogative-words and have appropriate subject-auxiliary inversion where possible. Likewise with the yes-no questions: although some are structurally deviant, all have subject-auxiliary inversion. Thus, the data given in Table 4 support our hypothesis with respect to the generalization in (8d). This is significant, since this cannot be accounted for in terms of the NL.

To recapitulate briefly, the IL data given or summarized in Tables 1-4 support in general the statements in (8), with (8c) being the only typological generalization where the data do not match perfectly. This being the case, we will now consider the question of whether any aspects of the IL rules which

TABLE 4

Japanese Subj Y.Y.	
Yes-No Questions	Interrogative-word Questions
1. Do you like chocolate apple?	1. What kind do you like?
2. Do you like money?	2. How many money?
3. Is this much money?	3. Who does it have? (Who has it?)
4. Are they family?	4. Where are they?
5. Is it basket?	5. What kind basket? (What kind of basket is it?)
6. Are they party?	6. How many child are they?
7. Is she smiling?	7. Why is she smiling?
8. Do you have apple?	8. What is picture do?
9. Does he have many present?	9. What kind do you like?
10. Do you like soccer?	10. What kind of sport? (What kind of sport is it?)
11. Do you like sports?	11. What does he have?
12. Is he happy?	12. What does it need a dumbbell? (Why does he need a dumbbell?)
13. Do you like circus?	13. What do you like play?
14. Do you like this picture?	14. What does he do?
15. Do you like flower?	15. What kind of this picture? (What kind of picture is this?)
16. Is there America?	16. Who does eat chocolate pudding?
17. Do you like family?	17. Who is taller?
	18. What are they doing?
	19. Where are they?
	20. What do you think?
	21. How many people do they? (How many people are there?)
	22. What is he doing?
	23. What is the reason?

produced these data are in violation of any statements in U_{pl}. That is, we shall consider the IL systems represented by the data in Table 1-4 in terms of the structural properties of the respective NL's and TL.

4. Discussion

In our interpretation of the data in Tables 1-4, we saw that in general the typological statements in (8) were supported. This means that in terms of the interlanguage data that we have considered thus far, we have found no significant violations of the statements in U_{pl}. This raises the questions of whether *all* IL's conform to the statements in U_{pl}, or whether there are some violations. In raising this question, we are addressing the issue of which of the interlanguage-types outlined in (5) actually occur.

Along this line of reasoning, let us consider the constraint in (10), which was proposed by Sanders (1979) and which will be shown to be violated by at least one IL.

(10) No language will have a grammar which contains a rule of final-vowel-insertion (paragoge).
(Sanders 1979)

The constraint in (10) is part of Sanders' (1972) equational grammar framework in which rules that are inverses of each other are metatheoretically excluded. Since rules deleting vowels word-finally can be motivated for at least some languages, rules inserting vowels in final position must in principle be excluded. The fact that there are no attested cases where such rules are motivated supports Sanders' theory.

By introducing (10) into our discussion at this time, we are implying that though both (8) and (10) represent statements in U_{pl}, they are in fact different types of statements. They are different in that on the one hand the generalization in (10) can be shown to be violated by IL's whereas the generalizations in (8) cannot, and on the other hand the statement in (10) refers to the *rules* of a language whereas those in (8) refer to the *forms* of a language. These two differences, we will argue, shed some light on the type of systems that interlanguages are. However, before we pursue these notions, let us consider which of the IL-types outlined in (5) actually occur.

Within this context, we can argue that the data in C of Table 1 represent a Type A interlanguage. More specifically, the IL forms in question exhibit only voiceless obstruents word-finally, and therefore these data are in conformity with the statement in (8a1). The reason that the IL conforms to this universal seems clear: The NL, Spanish, has only /ð/ and /s/ as the only allowable word-final obstruents. Thus, Spanish has no word-final voice contrast; the TL, English, on the other hand, has a word-final voice contrast. Given that a final voice contrast will be relatively difficult to acquire for a speaker whose native language does not have such a contrast (Eckman 1977), we can explain (a) the learner's ability to produce only voiceless obstruents finally, or equivalently (b) the learner's failure to maintain a final voice contrast in the IL in terms of the phonological structure of the NL and TL.

An example of an IL like Type B is represented by the data in A and B of Table 1, which contains forms exhibiting an alternation between a word-final /ə/ and null. In Eckman (1981), it was argued that such forms motivate an IL rule of Schwa Paragoge, formulated as in (11).

(11)   Schwa Paragoge (SP)

$$\emptyset \xrightarrow{\text{(opt)}} \partial / \begin{bmatrix} -son \\ +voice \end{bmatrix} _____ \#$$

(Optionally insert a /ə/ after a
word-final voiced obstruent)

Since a rule like SP is in violation of the universal constraint in (10), it seems that we have an instance where an IL grammar violates a constraint on primary-language grammars. What remains to be demonstrated is whether this violation can be explained in terms of the NL-TL contact.

The argument that the above can be so explained is essentially that put forth in Eckman (1981). Specifically, the NL's Japanese and Mandarin evidence only vowels and sonorants word-finally, whereas the TL has word-final voiced and voiceless obstruents in addition to sonorants and vowels. The learner, finding final voiced obstruents to be an area of difficulty (Eckman 1977), sometimes adds a word-final schwa to the underlying forms in (12a) to produce phonetic forms like those in (12b).

(12)   a.   /tæg/   'tag'   /ǰab/   'job'   /rɛd/   'red'
       b.   [tægə]   [jabə]   [rɛdə]

The rationale for such a rule, as discussed in Eckman (1981), is that the addition of a final schwa accomplishes two things. First, it places the problematic final consonant in a less marked position relative to a voice contrast, namely, medial position. Second, such a rule maintains the canonical form of the underlying representation, which, according to the analysis, the IL speaker has correctly learned. That is, if the learner dealt with the problematic final voiced obstruent by, say, deleting it, then the learner would be destroying some of what he/she has already learned: that 'tag' has a word-final [g]. On the other hand, adding a final vowel brings the TL word into conformity with the phonological constraints of the NL, places the voiced obstruent in an easier position and preserves the integrity of the underlying form. The SP rule can be explained then in terms of the discrepancy between the underlying forms in (12a), which contain final voiced obstruents, and the NL surface constraint which does not allow any obstruents finally.

Rules of paragoge do not exist in primary-language grammars because such languages do not have (and presumably, *could* not have) underlying forms with final voiced obstruents and also a surface constraint against forms with final obstruents. If the language contained such a surface constraint, underlying representations like (12a) could not be defended. Interlanguages, on the other hand, appear special in this sense, because they always involve language contact, and therefore the possibility exists that there will be underlying forms like those in (12a) along with a constraint against final obstruents as part of the same IL system. Thus, we consider the IL in Table 1B to be an example of a type B IL.

An example of an IL of Type C is represented by the data in Table 1D. Although the phonetic forms in Table 1D conform to the typology in (8a1), there is no accounting for this fact in terms of the language contact. Both the NL (Farsi) and the TL (English) exhibit both voiced and voiceless obstruents in word-final position. Consequently, the IL forms conform to the relevant statements of U_{pl} but are not directly explainable on the basis of NL-TL contact.

One possible explanation, which is independent of the NL-TL situation, is that learners tend to acquire simplified versions of the system that they are learning (Corder 1978). If we assume that phonologies with only voiceless word-final obstruents are simpler than those with both voiced and voiceless obstruents finally (Eckman 1977), then the data in Table 1D can be explained not in terms of the language contact but by the hypothesis that learners produce simplified forms of the systems they are acquiring.

Finally, an interlanguage of Type D is one which would be troublesome for the general framework which we are presenting. This type of IL would violate at least one statement in U_{pl} in a manner which could not be explained in terms of the structure of the NL and/or TL. Presumably, IL's of type D do not exist, since no data have ever been presented in support of such an IL. However, it would be worthwhile to examine the type of data which would constitute such an interlanguage, if it did in fact exist.

To take an example first from phonology, let us consider the rule of Schwa Paragoge (SP). We have argued that whereas such a rule is in violation of a statement in U_{pl}, that violation is explainable in terms of the phonological structure of the NL and TL involved. A Type D IL then would be an interlanguage which had a rule like SP, but where the NL and TL involved did not make it possible to explain the rule. That is, an IL which contained a rule like SP, where both the NL and TL exhibited a word-final voice contrast would be a Type D IL. Since we are hypothesizing that Type D IL's do not occur, we would never expect speakers of Arabic or Persian, both of which have a final voice contrast, to produce forms like (13) when learning English.

(13) *IL form*   *Gloss*

    tægə   tag
    rɛdə   red

Likewise, we would not expect Japanese and Mandarin learners of German, which has only voiceless obstruents in final position, to develop a rule like SP. Rather, such a rule should arise, according to our assumptions, only when the discrepancy between the TL and NL is great enough that the TL has *final voiced obstruents* and the NL has a constraint *against all final obstruents*. Thus, Japanese and Mandarin learners of German should never say (IL) forms like those in (14).

(14) *IL form*   *TL form*   *Gloss*

    takə   tak   day
    dɛkə   dɛk   deck

If such a rule did develop in this learning context, then that would characterize a Type D IL.

Turning to syntax, an example of Type D IL would be a Japanese speaker learning English, where the resultant IL was typified by forms like those in (15).

(15) a. You are going where?
     b. Are you going where?
     c. Is he going home?

(15a) represents a question where the interrogative word is not preposed; (15b and c) show that the inversion of the verb and subject occurs in the interrogative-word question and not in the yes-no question. Consequently, questions like those in (15) would violate (8d). Moreover, such violations would not be explainable in terms of the NL-TL contact, because Japanese has no inversion whatever in questions. Therefore, if questions like those in (15) characterized an IL, then that IL would be a Type D interlanguage.

The above hypothetical examples of Type D IL's are summarized in (16).

(16) a. NL = Arabic,   TL = English,   IL gives evidence
          which has final   which has final   of paragoge.
          voice contrast   voice contrast

      b. NL = Japanese,   TL = German,   IL gives evidence
          which has no   which has no final   of paragoge.
          final obstruents   voiced obstruents

      c. NL = Japanese,   TL = English,   IL has questions
          which has no   which has subject-   where interroga-
          obligatory in-   verb inversion in   tive is not initial
          version of subject- questions and ini-   but subject-verb
          verb in questions,   tial interrogative   inversion occurs.
          and no initial inter- words.
          rogative word.

In the above examples, we have argued that whereas the statements in (8) generally hold for IL's, the constraint in (10) is violated. Moreover, the generalizations in (8) refer to the forms of a language whereas the generalization in (10) refers to the rules of a language. We would like to speculate that the following situation will be true of interlanguages in general: IL's will not violate statements in U_{pl} which refer to the forms of a language; IL's will violate only those statements in U_{pl} which refer to the rules of a language. More specifically, the set of rules necessary for the description of IL's will be larger than those needed for the description of PL's.

The reason for this seems clear: whereas the development of PL's never requires language contact, the development of IL's always does. Consequently, the relationship between underlying and superficial representations that can occur in IL's is much different than that which can occur in PL's.

A case in point is the rule of Schwa Paragoge. Such a rule is necessitated by the large discrepancy between the underlying representations with final voiced obstruents and the phonetic representations with the general absence of final voiced obstruents. Schwa Paragoge attempts to resolve this discrepancy. But what is important is that this 'distance' between the underlying and phonetic representation can occur only in IL's where it is possible to have underlying forms with final voiced obstruents like English and surface constraints against final obstruents like Mandarin or Japanese. Thus, it is the languages coming into contact that necessitate the rule of Schwa Paragoge. Such a rule, however, would never be necessary for a PL because it would not be possible, without the language contact, to have *both* underlying representations with final voiced obstruents *and* a surface constraint against all final obstruents. Therefore, in PL's the discrepancy between the underlying and phonetic representation is less, and the set of rules necessary to resolve these discrepancies is smaller.

5. *Conclusion*
       The central question to which this paper has addressed itself is this: what do we conclude when we find that an interlanguage violates a universal statement which was formulated on the basis of data from primary languages? One possible conclusion we could draw would be that the universal is false and must be discarded; another would be that the domain of the universal must be restricted to apply only to PL's, thereby insulating statements in U_{pl} from falsification on the basis of IL data. The position that we have taken in this paper is essentially a modified version of the second alternative.
       The first alternative of discarding the universal is undesirable for several reasons, not the least of which is the fact that universals are highly valued and are not easily discarded. In addition, there is a natural domain over which the universal statement does hold, namely, all primary languages. Since we know that IL's and PL's differ in certain respects, then it would not be implausible for these languages types to differ structurally also. Consequently, instead of discarding the universal, we would simply designate it as pertaining only to PL's and develop a classification of universals in terms of the domain over which they hold: all language types, primary languages, or interlanguages.
       This is essentially the second alternative. However, restricting universal statements to certain domains can be very unenlightening if we merely classify these statements into arbitrarily-determined sets. On the other hand, such a classification can be very enlightening if we attempt to correlate the different structural aspects of PL's and IL's with other differences between these language types. This is the position that we have take in this paper. We have focused on one salient difference between interlanguages and primary languages — namely, that language contact is always involved in the develop-

ment of the former but not necessarily the latter — and we have attempted to correlate this difference with at least one structural difference between IL's and PL's. The fact that the grammar of at least two IL's contains a rule of paragoge, whereas this rule type is not contained in the grammar of any PL, is due, we have argued, to the language-contact situation.

At the same time, we have attempted to maintain the empirical nature of our inquiry by allowing our general framework to be falsified if it can be shown that structural differences between IL's and PL's cannot be explained on the basis of the language contact. We recognize that it is entirely possible — in fact, very plausible — that the differences in structure between IL's and PL's can be correlated with other differences between these language types. However, since this remains to be shown, the question must for now be left open.

NOTES

* Some of the ideas for this paper were developed through frequent and extended conversations with Edith Moravcsik and Jessica Wirth during the fall of 1981. The author wishes to thank Dan Dinnsen, Carol Lord, Edith Moravcsik, Gerald Sanders, William Washabaugh and Jessica Wirth for their comments and suggestions on some of the ideas in this paper. None of the above-mentioned necessarily agrees with the content of this paper, and should not be held responsible for any errors or inconsistencies.

1) The content and discussion of (3) are due to Edith Moravcsik.

2) This hypothesis is also tested in Schmidt (1980).

3) There may be other grounds on which the violations of/adherence to the statements in U_{pl} could be explained, such as psychological or social grounds. However, any such explanation of specific structural properties of IL's on grounds other than structural would have to be argued.

4) Resumptive pronouns are pronouns which occur in the position in the underlying representation from which an NP was relativized. For example, in the sentence

I saw the boy whom the dog bit *him*.

the italicized word is a resumptive pronoun.

REFERENCES

Adjémian, Christian. 1976. On the nature of interlanguage systems. *Language Learning 26*:297-320.

Andersen, Roger. 1979. Expanding Schumann's Pidginization Hypothesis. *Language Learning 29*:105-120.

Bailey, Nathalie, Carolyn Madden, and Stephen Krashen. 1974. Is there a 'natural sequence' in adult second language learning? *Language Learning* 24:235-244.

Beebe, Leslie. 1980. Sociolinguistic variation and style shifting in second language acquisition. *Language Learning 30*:433-448.

Corder, S.P. 1978. Language-learner language. In Jack C. Richards (ed.) *Understanding Second and Foreign Language Learning*. Rowley, Mass.: Newbury House Publishers.

Dulay, Heidi, and Marina Burt. 1973. Should we teach children syntax? *Language Learning 23*:245-258.

Dulay, Heidi, and Marina Burt. 1974a. Natural sequences in child second language acquisition. *Language Learning 24*:37-53.

Dulay, Heidi, and Marina Burt. 1974b. A new perspective on the creative construction process in child second language acquisition. *Language Learning 24*:253-278.

Eckman, Fred. 1977. Markedness and the contrastive analysis hypothesis. *Language Learning 27*:315-330.

Eckman, Fred. 1981. On the naturalness of interlanguage phonological rules. *Language Learning 31*:195-216.

Gass, Susan. 1979. Language transfer and universal grammatical relations. *Language Learning 29*:327-344.

Greenberg, Joseph H. 1966. Some universals of grammar with particular reference to the order of meaningful elements. In J.H. Greenberg (ed.) *Universals of Language* (Second edition). Cambridge, Mass: M.I.T. Press.

Greenberg, Joseph H. 1978. Some generalizations concerning initial and final consonant clusters. In Greenberg *et al* (eds.) *Universal of Human Language: Volume 2, Phonology*. Stanford, Calif.: Stanford University Press.

Hyltenstam, Kenneth. 1981. The use of typological markedness conditions as predictors in second language acquisition. Paper presented at the European-North American workshop on Cross-linguistic Second Language Acquisition Research. Los Angeles. September 7-14.

Keenan, Edward, and Bernard Comrie. 1977. Noun phrase accessibility and universal grammar. *Linguistic Inquiry 8*:63-100.

Lamendella, John. 1977. General principles of neurofunctional organization and their manifestation in primary and non-primary language acquisition. *Language Learning 27*:155-196.

Neufeld, Gerald G. 1979. Towards a theory of language learning ability. *Language Learning 29*:277-242.

Richards, Jack. 1971. A non-contrastive approach to error analysis. *English Language Teaching 25*:204-219.

Sanders, Gerald. 1979. Equational rules and rule function in phonology. In D. Dinnsen (ed.), *Current Approaches to Phonological Theory*. Bloomington, Ind.: Indiana University Press.

Schmidt, Maxine. 1980. Coordinate structures and language universals in interlanguage. *Language Learning 30*:397-416.

Schumann, John. 1978. *The Pidginization Process*. Rowley, mass.: Newbury House Publishers.

Selinker, Larry. 1972. Interlanguage. *IRAL 10*:209-231.

Tarone, Elaine. 1979. Interlanguage as chameleon. *Language Learning 29*:181-191.

Taylor, Barry. 1974. Toward a theory of language acquisition. *Language Learning 24*:23-36.

COMMENTS ON THE PAPER BY ECKMAN

CAROL LORD
University of California, Los Angeles

Eckman's terminology reflects his view of what universals should be: exceptionless statements about human language. If we require a statement to be exceptionless to qualify as a universal, we rule out a large number of observations, such as those made by Greenberg, which describe strong tendencies. For example, in about 99% of the world's languages the subject precedes the object in basic word order. This fact represents a statistically significant deviation from random patterning which it is the linguist's business to seek to describe and explain. Viewed in the context of universal tendencies then, an observation with no exceptions at all is just the extreme case of deviation from random distribution. (In fact, in his remarks at this conference Ferguson labels as a 'straw man' the position that universal statements must be true of all languages.)

A statement that is true of all languages without exception is called an absolute universal. A statement that is implicational in form — 'if X, then Y' — can also be exceptionless and therefore (at least in principle) an absolute universal. As Comrie (1981:19) points out, we can make a four-way classification of universals as either implicational or non-implicational in form, on the one hand, and as either absolute universals or universal tendencies on the other. In Eckman's paper, implicational universals are referred to as 'typological universals' or 'typologies'. The use of this label is confusing. In the interest of clarity, re-defining established terms should be avoided unless it is absolutely necessary. I would prefer to see the term 'typology' reserved for classifications or groupings of languages along broad parameters like word order, or subject-prominence vs. topic-prominence.

In his remarks at this conference, Comrie suggests that attested languages may comprise a skewed set due to historical accident, and second language acquisition may provide valuable evidence for delineating human language capacity as a whole. Eckman claims that a rule of Schwa Paragoge (his 10b) is necessary to describe interlanguage data. But he also accepts Sanders' assertion that this rule should be excluded from descriptions of primary languages on metatheoretical grounds. (Sanders' theory disallows rules that are inverses of each other, and there is evidence for including the inverse of SP: word-final vowel deletion.) Eckman regards Schwa Paragoge as an interlanguage phenomenon, inconsistent with primary language phenomena, and attributable to language contact.

The implications of this position are interesting to consider. Is there a set of features that characterize interlanguages but not primary languages? Are there communities of Mandarin and Japanese interlanguage speakers who share the Schwa Paragoge rule, violating a primary language universal? Do children in these communities acquire this phonological pattern — and if so, do we still exclude it from primary language universal status? It may be that certain universals are violated 'in passing' by interlanguage speakers due to the many factors involved in language learning, but that such violations are transient and are not maintained by actual speech communities.

The Schwa Paragoge data are from adult speakers. In view of Bickerton's discussion of the bioprogram hypothesis at this conference, it would be interesting to find out whether children's interlanguage shows the same pattern. Violation of the constraint by adults only would be consistent with the hypothesis that universals reflect a bioprogram, since this bioprogram may be exhausted before adulthood. Universal constraints would therefore not necessarily be reflected in interlanguages developed by adults.

REFERENCE

Comrie, Bernard. 1981. *Language Universals and Linguistic Typology*. Chicago: University of Chicago Press.

UNIVERSALS OF DISCOURSE STRUCTURE AND SECOND LANGUAGE ACQUISITION

T. GIVÓN
University of Oregon
Eugene, Oregon
and
Ute Language Program
Southern Ute Tribe
Ignacio, Colorado

1. Introduction

Recent studies in Pidgins and Creoles[1] have tended to emphasize the systematic, regular, language-universal nature of Creoles, while at the same time downplaying the systematicity of Pidgins — and thus of early second language acquisition by implication. Pidgins are viewed in these studies as 'variable', 'non-categorial', 'lacking syntax', 'reduced' or 'simplified'. I myself have tended earlier on[2] to accept this emphasis uncritically, concentrating my energies with the rest of my colleagues on the more promising, indeed exciting study of Creoles as a rich source of language universals. Later on, when studying the relation between discourse and syntax,[3] it began to dawn on me that in certain respects the 'reduced' structure of Pidgins and early second language competence displayed a number of highly systematic features of grammatical structure, ones with rich potential for the study of linguistic and communicative universals. These features corresponded, at least to some extent, to those characterizing informal or 'unplanned' registers (Ochs, 1979), to early stages of first language acquisition, and to the earlier paratactic sources of diachronically-rising syntactic constructions. These correlations were summarized (Givón, 1979, Ch. 5) as:

(1)   *pre-syntactic modes*   *syntacticized modes*

    a. diachronically-earlier   ⟹ diachronically-later
       paratactic constructions   syntactic constructions
    b. early child language   ⟹ later adult language
    c. Pidgins   ⟹ Creoles
    d. informal register   ⟿ formal/written register

The paired relations (1a,b,c) above are *developmental* relations, while (1d) is
a synchronic *variability* within the communicative competence of adults, presumably arising from the survival of early childhood communicative modes.[4]
In attempting to characterize more specifically the difference between the two
communicative modes, the following contrasts then suggested themselves:[5]

(2)   *pre-syntactic mode*[6]   *syntacticized mode*

    a. topic-comment structure   subject-predicate structure
    b. loose conjunction   tight subordination
    c. slow rate of delivery   fast rate of delivery
    d. pragmatic government   semantic government
       of word-order   of word-order
    e. low noun/verb ratio   higher noun/verb ratio
       within clauses   within clauses
    f. scant use of grammatical   extensive use of grammatical
       morphology   morphology

And there matters rested for a short spell.

    There was one clear attraction to the earlier — particularly Bickerton's[7]
— discussion of Pidgins as variable, chaotic, and lacking in real grammar: It
suggested the crucial *motivation* for the rise of Creoles, via the natural syntac-
ticizing ability of young children. If the Pidgin input of the parent speech community furnished so little syntactic input, in terms of both structure and regu-
larity, the children must strike out on their own, utilizing their universal syn-
tacticizing capacity to create semantically-based word-order, tight/subordi-
nate constructions and grammatical morphology. However, as Bickerton and
myself were engaged in revising and re-revising the now apocryphal Island
Project, it became clear that over-emphasis on the chaotic, variable nature of
plantation Pidgins — and thus of the early stages of the acquisition of second
language — had in fact yielded one undesirable consequence: the masking of a
potentially large set of important language universals, those of *discourse-
pragmatic* or *pre-syntactic* communication.[8]

2. *Topicality and topic continuity in discourse*

Of the 6 properties (2a-f) which characterize the pre-syntactic mode of communication, (2a) — topic-comment structure — was both the most promising and the most frustrating. The early Praguean works,[9] which many of us followed in the early seventies,[10] suggested a binary distinction, with a constituent either being or not being 'topic'. Eventually, the data from sentences in which many arguments appeared and were in some sense all 'topics' — especially when all equally definite and thus in the discourse 'register' — began to suggest that one was not dealing with an either/or property but rather with a graded one, which I myself began to refer to as *degree of topicality*.[11] Thus, consider the following sentence, in which four NP's appear that are clearly old-information and thus 'topical':

(3)   As for **Joe**, **he** gave **that one** to **Mary**

Contemplating data of this kind had finally convinced me that the graded property we were looking for was not 'topicality', which was psychologically and functionally rather opaque, but rather *topic continuity* or *ease of topic identification*, which could be demonstrated in discourse as well as have clear psycholinguistic potential. And the earlier formulations of these two[12] finally yielded a massive cross-language study where this graded property of nominal arguments in discourse has been studied quantitatively in a reasonably diverse sample of natural languages.[13] This study involved three quantitative measurements whose relation to both topic continuity and ease of identification is rather transparent:

(4)   a. *Referential distance to the left*: "The distance from the present mention of a topic NP and the last clause where the same referent was a semantic argument within the clause, in terms of *number of clauses*".

       b. *Potential ambiguity*: "The number of other referents within the immediately preceding environment (3 clauses to the left) which could qualify in terms of their semantic/syntactic selectional restrictions to compete for referential identification with the topic/argument under study".

       c. *Topical persistence*: "The number of clauses to the right, from the locus under study, in which the same topic/referent persists in the discourse register as argument of some clause".

The correlation between *topic continuity* and *ease of topic identification* is rather transparent with respect to the first two measurements, (4a,b):

(5)   a. The wider the gap between present and preceding appearance
         of the referent/topic in the discourse register, the harder it
         would be for the *hearer* to identify it.
      b. The more competing topics/referents are present in the im-
         mediately preceding discourse environment of a topic/referent,
         the harder it would be for the hearer to identify it.

Topic continuity without interfering *gaps* or *other topics* thus yields easier
topic identification; inertia and routine-continuity are easier to process; while
breaking the continuity or disrupting the routine presumably results in processing difficulties. Measure (4c) is related to continuity in a less-direct way,
since it assesses the *importance* of the topic in terms of its *length of survivabil-
ity* in the register.[14]

While each language studied has some topic-identification devices
idiosyncratic to it, on the whole a great degree of comparability was evident in
our study. The comparability involves both the relative ranking of the various
devices on the scale of continuity and also many of the actual numerical values
obtained for comparable devices. The following ranking involves the devices
that are cross-linguistically more common:

(6)   *most continuous/predictable*

       Zero anaphora
       Clitic/unstressed/agreement pronouns
       Independent/stressed pronouns
       R-dislocated DEF-NP's or comment-topic word-order
       Simple DEF-NP's in the neutral/fixed word-order (if any)
       L-dislocated DEF-NP's or topic-comment word-order

                 least continuous/predictable

To demonstrate typical numerical values obtained in our cross-language
study, consider the following data from Bibilical Hebrew,[15] a language with
pragmatically flexible VS/SV word-order, a flexibility functionally comparable to the use of R- and L-dislocation, respectively, in spoken English.[16] There
is no zero-anaphora for subjects in Biblical Hebrew, since subject agreement
is obligatory. In the data on human subjects presented below, subject agreement (i.e. clitic pronouns) covers functionally both zero anaphora and unstressed (anaphoric) pronouns in (6).[17]

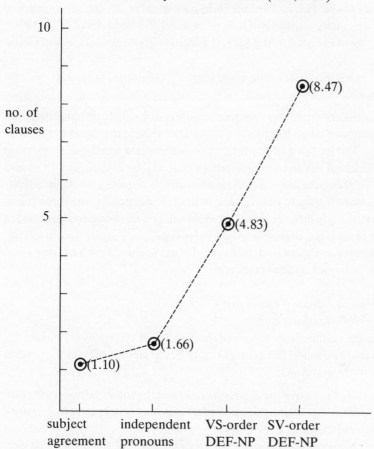

CHART I: Referential distance for human subjects
in Early Biblical Hebrew (Fox, 1983)

3. *Methodology and data-base*

Of the three measures developed in Givón (1983a, ed.), only one — referential distance — was used in this study. It is the easiest to apply, in terms of
making tricky judgments in live-discourse contexts, and that is especially important given the often chaotic nature of the early second-language acquisition texts. This measure was applied to three transcripts:

(a) *Stage-I Hawaii Pidgin English/Korean speaker*: About seven pages of
transcript originally elicited by D. Bickerton (cf. Bickerton and Odo, 1976),

one of the speakers used in the Stage-I Pidgin study of Bickerton and Givón (1976).[18]

(b) *Stage-I Hawaii Pidgin English/Philippine speaker*: About seven pages of transcript originally elicited by D. Bickerton (cf. Bickerton and Odo, 1976), one of the speakers used in the Stage-I Pidgin study of Bickerton and Givón (1976).[19]

(c) *Early Stage English/Spanish speaker*: A transcript provided by John Schumann.[20]

All three speakers are rather rudimentary users of English, although they are old and have been using English as a Pidginized vehicle for anywhere from 10 to 60 years. The first two transcripts are narratives, for which the application of our referential distance measurement is straightforward. The third is a transcript of short-exchange conversation, which required a certain adjustment in the measurement (see further below). Superficially, the three transcripts are strikingly different, and it would thus be advantageous to present each study separately, illustrating the kind of topic-marking devices involved. Once the results are tabulated, however, I hope to show how a striking measure of similarity nevertheless emerges.

4.   *The Hawaii Korean-English transcript*
    4.1.   *Topic-marking devices*
    Given the rudimentary nature of the English of this speaker, certain adjustments must be made as to categories of her grammar. The more general adjustments are as follows:

(a) *Predicates*: Transitive predicates include a verb plus some non-verb complement (see below). Intransitive complements may be either verbal or nonverbal (nominal, adjectival, or other).

(b) *Object*: No attempt was made to separate indirect from direct object, since no prepositions are used in the transcript. Objects may be also manner adverbs, which are then counted perforce as *non-referential*. Further, objects may also be verbal phrases, in which they are again counted as *non-referential*.

    The following are the categories that were found and counted:[21]

(i) *Zero-anaphora (subject or object)*:

    (7)   ...He like Ø OK. Ø marry. Ø come Hawaii...'
           '...He liked it well. So we married, and we came to Hawaii...'

In the counts, 1st person was separated from 3rd person, in order to facilitate the comparison with pronouns (see below).

(ii) *Independent subject pronouns*:

> (8) ...I like Hawaii come...
> '...**I** liked coming to Hawaii...'
> (9) ...He like OK...
> '...**He** liked (it) well'

In the transcript counted, only subject pronouns were found, although many zero-anaphora objects were found, as in (7) above.

(iii) *DEF-NP subjects*:

Only the SV word-order was found in the transcript, either with *transitive* predications, as in:

> (10) ...Husband picture me see...
> '...**My husband** saw a picture of me...'
> '...**My husband** saw me in a picture...'

or in an *intransitive* predication ,as in:

> (11) ...Husband only work...
> '...**my husband** just worked...'

The overwhelming majority of DEF-NP subjects were *unique* NP's, such as kinship terms ('my husband', 'my son', 'his daughter') or place names ('Korea', 'Hawaii', 'Honolulu'). Even the few technically non-unique ones, such as 'the boat' below, are in fact unique by virtue of general cultural presuppositions. Thus consider:

> (12) ...no, only me come; Japan first time, ship Japan come...
> '...No, I came alone; I first went to Japan, **the ship** came to Japan first...'

In the context of travel from Korea to the US, 'ship' needs no antecedence in order to be considered unique.

(iv) *DEF-NP OV-ordered objects*:

These may be semantically *patients*, as in:

> (13) ...my brother children see...
> '...(so that I can) see **my brother's children**...'

Though the great majority in this transcript are actually *locatives*, as in:

(14) ...ship Japan come...
   '...the ship came **to Japan**...'

Again, the great majority of DEF-NP objects are unique NP's, such as kinship terms or place-names, as above.

(v) *DEF-NP VO-ordered objects*:

These may be again semantically *patients*, as in:

(15) ...Husband pay help husband better...
   '...My husband's pay was better (and) that helped **my husband**...'

Or they may be, as the overwhelming majority is, *locatives*, as in:

(16) ...Boat come Hawaii...
   '...(then) the boat came **to Hawaii**...'

Again, the overwhelming majority of these DEF-NP's are referentially unique, i.e. kinship terms or place names.

(vi) *Indefinite NP's — referential*:

The overall count for these is exceedingly small in this transcript. Most of the subject REF-INDEF NP's are referentially *tainted* by being kinship terms as well, as in:

(17) ...one brother dies...
   '...**one of my brothers** died...'

The object REF-INDEF's may come either in the *OV order*, as in:

(18) ...office work...
   '...he works in **an office**...'

Or they may come in the VO order, as in:

(19) ...one girl he get...a...gran...grandaughter...
   '...one of my girls has **a grandaughter**...'

(vii) *Indefinite NP's — non-referential*:

These may come either in the VO or OV word-order, and we count here primarily *manner adverbs*, as in:

(20) ...He like OK..
   '...he liked (it) **well**...'

or *verbal-phrase complements*, as in:

(21) ...I like Hawaii come...
'...I liked **coming to Hawaii**...'

The referential distance measure is obviously irrelevant for indefinites (referential or non-referential), so that only the total number of occurrences was recorded for these categories.

(viii) *L-dislocated DEF-NP's*:

The few instances found may be divided into *subject L-dislocation*, as in:

(22) ...Satari they Japan...
'...**Satari, it** is in Japan...'

and *object L-dislocation*, as in:

(23) ...diploma my son highschool get...
'...**diploma**, my son got **a highschool diploma**...'[22]

(ix) *R-dislocated DEF-NP's*:

The few instances found may be divided into *subject R-dislocation*, as in:

(24) ...now this man die thirty three yeah, second husband...
'...**this man** died thirty three years ago, **my second husband**...'

and *object R-dislocation*, as in:

(25) ...diploma my son highschool get, yes, yes, Farrington highschool...
'...my son got his **highschool diploma**, yes, yes, **at Farrington high-school**...'[23]

(x) *Topic NP without any predication*:

As we shall see later on, this is an important category, both numerically and functionally, in the kind of text studied here. It is akin to but not identical with L-dislocation, in the sense that the speaker attempts to introduce a (new) topic by such a device, but often has severe difficulty in launching the topic into the register. In this text, the use of the device was characterized by multiple repetition of a new topic NP, as in:

(26) ...yes, one brother, six sist...one brother, three sister, all together...'
'...yes, we were one brother and three sisters all together...'

Or again as in:

(27) ...highschool, highschool diploma, diploma, highschool, diploma, my son highschool get...
'...speaking of highschools and diplomas, my son got his diploma...'

Although my transcripts do not indicate this, I suspect many if not all the instances in which this device was used involved an introduction of the new topic *by the interviewer*. As we shall see further below, this is also the case in the Spanish-English text, where the role of the interviewer is documented explicitly.

4.2. Numerical results

The results of our referential distance measurement for definite topics of all types are presented in Table I, below. The number above the line in each box is the *average* referential distance per token, in terms of number of clauses to the clause where the same referent was last serving as an argument. The minimal possible value is thus *one* (1). Rather than deal with computations involving infinity, I have arbitrarily assigned the value *twenty* (20) as the maxi-

TABLE I: Referential distance for definite topics in the Korean-English text

	zero anaphora	indep. pronoun	DEF-NP	left-disloc.	right-disloc.	pred-less repetition
SUBJECT 1st pers	1.11^{25} (38)	3.46 (26)				
			8.84 (19)	7.00 (5)	1.00 (5)	
3rd pers.	1.00 (50)	1.00 (14)				16.30 (41)
OBJECT OV-order			11.86 (22)			
	1.4^{26} (5)	/		15.8 (3)	1.00 (2)	
VO-order			8.23 (11)			

TABLE II: The numerical distribution of indefinite NP's in the various categories of the Korean-English text

category	referential indefinite	non-referential indefinite
SUBJECT	5	/
OBJECT-OV	7	21
OBJECT-VO	3	14
pred-less repetition	10	

mal referential distance that can be assigned, thus not counting further to the left beyond twenty clauses. The justification for this practice is discussed elsewhere.[24] The numbers in parentheses below the line in each box represent the number of tokens counted in the category. The numerical results for indefinite NP's are presented in Table II. Only total counts in the text are presented, and some of those will be discussed later on.

One fairly striking feature of the referential distance figures presented in Table I is the progression — in very much the same direction although with one additional category — from zero-anaphora upward. The values for zero anaphora hover around 1.00, the minimal value possible. This is, predictably, the most *continuous* topic-marking device. The value rises, at least with the use of *1st person* subject pronoun, to 3.4.6. This speaker thus makes a significant difference between her use of zero-anaphora and independent pronoun at least when referring to herself. The values rise again to 8.84 (subject) and 11.86/8.23 (OV/VO objects) for definite NP's. The highest *discontinuity* is found for the last device, repeated predicate-less topics, with values averaging 16.30, or quite close to the maximum of 20.

The OV-VO dimension does not seem significant in terms of the measure of referential distance. The same 2/1 OV/VO ratio found with definite objects is also found with indefinite ones (see Table II). It may be that these figures represent the frozen variability observed by Bickerton and Givón (1976) for the Japanese/Korean-English sample, and this variability is thus seemingly non-functional. It may also be that other measures, such as potential ambiguity or decay (see section 2, above), may reveal a functional difference. And it may also be that more subtle and hitherto undeveloped measures of *thematic continuity/discontinuity* will in the future reveal a functional difference between the use of OV and VO in this text.[27]

Finally, while the counts are rather small, the difference between L-dislocation and R-dislocation is striking, with the latter representing a much more *continuous* topic-marking device, and the former a much more *discontinuous* one. This is consistent with the predictions made in (6) above and with word-order and dislocation studies found elsewhere.[28]

5. *The Hawaii Philippine-English transcript*
   5.1. *Topic-marking devices*
   The same devices were studied as in the Korean-English transcript above, so that I will forego citing examples again. Two adjustments relevant to this particular text were:

(a) The use of 2nd person pronouns ('you') was added to the 1st person pronoun ('I', 'me'), both for zero anaphora and independent pronouns;
(b) Due to the native language here (Philippine, probably Ilocano), the OV order is insignificant, although two tokens were actually recorded;

5.2. *Numerical results*
The results of our referential distance measurement for definite topics of all types are given in Table III, below. The number above the line in each box again represents the average referential distance for the category in terms of number of clauses to the left (again minimally 1 and maximally 20). The integer in parentheses below the line again represents the number of tokens counted for the category.

The overall correspondences with the Korean-English data in section 4, above, are rather striking. Again, the *most continuous* category, with the lowest referential distance, is zero anaphora. Independent pronouns again represent an intermediate case. However, here some language-specific differences pertaining to L1 of the speakers begin to appear. In Bickerton and Givón (1976) we noted that there was a much higher overall frequency of pronouns in the Philippine texts as against the Korean and Japanese texts. This is again borne out in the data in Table III, where the Ø/PRO ratio was 32/60 for 1st and 2nd persons and 6/35 for 3rd persons in the Philippine-English data. In contrast, the Korean-English data in Table I yield the ratio of 38/26 for first persons and 50/14 for 3rd persons. Clearly, some of the functional load carried by zero-anaphora in the Korean-English text is borne by (unstressed) pronouns in the Philippine-English text, at least for 1st/2nd persons, perhaps accounting thus for the *lower* (i.e. more continuous) referential distance of those pronouns in the Philippine-English data (1.80 vs. 3.46). The opposite tendency is seen for the 3rd-person pronouns, where the Korean-English use (subjects) is indistinguishable from the zero-anaphora values, while the Philippine-English use is the *highest* (i.e. least continuous) for this category (3.60).

TABLE III: Referential distance for definite topics in the
Philippine-English text

		zero anaphora	indep. pronoun	DEF-NP	left-disloc.	right-disloc.	pred-less repetition
SUBJECT	*1st/2nd person*	1.00 (23)	1.80 (60)				
				8.00 (6)	16.10 (7)	1.00 (2)	
	3rd pers.	1.00 (6)	3.60 (35)				
							17.4 (5)
OBJECT VO	*1st/2nd person*	/	1.80 (5)	/	/	/	
	3rd per.	1.00 (3)	/	15.20 (26)	/	/	
OV		/	/	10.10 (2)	/		

TABLE IV: Numerical distribution of indefinite NP's in the
            Philippine-English text

category		referential indefinite	non-referential indefinite
SUBJECT	VS	3	1
	SV	/	1
OBJECT	VO	11	21

The rest of the Philippine-English data correspond rather closely to the results of the Korean-English study. Again the least-continuous category is that of predicate-less repetition (17.40), although L-dislocated subject NP's assume values almost as high (16.10). And definite *objects* are not far behind (15.2). The much more continuous nature of R-dislocation is again confirmed, although the counts are again low.

The results of the indefinite-NP distribution in the text are given, for the sake of completeness, in Table IV. There is no significant word-order variation in this text to warrant further comment on these data.

6.   *The Spanish-English transcript*

6.1.   *Methodological adjustments for conversation data*

The short-exchange conversational nature of our third text, where in many cases topics are initiated by the (English speaking) interviewer, contrasts sharply with the largely narrative, monolog nature of the two previous texts. The conversational text, combined perhaps with the particular style and/or competence level of our Spanish speaker, requires a number of adjustments in our *measurement methodology* before it could be applied here. Further, it also necessitated some *re-categorization* of what appeared in the text. I will discuss the methodological adjustments first.

(i)   *Definition of a clause*: I have adopted a much more lax definition of what is to be counted as 'clause' in measuring referential distance. Extremely short exchanges with no pauses included are counted as single clauses. In longer contributions from the *subject*, pauses are taken to separate 'clauses', and the latter could easily be single-words, either 'topic' or 'comment', which may also include *repeated topic* for lack of understanding, or *WH-question* either confirming the topic or expressing misunderstanding.

(ii) *Counting across-speakers*: In cases — and they are numerous — when the topic was introduced by the interviewer, the referential distance is *not* counted from the *subject's* first mention of the topic, which would most commonly be a repetition of the topic, but rather from the *interviewer's point of raising the topic* in the preceding line (on the right side of the transcript; see appendix 3). The motivation for this adjustment is transparent. It allows the application of the same quantitative methods to the study of conversation as initially applied to narrative.

(iii) *Topic/comment vs. subject/object*: The José text makes it virtually impossible, due to the shortness of most exchanges and the extremely elliptic nature of even the more continuous short clauses, to deal in terms of categories such as 'subject', 'object' or 'verb'. Rather, it makes it necessary — and surprisingly easy once the discourse/communication is understood — to describe the text in terms of 'topics' and 'comments' only. The *topic* will correspond in a fairly straight-forward way to the 'subject' of the preceding two texts, while the 'comment' will take any new information category, be it verb, adjective, noun or adverb. There are no grounds available in this text for making further discriminations.[29]

6.2. *Topic-marking devices*
The following six categories were measured in this text:

(a) *Overtly-expressed incomprehension*:
   (28) *Interviewer*: What's it like there? Describe it to me.
       José: No stand
           'I don't understand'

(b) *Repetition of a topic introduced by the interviewer, again indicating incomprehension*:
   (29) *Interviewer*: Tell me about Mexico. Where did you live there?
       José: Me?
           'Who, me?'

(c) *Topic repetition plus an attempted comment*:[30]
   (30) *Interviewer*: The movies? *Cine*? Do you go to them?
       José: *Cine*? Me no. No like *cine*. *Ni* in Mexico *ni* in California.
           'Movies? Me no, I don't like the movies, neither in Mexico nor in California'

(d) *SV or T-C word-order with full "NP's"*:[31]
     (31) *Interviewer*: **Ramón** in school Los Angeles...
           José: No. **Ramón** in school Los Angeles...
           'No. **Ramón** is at school in Los Angeles...'
(e) *SV/T-C order with pronominal ('I', 'me') topic*:
     (32) *José*: ...**me** sí, **me** come-back Mexico in nineteen seventy four...
           '...**as for me**, yes, **I** came back from Mexico in 1974...'
(f) *VS or C-T word-order with full NP's*:
     (33) *José*: ...(me come-back Mexico in 1974), is come **my family**...
           '...(I came back from Mexico in 1974), they came too, **my family** did...'
(g) *Zero-anaphoric topic*:
     (34) *José*: ...(no time for me). In Saturday Ø no like, Ø no time. Ø
           watch TV...
           '...(there's no time for me). On Saturday I don't like (to go to
           the movies), I don't have any time. I watch TV...'

6.3. Numerical results

The results, in spite of the methodological and categorization adjustments, are again striking, and they are given in Table V. The most *continuous* topic-marking device is again *zero-anaphora*, with the average 1.00 value, just as in the Korean and Philippine-English texts. The *VS or comment-topic word-order* is again next, with a value of 3.42 — higher than in the previous text but with higher and thus more reliable counts and a value almost coming to the level recorded for the VS word-order in Biblical Hebrew (4.83 there; see Chart I, above). Next is the *SV word order with pronouns*, the only word-order for pronouns in this text, with a 4.83 average value, corresponding fairly closely to the 3.48 value recorded in the Korean-English text for first-person subjects or the 3.60 value in the Philippine-English text for 3rd-person subjects. Next is the *SV word-order for full NP's*, with an average value of 13.00, corresponding to the subject L-dislocation value of 16.10 in the Philippine-English data or the object L-dislocation value of 15.8 in the Korean-English data, and in the same relative position on the continuity scale as the SV word-order in Biblical Hebrew (8.47 value there). Finally, the three most *discontinuous* devices — incomprehension or topic repetition, with numerical values approaching the maximum (18.10, 20.00, 20.00 here) — correspond closely to the repetition device in the Korean-English data (16.30, highest on the scale) and Philippine-English (17.40, highest on the scale).

TABLE V: Referential distance of topic-marking devices in the Spanish-English text

category	result
(a) Incomprehension	18.10 (10)
(b) Repeated topic with incomprehension	20.00 (9)
(c) Repeated topic plus attempted comment	20.00 (5)
(d) SV/T-C order—NP's	13.00 (36)
(e) —PRO	4.83 (18)
(f) VS/-C-T order (NP's)	3.42 (14)
(g) Ø-anaphora	1.00 (91)

7. *Discussion*

7.1. *Comparison of coding-points on the topic-continuity scale*

The values for subjects/topics from Tables I, III, and V above are represented for comparison in Chart II below, together with the Biblical Hebrew values reproduced from Chart I. One could see without further elaboration the striking cross-language similarities that the three foreign-English 'dialects' project, in spite of the native-language typological variability (SOV-Korean, V-first Philippine, VO, SV/VS-Spanish), in spite of the relatively small body of text counted (7-10 pp. each), in spite of the genre variation (narrative vs. conversation), in spite of the different methodology and personality of the interviewer (Bickerton vs. an ESL graduate student of Schumann's), and in spite of the extreme variation in culture, personality and English-fluency among the subjects. The curves are inherently parallel, their close parallel to the Biblical Hebrew curve is striking, and the marked instances of deviation are all instances where second-language users use a more-marked device — one normally involving more *discontinuity* — at a much less marked functional point (i.e. in environments of much higher topic-continuity) than one would expect in 1st-language users of comparable devices. This over-use of more marked devices is also a major facet of early *child language*, and also figures prominently in *diachronic change* toward *demarking* erstwhile marked constructions.[32] The cross-language data in Givón (1983a ed.), representing only 1st-language data, show much closer curves, but that is only to be expected. It is very clear we are dealing with a stable phenomenon that supersedes cross-language diversity (for first languages) and the 1st-language diversity (for second-language acquisition). What we deal with is dis-course-structure universals of topic-continuity marking.

7.2.   *The gist of the topic-marking universals*

In the *pre-syntactic* universe of no grammatical morphology and no semantically-based word-order, what are the *rock-bottom universals* of cod-ing the degree of topic continuity? It seems to me that the juxtaposition of the cross-language study in Givón (1983, ed.) and the data presented here makes it possible to list these universals rather unambiguously. To wit:

(i)   *Quantity universal*: "More continuous, predictable, non-disruptive topics will be marked by *less marking material*; while less continuous, unpredictable/surprising, or dis-ruptive topics will be marked by *more marking material*".

For 'marking material' one could well substitute 'length of phonological se-quence used to code the topic'. This universal yields the following hierarchy:

(35)   zero   > unstressed PRO/   indep/stressed   > full-NP   repeated full-
       anaphora > verb-agreement > PRO   > topic > NP topic

(ii)   *Word-order universal*: "Of topics that are fully expressed as an indepen-dent word or pronoun, those that are most con-tinuous/predictable will display COMMENT-TOPIC (VS, VO) word-order; while those that are less continuous/predictable will display TOPIC-COMMENT (SV, OV) word-order".

CHART II: Overall comparison of referential-distance values for
           subjects/topics of four texts

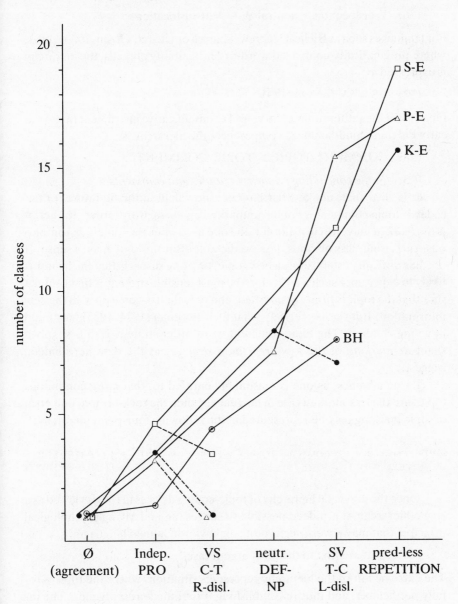

For languages with a fixed word order such as English (SVO) or Korean (SOV), the more common expression of this universal is in the hierarchy:

(36)   L-dislocation > neutral W-O > R-dislocation

For languages such as Biblical Hebrew, Spanish or Ute (cf. Givón, 1983a, ed.), where pragmatically-controlled word-order flexibility prevails, the hierarchy is expressed as:

(37)   VS > SV (or VO > OV)

Finally, for the rather rudimentary, frail communicative instrument that is the early Pidgin/second-language competence, the hierarchy is:

(38)   COMMENT-TOPIC > TOPIC-COMMENT

7.3.   Some concluding remarks on topics and comments

It is clear that, unlike what has been prevalent in the literature for decades,[33] topic-comment is *not* the unmarked universal word-order. Rather, it is the *marked* universal word-order, the one used when the topic is discontinuous, surprising, less obvious, less predictable. But this only makes sense. If one has difficulty establishing a new topic, or if one suspects that the hearer is likely to experience such a difficulty, the most sensible strategy is first to make sure that the topic is *firmly established*, and only then to come up with the new information. But this is precisely what Ochs/Keenan (1974, 1975) has found in young children. The topic-comment word-order strategy is thus simply a slight *de-marking* of the *topic repetition strategy*, as the data here indeed suggest.

If one assumes, as one is reasonably entitled to, that more continuous topics are the less-marked case in language,[34] then the rock-bottom universal of topic marking may be represented in the following four-point hierarchy:[35]

(39)   COMMENT $>$ COMMENT-TOPIC $>$ TOPIC-COMMENT $>$ REPEATED TOPIC
       (ZERO TOPIC)   (ZERO COMMENT)

Once the universal hierarchy of topic-coding devices in (39) is viewed as a single hierarchy, it is indeed possible to suggest an underlying psychological principle that may govern such coding behavior in human language:

(40)   "Attend first to the most urgent task"

The extreme left of the hierarchy represents situations where the topic is totally predictable, and thus re-establishing it is of the *lowest* urgency. The remaining urgent task is to process the comment or new information. The extreme right of the hierarchy represents the opposite situation, where the topic is extremely *unpredictable*. Communication could not therefore proceed without first firmly establishing the topic, and this is then the most urgent task. The large amount of topic-repetition found in child language (Ochs/Keenan 1974, 1975) as well as in our transcripts of early second language acquisition is clear illustration of the latter extreme situation, where the communicative stress characterizing the system manifests itself primarily as paucity of available *routinized means* of identifying the clausal topic.

Within the framework of principle (40), above, it is possible to view the relationship between topic-comment and comment-topic word order — in languages where discourse-pragmatics rather than case-role semantics controls word-order variation — as a reflection of a general psychological principle of *task performance*, rather than a relatively 'structural' question of abstract 'markedness'.

7.4. *Variability and non-grammaticality in Pidginization*

When one approaches Pidgins and Early 2nd Language data trying to assess their syntax (as in, for example, Bickerton and Givón, 1976), they seem indeed chaotic, variable and non-systematic — a baffling melange of randomly-used devices. Once one divests oneself of syntactic prejudice and proceeds to investigate the use of discourse-pragmatic devices, a greater measure of systematicity and universality begins to emerge. It is thus the syntacticized level of language that reveals, in 2nd language acquisition, the stronger traces of 'error' and '1st language interference'. On the other hand, discourse universals tend to be 'more universal' than syntactic structure. It is thus only to be expected that when communication is under severe stress, speakers of varying linguistic background revert to this more common communicative mode. It has persisted subterraneanly in some registers of linguistic-communicative behavior, those which hark back to early childhood and pre-syntactic communication. Rather than 'making errors vis-à-vis a syntactic target-L', one must consider early 2nd language communication as a coherent instrument utilizing universally available devices under appropriate circumstances.

NOTES

1) Eg. Bickerton (1975, 1977a, 1977b), Bickerton and Odo (1976), Bickerton and Givón (1976), Kay and Sankoff (1974), Traugott (1977), Ferguson and DeBose (1977), *inter alia*.

2) Cf. Givón (1973/1979).

3) Givón (1979, Ch. 5).

4) Ochs (1979), Givón (1979, Ch. 5).

5) Givón (1979, Ch. 5).

6) This was initially named 'The pragmatic mode', but I suspect now the earlier term has some potential for confusion.

7) Bickerton (1975, 1977a, 1977b), Bickerton and Odo (1976).

8) Pre-syntactic communication is evident in the speech of early childhood and in the data of early second-language acquisition. As we shall see below, discourse-pragmatic data are available independently from the study of any natural language.

9) Firbas (1966a, 1966b), *inter alia*.

10) Hawkinson and Hyman (1975), Li and Thompson (1976), Givón (1976a), *inter alia*.

11) Givón (1976a, 1976b, 1979 Ch. 2, Ch. 4).

12) Givón (1979, Ch. 2) and (1980, Ch. 17).

13) Givón (ed., 1983a). The languages investigated were Spoken and Written English, Spanish, Biblical Hebrew, Amharic, Hausa, Japanese, Ute and Chamorro.

14) This measure does not always correlate to (4a,b), for reasons that are discussed in detail elsewhere (Givón, 1983a, ed).

15) Fox (1983).

16) Givón (1983b).

17) In all the studies in our volume (Givón, 1983a, ed.), subject as well as various object NP's were investigated across the range of grammatical devices, to the extent that those were available across the case-role scale. Indeed, the topic-hierarchy of semantic case roles — AGT>DAT/ BEN>PAT>LOC>INSTR>MANN — as discussed in Givón (1976a), *inter alia*, correlates rather directly to our continuity dimension as revealed in the cross-language study.

18) Bickerton's tape 23-CHL (efk) FK-79, beginning from p. 28 of Bickerton's transcription. A sample page can be seen in *Appendix 1*, below, together with a suggested running translation into standard English.

19) Bickerton's tape BI-16 (MK/KN) AA, MF-77, beginning from p. 1 of Bickerton's transcription. A sample page together with standard English translation can be seen in *Appendix 2*, below.

20) Transcript labeled 'José no. 1, Jan 21, 1979, 1 pm' [Restaurant where J. has just gotten off work], supplied by John Schumann. A sample page may be seen in *Appendix 3*, below. The first 10 pages were analyzed.

21) The nature of the text is such that one must allow for anywhere from 10 to 20 percent of uncategorizable output. In Bickerton and Givón (1976), where a more syntactic categorization was sought, the percent of such 'garbage' was much larger.

22) Given the nature of the text, I have chosen to relax the definition of dislocation, either R or L, to include both repeated NP's as well as repeated pronouns.

23) Again, given the nature of the text, I have chosen to relax the definition of dislocation here to allow non-strict-one-to-one referential relations, i.e. 'highschool diploma' and 'Farrington highschool'. There are general theoretical grounds for allowing such relaxation (see Givón, 1982).

24) See Givón (1983a ed., introductory chapter).

25) The deviation from the expected 1.00 average value here is due to only three (3) tokens out of the entire sample of 38.

26) The deviation from the expected 1.00 average value here is due to only one (1) token out of the sample of 5.

27) For example, the difference between zero anaphora and unstressed pronouns in English is expressed not in terms of referential distance (both 1.00 on the average) and not so much in terms of potential ambiguity (both low values), but rather in terms of *thematic* continuity. For further detail, see Givón (1983a ed.).

28) Givón (1983a ed.).

29) Whether this is a function of the text type (short exchanges across two speakers), José's individual style or José's lower proficiency in English remains to be assessed, obviously not in this study. My own suspicion centers on a combination of the first and the third factors.

30) It was deemed unimportant, for the purpose of this study, to try and determine whether José 'correctly identified' the topic introduced by the interviewer and thus supplied the 'relevant comment'. The interviewer herself was rather intrusive, over-controlling the interaction and introducing new topics rather abruptly, I suspect from a pre-determined checklist. Felicitously, that generated a lot of data concerning José's use of various devices indicating *topic discontinuity*.

31) The term 'NP' is just as meaningless for this transcript as are 'subject', 'object', or 'verb'. What is meant in 'full NP' is then a *word/constituent* excluding pronouns.

32) See discussion in Givón (1979, Ch. 5), *inter alia*.

33) The history of topic-comment being considered the unmarked word-order is rather curious, starting with early Praguean attention to *marked* topicalization devices in Indo-European languages, such as contrastive-topicalization and L-dislocation, continuing with similar misapprehensions in Givón (1976a) and many other contributors to the Li (1976) volume, and thus being passed on uncritically via Givón (1979, Ch. 5) and onward to Bickerton (this volume), *inter alia*. This is an obvious point for me to apologize for my part in this chain of transmission.

34) To the extent that multi-propositional discourse should be considered the unmarked norm for human disocurse, a discourse where many comments in a row are made about the same ('continuous') topic, then obviously discontinuous-topic devices are to be considered 'marked'. This point has been belabored beyond the need to further support it.

35) It may very well be that when one deals with the very early stages of first or second language acquisition, where discourse is nearly *mono-propositional* and thus topic continuity in the discourse is very low *as a rule*, one is perhaps justified in arguing that grammatical devices which code more *discontinuous/unpredictable* topics are the 'unmarked' case in such discourse type. The same may be true about some genres of extremely disjointed conversation. Markedness thus cannot be defined independently of discourse normativity, i.e. text frequency (cf. Givón, 1979, Chapter 2).

REFERENCES

Bickerton, D. 1975. Creolization, linguistic universals, natural semantax and the brain. Unpublished paper, University of Hawaii.

Bickerton, D. 1977a. *Change and Variation in Hawaiian English*, vol. II, *The Creole*. NSF Report, University of Hawaii.

Bickerton, D. 1977b. Pidginization and creolization: Language acquisition and language universals. In A. Valdman (ed.) 1977.

Bickerton, D., and T. Givón. 1976. Pidginization and syntactic change: From SXV and VSX to SVX. *Parasession Volume on Diachronic Syntax*, CLS no. 12. Chicago: Chicago Linguistic Society, University of Chicago.

Bickerton, D., and C. Odo. 1976. *Change and Variation in Hawaiian English*, vol. I, *The Pidgin*. Final Report on NSF Grant No. GS-39748. University of Hawaii.

Ferguson, C., and C.E. DeBose. 1977. Simplified registers, broken language, and pidginization. In A. Valdman (ed.) 1977.

Firbas, J. 1966a. Non-thematic subjects in contemporary English. *Travaux Linguistiques de Prague 2*:239-256.

Firbas, J. 1966b. On defining the theme in functional sentence analysis. *Travaux Linguistiques de Prague 2*:267-180.

Fox, A. 1983. Topic continuity in Early Biblical Hebrew. In Givón (ed.) 1983a.

Givón, T. 1973/1979. Prolegomena to any sane Creology. In I. Hancock (ed.), *Readings in Creole Studies*. Ghent: Storia-Scientia.

Givón, T. 1976a. Topic, pronoun and grammatical agreement. In Li (ed.) 1976.

Givón, T. 1976b. The VS word-order in Israeli Hebrew: Pragmatics and typological change. In P. Cole (ed.), *Studies in Modern Hebrew Syntax and Semantics*. Amsterdam: North Holland Publishing Co.

Givón, T. 1979. *On Understanding Grammar*. New York: Academic Press.

Givón, T. (ed.). 1979. *Discourse and Syntax: Syntax and Semantics vol. 12*. New York: Academic Press.

Givón, T. 1980. *Ute Reference Grammar*. Ignacio, CO.: Ute Press.

Givón, T. 1982. Logic vs. pragmatics, with human language as the referee: Toward an empirically viable epistemology. *Journal of Pragmatics 6.1*.

Givón, T. (ed.). 1983a. *Topic Continuity in Discourse: A Quantitative Cross-Language Study*, vol. 3 of *Typological Studies in Language*. Amsterdam: John Benjamins.

Givón, T. 1983b. Left and right dislocation in spoken American English. In Givón (ed.) 1983a.

Hawkinson, A., and L. Hyman. 1974. Hierarchies of natural topic in Shona. *Studies in African Linguistics* 5:147-170.

Kay, P., and G. Sankoff. 1974. A language-universal approach to Pidgins and Creoles. In D. DeCamp and I. Hancock (eds.), *Pidgins and Creoles: Current Trends and Prospects*. Washington, D.C.: Georgetown University Press.

Li, C. (ed.). 1976. *Subject and Topic*. New York: Academic Press.

Li, C., and S. Thompson. 1976. Subject and topic: A new typology of language. In Li (ed.) 1976.

Ochs [Keenan], E. 1974. Again and again: The pragmatics of imitation in child language. Unpublished ms. University of Southern California.

Ochs [Keenan], E. 1975. Making it last: The use of repetition in children's discourse. *Berkeley Linguistic Society* vol. I. University of California, Berkeley.

Ochs [Keenan], E. 1979. Planned and unplanned discourse. In Givón (ed.) 1979.

Traugott, E. 1977. Pidginization, Creolization and language change. In Valman (ed.).

Valdman, A. (ed.). 1977. *Pidgin and Creole Linguistics*. Bloomington: Indiana University Press.

APPENDIX I: *Transcript page of the Korean-English text*

...Picture marry.
Husband picture me see girl-time Korea.
He like OK. Marry. Come Hawaii.
Husband pay help husband better.
That's why Hawaii come.

I like Hawaii come.

My father, my mama, all said "go",
   "you like, go",
That's why come Hawaii.

Yes, one brother, six sist...
no, one brother, three sister, all together.
no, only me come.
Japan, first time, ship Japan come,
second come Hawaii.
This steamer... name Chang-Yang-Hwang...

he said...a...
Some people they...ah...american boat come.
Too big. My come-time up boat...ah...too big.

America boat come,
first time in *made* [?]...Satari come,
Satari they Japan,
Japan come one...ah one month time,
boat come Hawaii.

Running translation: 'I married through a picture. My husband saw my picture
when I was a girl in Korea. He liked it fine, so we got married and came to
Hawaii. My husband would have been better paid here, that's why we came to
Hawaii. I liked going to Hawaii. My dad and mom said "Go, if you like to,
go". That's why I came to Hawaii. [Gap presumably with interviewer's ques-
tion] Yes, I have one brother and six sist... I mean one brother and three sisters altogether. [Gap, presumably interviewer's question]. No, only I came to
Hawaii. We went first to Japan, the boat came first to Japan, then next stop to
Hawaii. This steamer, its name was C-Y-H... [Gap, presumably with interviewer's comment]. He said, uh...Some of the people, they came over on an
American boat, but it was too big. When I came up to it, it was too big. [gap].
The American boat came, first to made [? place name ?], then to Satari. Satari
is in Japan. So it came to Japan first... then in one month it made it to Hawaii.'

APPENDIX II: *Transcript page of the Philippine-English text*

...me before ah... *amaulu* ['camp'] number one,
strike-time Filipino, nine, nineteen-twenty-four.
And then I go make he special place.
I no, I no strike.
Filipino all he go strike.
Special place *amaulu*.
I sayin' for he special place,
I go *ama*... ah, I go Ola.
I go *dak* ['cut'] the sugar,
and then *pau* ['finish'] *pau* cut cane,
no more job,
ah, I go Kalapana side, I go plant taro,
one bag only three dollar;
one *hemo* [?] time one year.
One acre *hemo* oh, oh one acre make over thousand.
But no more he sp(end)... no more keep.
All he spend...
Spend good girl. Girl anykind, shit.
I go volcano, cut wood.
Five, five dollar one, one co... one cord.

Running translation: '...before that, I was a camp foreman, during the time of
the Filipino strike, in nineteen-twenty-four. I was going to make it a special
place then. No, I didn't go on strike, although all the Filipinos did. That camp
was a special place, that's what I say, a special place... So from there I went to
Ola, I went cutting sugar-cane. Then cane-cutting ended, it was finished, no
more work. So I went to a place around Kalapana and worked in planting
Taro. One bag (of Taro) was only three dollars then. So on one acre you could
make a thousand dollars or over. But that money didn't last, I spent all of it, on
good girls, on any kind of girls, shit.... So then I went up around the volcano,
cutting wood. For five dollars a cord...'

APPENDIX III: *Transcript page of the Spanish-English text*

JOSÉ	INTERVIEWER
	So tell me something about yourself. Tell me about your family, tell me about Mexico. Tell me about where you live.
Oh, Mexico.	
	OK, tell me about Mexico, where you lived there.
Me?	
	Where did you live in Mexico?
Mexico. On the Colima.	
	Colima? Where's that?
A state. Comila.	
	What's it like there? Describe it for me.
No stand.	
	Are there mountains, water, farms, cities?
Colima. Noun...? Oh. In the moun... Is the... I don't know.	
	What are you trying to say? Mountains?
No, *no puedo decir*.	
	Are there mountains?
Mountains, *está bien*.	
	Montañas?
Oh yes, *Si*. Yeah. *Montaña*.	
	Mountains.
Montaña.	
	Uh huh. Water?
Yeah. Water in the...oh, in the Colima.	
	Uh huh.
And the *agricultura*. *Agricultura*. Make and the *cocayn*...[cocconuts] and everything.	
	When did you come here?
Me? In the nineteen-seven-o, seven-o.	

COMMENTS ON THE PAPER BY GIVÓN

JOHN SCHUMANN
University of California, Los Angeles

When we first studied early second language acquisition (SLA), or the basilang as we've come to call it, we treated this interlanguage (IL) as though it were syntax without morphology. But as more and more data were recorded, transcribed, and analyzed it seemed that basilang speech often lacked anything that could be considered syntax. I mentioned this to Givón about two years ago, and he suggested that we might want to view this language as pragmatic or (what he's now calling) pre-syntactic speech. This seemed like a good idea and we began to pursue that direction in our research. What soon became clear, however, was that in order to work within his perspective we would have to abandon our 'syntactic prejudice and ... investigate the use of discourse-pragmatic devices.' Any such re-orientation takes time and thus the analyses have proceeded slowly.

At about the same time, at the level of syntax and morphology, Bickerton (1981) presented a strong criticism of the supplied-in-obligatory-context (SOC) and target-like use (TLU) analyses that have been employed in SLA studies. In response to this criticism we have begun to use a version of his semantic analysis to study tense, aspect, and modality in interlanguage. This effort has led us to tentatively hypothesize that there may be a sequence of development in IL from no grammar in the basilang to an aspectual system in the middle stages to a tense system in the later stages. Thus a Bickerton type analysis seems to be most appropriate with subject in the middle of the continuum, and the traditional SOC and TLU analyses may be more appropriate at upper levels of the continuum where the subject approaches targer language proficiency. However, none of these analyses reveal much about the lower basilang because at this stage learners essentially have no grammar. Thus it would appear that the earliest stage of SLA may best be studied from the perspective of Givón's notion of pre-syntactic speech modalities.

The non-syntactic agrammatical nature of José's speech has been established in a series of previous studies. Noble (1979) showed that he had 100% pre-verbal (*no*+verb) negation. Stauble and Schumann (1983) assessed his verb phrase morphology according to its TLU and found that no forms other than *is* (copula) and *base* were used correctly in excess of 20%. Schumann (1982) demonstrated that approximately 50% of José's utterances were non-syntactic and that about 92% of these were topic-comment forms. Schumann (1983) found that in a sample of 100 of José's utterances, subjects were absent 25% of the time and verbs were missing 53% of the time.

In spite of the clearly agrammatical nature of José's speech, he does communicate, but he does so through discourse-pragmatic means. As Givón has pointed out, such speech allows us to view rock-bottom universals of topic marking. In other words, although the hierarchy of devices for topic-continuity marking that he presents is maintained across numerous languages, the incipient process of such marking is available for study in second language acquisition both in the form of a pidgin language and a pidginized second language. Now since pidgin languages, i.e. true tertiary hybrids, are extremely rare, whereas early SLA is constantly renewed in immigrant situations, basilang data become especially useful for studying the language universals of pre-syntactic communication.

Finally, I'd like to comment on Givón's unambiguous equation of early SLA with pidginization. Of course I find this equation eminently reasonable. Although the essential identity of the two processes has been demonstrated in the areas of grammar and syntax (Andersen, 1981), it may emerge even more clearly in investigations of the discourse-pragmatic domain.

REFERENCES

Andersen, R.W. 1981. Two perspectives on pidginization as second language acquisition. In R.W. Andersen (ed.), *New Dimensions in Second Language Acquisition Research*. Rowley, Mass.: Newbury House Publishers.

Bickerton, D. 1981. Discussion of 'Two perspectives on pidginization as second language acquisition.' In R.W. Andersen (ed.), *New Dimensions in Second Language Acquisition Research*. Rowley, Mass.: Newbury House Publishers.

Noble, S. 1979. An interlanguage analysis. Unpublished paper (English Dept., TESL). University of California, Los Angeles.

Schumann, J. 1982. Simplification, transfer and relexification as aspects of pidginization and early second language acquisition. *Language Learning* 32:336-366.

Schumann, J. 1983. Utterance structure in the basilang. Paper presented at the Seventeenth Annual Convention of TESOL, Toronto.

Stauble, A.E., and J.H. Schumann. 1983. Toward a description of the Spanish-English basilang. In K. Bailey, M. Long, and S. Peck (eds.), *Second Language Acquisition Studies*. Rowley, Mass.: Newbury House Publishers.

THE LANGUAGE BIOPROGRAM HYPOTHESIS
AND SECOND LANGUAGE ACQUISITION

DEREK BICKERTON
University of Hawaii

1. *What are linguistic universals?*

Hitherto, work on language universals, whether from a Greenbergian, Chomskyan, or Keenan-Comriean perspective, has mostly been based on what might seem to be the unimpeachable assumption that a language universal is something that is found in all languages. It is true that there has been work on what have been called 'implicational' or 'partial' universals, but the existence of such things hardly affects the truth of my opening sentence. Implicational universals are assumed to exist throughout language of certain types, or wherever some particular diagnostic feature is satisfied; they are, so to speak, only 'universal universals' in limited domains. Partial universals are supposedly features which occur in languages with more than chance frequency, although how one computes the chances is quite beyond me; to my knowledge, no one has ever claimed that any partial universal resulted from the biological make-up of the species. Thus, to claim, as I am going to, that there are biologically-based universals which, in their pure form, occur in hardly any languages at all, must seem, at first sight, a paradoxical and wholly gratuitous piece of perversity.

That it should so seem is due to a number of assumptions which, although widely endorsed by linguists, are quite baseless. The first is that all languages are developmentally equal — often expressed in the proposition, 'there are no primitive languages.'[1] The second, closely associated with this, is that there has been no evolutionary development in language — that 'stone age man spoke languages like ours' (Chomsky 1979:55). The third, which follows from these two, is that language can be studied (and perhaps can best be studied, or even can only be studied) in a static, aprocessual framework. This triad of assumptions had the inbuilt advantage that it confirmed and hallowed the traditional practices and prejudices of linguists, who from Panini on have been engaged mainly in the writing of grammars of individual standardized native adult languages, and who have regarded the study of other language phenomena, or those phenomena from different perspectives, as some inferior species of activity.[2]

Within this framework of unsupported assumption and timid conservatism, the belief that the central secret of language was just what all languages shared could live in comfort and, indeed, without serious challenge.

The best way to test the hollowness of this conventional linguistic wisdom is to ask, 'if language universals exist, why should they exist?' I can think of only three possible answers to this question. The first ('They exist because they exist, our business is merely to describe them') seems to me to refute the whole purpose of scientific inquiry. The second ('They exist because the nature of intelligent communication must always and everywhere be the same'), if viewed in the context of the fact that we know of only one species, our own, that communicates intelligently, seems to me as arrogant as it is empirically baseless. The third ('They exist because language is controlled by neuro-biological structures unique to, but universal among, our species') was, to the best of my knowledge, first made explicit at another conference on universals and second language learning (Howard 1971),[3] and represents the only possible intelligent answer.

1.2. Universals and their neuro-biological infrastructure

Now if what is universal in language is dependent upon species-specific neuro-biological structures, does it automatically follow that this will emerge in the structure of all adult human languages? Most people would answer automatically that it does. But why would they answer in this way? I think because of the confusion that is caused by the term innate, when this is introduced into the essentially static framework that I sketched in my opening paragraph.

If we are talking about innate mental structures, just what are we talking about? A partial answer may begin by considering what people once thought, and what they now think, about innate physical structures. Two or three centuries ago, most learned men found it impossible to believe that anything so complex as a human being could develop out of anything so simple as a fertilized human egg. Therefore the conventional wisdom of that day was preformationism, the belief that there existed, in forms too subtle for the instruments of the day to perceive, a miniature full-fledged chicken in the chicken egg, and a miniature adult human being in the human egg. Neither chicken nor man 'really' changed in the maturational process; all that happened, contrary to appearances, was that the miniature grew bigger and bigger and less and less subtle.

Nowadays we are more sophisticated. We know enough about biology and genetics for physical preformationism to seem as bizarre and arbitrary as the four humors, or phlogiston, or the geocentric universe (all good ideas in their day). We know that the instructions for making an adult species member, whether chicken or human, are encoded in DNA molecules in the form of a bioprogram which then evolves through time, changing as it evolves. But we are a good deal less sophisticated as we approach the central human problem of the linkage between the 'physical' neocortex and the 'mental' world of thought and language. Moreover, in this area there is not even any counterevidence, any equivalents of the embryos and neonates that physical preformationists had to explain away, to get in the way of mental preformationism. Thus, though it now seems demonstrably absurd to suppose that physical features remain unchanged throughout ontogeny, the same does not seem to hold for the innate structures that presumably underlie phenomena of the mind.

Tacit acceptance of some brand of mental performationism seems to be shared both by those who defend innate mental structures (cf. Chomsky's [1965] endorsement of Leibniz's 'figure in the marble' image) and those who, like Luria, Piaget and many others, find in innateness a mere evasion of the psychologist's responsibility.[4] In fact, preformational innateness is as unnecessary a concept for mental as it is for physical structures. Rather, it is much more plausible, in light of all we have learned about the functioning of animate organisms, that a bioprogram for mental features would follow a path very similar to that of a bioprogram for physical features. That is to say, instead of the mental structures that underlie language being present, in some elusive sense, from the moment of conception, or at least birth, we will regard only the DNA instructions for those structures as being present. Then, those instructions, just like the physical instructions for standing, walking, becoming sexually potent, etc., will become available *consecutively* rather than *simultaneously*. However, each instruction will by no means be part of the finished set of instructions. If bioprograms worked in this way, then the male voice of childhood would give way without incident to the male voice of adulthood. But we know that it does not, that it characteristically gives way to an intervening phase in which the male voice is a cracked falsetto of unstable pitch — a phenomenon popularly described as 'the voice breaking.' It is a good metaphor. Things have to break before they can be remade.

Thus we would expect that a genetic bioprogram for language would pass through a series of stages during the developmental cycle of the human child; that the instructions of that bioprogram at age two might differ significantly from the instructions at age four; and further, that the age two instructions need not necessarily be even a subset of the age four instruction, but could, in theory, differ from them in ways as unpredictable as the ways in which the butterfly and caterpillar differ.

2. *The nature of the language bioprogram*

But then, of what kind are these mysterious instructions? Again, we have to do battle with a horde of baseless yet all-but-unquestioned assumptions.

It is generally assumed that children learn their first languages. If we assume this, we must further assume that they do not already know a language, even though Fodor (1975) has conclusively shown that one must already know a language in order to learn a language.[5] If we thus implicitly rule out the possibility that the instructions of the bioprogram could be instructions on how to start a language, we are left with no option but to assume that they must be instructions on how to *learn* a language. Such is the assumption underlying the Chomskyan 'Language Acquisition Device' (Chomsky 1962): the child is supposedly programmed with a set of universal categories and a set of universal constraints which, together, sharply limit the types of (theoretically possible) language that the child might expect to have to learn, and thereby make his learning task — a task Chomsky usually refers to as one of 'selecting from a range of possible grammars' — that much easier.[6]

But if all our innate bioprogram tells us is how to learn something, it is unique in the whole of nature. Bioprograms of other creatures do not enable them to learn things, but rather present the things themselves, in ways such that there is no necessity for anything you could call learning. The European swift does not learn the way to South Africa; the Canadian salmon does not learn the way to the rivers of British Columbia; the Arctic tern does not learn the path between the Poles. These routes are, in ways still not fully understood by us, imprinted on these creatures' neural circuitry. In the same way, even our own bioprogram, insofar as it is physical, does not involve learning. We do not learn how to change the pitch of our voices, or how to grow pubic hair. Why then should we assume that the bioprogram which governs those aspects of our life that we label 'mental' should operate any differently? Parsimony alone would suggest that the bioprogram provides specific instructions for a sharply restricted type of language, rather than obscure and highly complex constraints on what can and cannot be learned. In other words, the language bioprogram ensures that people will have a particular type of grammar in just the same way as the physical bioprogram ensures that they will have a particular skeletal structure or a particular distribution of body hair.

Moreover, the suggestion that the bioprogram is of just this concrete and specific nature is no mere matter of speculation. Massive evidence in favor of it can be found in at least five distinct fields: creole languages, first-language acquisition, language origins, sign language, and linguistic change. The first three of these are discussed in some detail in Bickerton (1981). I shall briefly summarize the main findings of that work.

3.   Evidence for the bioprogram
3.1.   Creoles
With regard to creoles, these languages have frequently arisen under conditions which precluded any normal 'learning' process. They have arisen in colonies with a largely or exclusively immigrant population speaking a dozen or more mutually unintelligible languages, where the only means of communication common to all speakers was an immature pre-pidgin continuum. Children born under such circumstances did not acquire the set of competing immigrant languages or any subset of that set; often they did not acquire even the rudiments of their parent's language(s). But they did not acquire the pidgin either. The latter was both too variable to be learned (in Hawaii, this variability extended even to major word-order differences, some speakers having predominantly VO, others, predominantly OV, and still others, at least partially VS orders) and too deficient to be worth learning (the vast majority of pidgin speakers at the time of creole formation had not progressed beyond single-clause sentences). A new language, a creole, was therefore 'invented' in every case; but all of such 'inventions' exhibit grammatical structures of such close similarity that, as Douglas Taylor pointed out more than a decade ago (Taylor 1971), morph-for-morph translation can often be carried out on creoles with superficially quite different ancestry.

For facts such as these there is no explanation within the traditional frameworks. However, they follow naturally if there is a linguistic bioprogram of the kind I have suggested above. Then, a creole language is simply the realization, with minimal cultural admixture, of the instructions of that bioprogram.

Note that the birth of creoles falsifies any predictions that would follow from a Chomskyan LAD-type bioprogram. Chomsky (1968:76) has defined the child's learning task as 'to search among the possible grammars [i.e. those not explicitly ruled out by the structure of the internal schema, D.B.] and select one that is not definitely rejected by the data available to him.' Neither Chomsky nor anyone else (apart from the present writer) has ever seriously considered what would happen to such a child under the conditions sketched in the preceding paragraph. For under those conditions, the data are too rudimentary and too variable to reject ANY possible grammar that the LAD might make available. Would the child hesitate, like Buridan's ass, between those possible grammars, and end up learning no language at all? Or would he merely learn to replicate the pidgin of his elders? Even if such a theory were to bestow on the child the capacity to invent rules without any data to induce them from, it is hard to see how it could do more than predict that the resultant novel language would not violate any universal constraints. In fact, a much stronger prediction is supported by the facts: that languages formed under such conditions will be all but identical, save for the surface forms in the lexicon. Only the language bioprogram hypothesis makes such a strong prediction.

3.2. *First language acquisition*

In the second field explored in Bickerton 1981, first-language acquisition by children — or, more precisely what Lamendella (1977) describes as 'primary language acquisition' — there are, as has long been known, many phenomena for which no satisfactory explanation has ever been provided. In the primary acquisition of English, for example, certain things — the distinction between specific and nonspecific NP, or the correct use of the progressive form, for instance — seem to be acquired very quickly, very early, and with hardly any mistakes; while certain other things, not obviously more difficult — subject-aux inversion in questions, negative placement — are acquired considerably later, far more slowly, and with large numbers of utterances which are quite ungrammatical according to the rules of adult English. Since it so happens that the things which are learned early and effortlessly are those in which English grammar most closely resembles creole grammar, while the things which provoke systematic error are those in which English grammar is furthest from creole grammar (the errors themselves being perfectly good creole sentences!), the evidence again points to an innate bioprogram which directly furnishes certain distinctions and certain structures.

Further evidence from primary acquisition can be found in psycholinguistic studies such as those of Bever (1970). Bever found that between the ages of two-and-a-half and four, children's capacity to understand passive and cleft sentences not merely did not improve but actually declined quite sharply. Bever attributed this to a change in the child's basic 'learning strategy' from 'Principle C' — roughly, 'interpret syntax in terms of semantic probabilities' — to 'Principle D' — 'interpret N__V__N sequences as actor-action-patient.' Such abrupt changes of course, triggered by maturation (which is the same for everybody) rather than by experience (which is different for everybody), are typical of changes in bioprograms of other creatures; one is reminded of the African hornbill, which spends a large part of its infancy in narrowing the entrance to its nest, and yet suddenly, overnight, turns to widening it.[7] Moreover, this particular switch is explicable in terms of the third area.

3.3. *Language origins*

The third area explored by Bickerton (1981) is that of the origin of language. While any evidence from this field must have a much more tentative status than that drawn from other fields, it is possible to show that many of the semantic distinctions most basic to creole languages and primary acquisition can be provided with a plausible ancestry in terms of the development of mammalian nervous systems;[8] while the syntactic structures most basic to creoles can be derived if we attempt to reconstruct the most probable course for the evolution of human language from a primitive one-word stage to its contemporary complexity. The 'Principle C-Principle D' switch referred to in the last paragraph results quite naturally from such an evolution. If we assume, as seems reasonable, that the earliest human utterances were asyntactic, in the 'pragmatic mode' of Givón (1979), the most probable ordering was topic-comment and the only way to process sentences that were not interpretable in terms of the direct visual field would have been one based on semantic probabilities (if a man and a tree occur in the same utterance, the man is more likely doing something to the tree than vice versa, and so on). However, as soon as two-clause utterances began to appear (if not before), the multiplication of ambiguities and the increase in real-time processing (not to mention the accidents) that resulted from this would have led to a hardening of sentence-order in terms of a hierarchy of participants (case roles, arguments) in any given action.

Now the most plausible explanation for the origin of a bioprogram is that of Lamendella (1976), who suggested that developments in the evolution of human language were hard-wired into the genotype in such a way that the ontogeny of language in the child replicates, to a large extent, the phylogenetic development of language across time. If this is indeed the case, we have a natural explanation of why a child should move from 'Principle C' to 'Principle D' in the course of its linguistic development.

Two further areas provide independent evidence for the existence of the bioprogram. Studies in American Sign Language (e.g. Goldin-Meadow 1979) have shown that deaf children of hearing parents (non-ASL users) are capable of inventing sign language for themselves, and as yet unpublished research by Viv Edwards in England (p.c.) claims to have detected similarities to creole structure in naive sign. The theory also predicts that at least some bioprogram features may emerge when languages undergo extreme forms of change such as that from SOV to SVO basic order (or the reverse). For example, verb serialization, a common feature of creoles, is found also among the Kwa languages of West Africa, which have recently undergone a change from SOV to SVO, and among Papuan-influenced Austronesian languages in Papua-New Guinea, which are presently changing from SVO to SOV. Much further research will be required in both these areas, but it seems highly probably that such research, even if limited to a review of existing descriptions, will lend strong support to the bioprogram hypothesis.

If a bioprogram for language underlies and steers the primary acquisition of language, are we to conclude that it plays any role at all in second-language acquisition by adults?

This is, ultimately, an empirical question. The most that can be done at present is to re-examine some relevant issues and indicate the courses that such empirical research may follow. The most obvious issue involved is that of the so-called 'critical period' of language acquisition. This has, of course, long been a bone of contention in acquisition studies, but there seems to be a general consensus, shared even by those who take differing viewpoints (e.g. Scovel 1981, Seliger 1981) that the strongest evidence for a critical period comes from nonprimary acquisition of phonology; in other words, it is a good deal less than certain that there *is* any critical period with regard to secondary acquisition of syntax and semantics. What we have to ask is whether there *should* be such a period, if the bioprogram hypothesis is correct.

4.   The bioprogram and the critical period

If a bioprogram for language exists, then the infrastructure of that bioprogram can only be a particular set of neurons linked by a particular set of synaptic connections (or, to be more precise, the progressive growth of such a network over the period between birth and approximately age four). At the end of the growth period, that network is in place. What, subsequently, happens to it?

The issues to be resolved will become clearer if we look at the primary acquisition process as the hypothesis envisages it. As the network builds, the child becomes capable of making abstract distinctions — among the most salient are those between states and nonstates, causatives and noncausatives, punctual and nonpunctual actions, specific and nonspecific referents — which he then proceeds to try to impose upon the (to him) still inchoate language data with which he is confronted. In creoles, where the instructions of the bioprogram are minimally suppressed, these distinctions are mapped directly and biuniquely onto the syntax. In the vast majority of natural languages, however, these distinctions are neither directly nor biuniquely mapped, and may be cross-cut and partially or wholly overlaid by other, language specific, distinctions. What the child then has to do is modify the grammar with which the bioprogram endows him until it matches the grammar of the community in which he is raised.

What there is as yet no way of knowing is how this process of adaptation affects the neural network which serves as the infrastructure of the bioprogram. Clearly, either the function of the original network must change as it is taken over by the representational model of the primary natural language, or a new network must be forged alongside or on top of it in order to accommodate that new model.

If the first development took place we would expect the bioprogram to be entirely erased, by around the end of the fourth year, with a concomitant change in the capacity to acquire language. Although this would accord with Lamendella's placement of the end of the primary acquisition period at age five, I know of no decisive evidence which would lead us to accept any sudden and qualitative change in capacity at so early an age. Rather, the evidence, equivocal as it is (and in a moment I shall try to show *why* it is equivocal), would seem to indicate a much slower and more gradual decline over the period between four and puberty. Of course a relatively sudden change might be masked to some extent by the growth of general cognitive powers. But in general, sketchy as it is, the picture seems more to support the forging of a second, parallel network to support the representational model of the so-called 'native' language.

However, it is at best highly questionable whether the original network — the infrastructure of the bioprogram grammar — survives intact into adulthood. If it did, there would be no need for people in a pidgin-speaking community to await the growth of the first locally-born generation in order to generate a fully viable human language. They could produce such a language themselves. But the very existence of pre-pidgin continua indicates that this is impossible for the adult. He is forced to tolerate an unstable and inadequate makeshift language; more than that, even when the creole comes along, he is incapable of learning it. In Hawaii, although the creole has been in existence for around seventy years, there are still many immigrants whose speech is wholly uninfluenced by it, and there are NONE who have completely mastered its rules!

There is space for only a single example of this. In Hawaiian Creole, as in all creoles that failed to develop an equative copula, there is a rule (applied by some speakers as often as thirty times an hour) which fronts focused constituents and which in the case of subjects — since these are already sentence-initial — marks them by immediately following them with a pronoun copy. When the subject is qualified by a relative clause, this copy follows the clause, i.e. marks the highest node in the derivational tree.[9] These rules are followed by all speakers of Hawaiian Creole who have not undergone substantial de-creolization. But of all the pidgin speakers we studied, only one had even an approximation to the correct rules, and even he, although he sometimes placed the copy after the relative clause, also produced sentences without any copy at all (where discourse rules demanded them), sentences with copies *before* the relative clause, and double copies — one before and one after the clause! It by no means appears, therefore, that what is natural in every sense for children is natural for adults in any sense, at least in this case.

However, because *some* natural rules cannot be acquired by adults we should not conclude that *no* such rules are accessible to them. One rule that may be accessible is negative placement. Mature creole speakers, children in Klima and Bellugi's (1966) State II of negative placement acquisition, and pidgin speakers all share the same rule — place the negative morpheme (*no* or mutated forms thereof in all English-based pidgins and creoles and in English primary acquisition) immediately before the first verbal element, whether main verb or auxiliary. In Hawaii, it would be impossible to tell whether pidgin speakers independently invented this rule or learned it from creole speakers, but in other situations, such as the transient pidgins created by servicemen and bar-girls in the Far East described by Howell (1976), the possibility of any child intervention can be satisfactorily ruled out.

This would suggest that second language learners may have some limited degree of access to bioprogram universals. Such a state of affairs would still be consonant with the second suggestion as to what happens to the bioprogram's infrastructure. Brain cells, and the synapses that link them, are not immortal. If a network is not used, it may decay.[10] Until we are able to trace and interpret neural pathways, and we are a long way from being able to do this, we can only look for oblique and inferential evidence on this issue.

5. *Primary versus secondary acquisition*

I said earlier that evidence of the relationship between primary and non-primary acquisition was equivocal. There has been much discussion of whether first and second languages are acquired in the same way or in different ways, without any strong consensus having been achieved. To a considerable extent, this state of affairs has been due to the dominance of the 'order of acquisition' approach.[11] This approach looks only at the *target* of acquisition — the point at which a given form or structure is used more or less as a native speaker of the acquired language would use it — and ignores the *path towards* acquisition — the ways in which the learner first uses the novel form or structure, long before he reaches the so-called 'criterion point,' and the kinds of modifications he makes in those initial uses in order to reach criterion. Even if it could be shown that both first and second language learners acquired the features of a given target language in an identical order (and there have been conflicts of evidence on this score too), we would by no means be entitled to conclude from this that the *paths* of acquisition in both cases were identical or that the overall acquisition process was steered by the same set of principles. Determination of these points awaits systematic studies of the pathways followed in both primary and nonprimary language acquisition.

What we badly need now are longitudinal research programs that will adequately describe, compare, and interpret (a) primary acquisition of a first language, (b) primary acquisition of a second language, (c) secondary acquisition between age five and puberty, and (d) post-pubertal secondary acquisition. Many previous studies have suffered from the defects already mentioned; all have suffered from the lack of any single unifying principle which would enable comparisons to be made at a non-superficial level.

The language bioprogram hypothesis provides just such a unifying principle, and in addition it sheds light on why there should be both similarities and differences between primary acquisition and secondary acquisition.

There is at least one sense in which we might claim that there is no such thing as the acquisition of a first language and that both primary and secondary acquisition, although differing perhaps in mode, are both really cases of second-language acquisition. The child between one and four years already 'knows' the grammar of the bioprogram; and if objection be taken to this use of 'know', because the child does not know that he knows it, it can be pointed out that he equally will not know that he knows the grammar of the so-called 'native' language that he is destined to acquire. In both primary and secondary acquisition, then, a speaker can be regarded as moving from a known grammar to a novel one: in primary acquisition, from the bioprogram grammar to the 'native language' grammar, and in secondary acquisition, from that 'native' grammar to the second-language grammar.

Much has been written about 'transfer' or 'interference'; unfortunately, many writers on the subject have failed to perceive acquisition as a longitudinal process in which transfer may play differing roles and occur to differing extents at different stages of the process. However, there is not space to discuss such matters here. I merely want to point out that, in light of the hypothesis put forward here, the child who insists on saying *Why they don't know?* instead of *Why don't they know?* and the Spanish learner of English who persistently says *Is better now* instead of *It is better now*[12] may be doing exactly the same thing — transferring rules of grammar from the grammar they already have to the grammar they are seeking to acquire.

In fact, the account that the present theory gives of first-language acquisition differs from conventional accounts of first-language acquisition (and more resembles conventional accounts of second-language acquisition) in the following manner. In traditional accounts of first-language acquisition, the child had, at most, only a device for restricting the nature of possible hypotheses about the target language, and was supposed to test hypotheses about the grammar of that language against the primary data provided by caregivers, elder siblings, etc. These hypotheses, where incorrect, could then be progressively rectified by application of the same process to a richer body of data. In the present account, a set of specific hypotheses is furnished by the bioprogram in the earlier stages of the acquisition process and the child proceeds to act on these hypotheses. It is not until a 'hypothesis' is shown by richer data to be incorrect that inductive processes take over. In the case of second-language acquisition, too, the initial hypotheses do not have to be induced from input, but are rather given, in this case by the natural-language grammar(s) derived from the primary acquisition period (and perhaps also in part by the bioprogram if there is anything left of it at this stage). To the extent that these initial hypotheses are subsequently falsified, inductive processes will again take over. Thus, the bioprogram hypothesis not only claims a degree of similarity in the two processes, but additionally specifies, as no previous account has done, just what that similarity consists of and why it should be there.

However, 'similar' should not be read as 'the same'. The bioprogram suggests also some ways in which the two kinds of acquisition would diverge from one another.

Primary acquisition (that is, acquisition of a first or a second language in infancy) draws its initial hypotheses from a base which is relatively simple, while nonprimary acquisition draws its initial hypotheses from a base which is relatively complex. Since words like 'simplicity' are anything but simple and have led to endless controversy, I had better make it as plain as possible what I mean. I begin from the assumption that there is no such thing as species-free simplicity. What is simple for any species is what that species can do without any learning and as a result of its genetic inheritance. Walking, for humans, is simpler than riding a bicycle, in this sense. Thus, since the child's earliest grammar is that (or rather those)[13] made available by the bioprogram, it must be simpler than the grammar of any so-called natural language, which is the product of milennia of cultural evolution as well as of biological evolution. If we can assume that movement from a simple system (based on bioprogram-med universals) to a more complex one (viz. the primary language) is easier than movement between two systems of equal but differing complexity (i.e. primary language to secondary language), we can see why primary acquisition should be easier than nonprimary acquisition.

A second difference arises for rather subtler reasons, which may be roughly characterized by saying that while the base for primary acquisition is serially accessed, the base for nonprimary acquisition is simultaneously accessed. Again, a word of explanation is in order. Let us start with a counterfactual thought-experiment. Let us suppose that the primary acquirer waited until the instructions of the bioprogram were complete before launching upon the change from the bioprogram grammar to first-language grammar. Such a child would take from his parents only such lexical items as he needed and would persist, up to the age of four or so, in using only structures such as *He no can fix it*, *Where the boy must go?*, *I flatted the paper*, *The dog running*, *I want you give me toy*, and so on. At age four he would have a complete language system, rather like that of a creole, but quite distinct from the system he was supposed to be 'learning'. He would then undertake the task of moving from this complete system to another equally complete but more complex.

If this were the natural course of development, then primary and non-primary acquirers would be even more like one another than they at present are. For the acquirer of a second language has (subsequent to the primary acquisition period) just such a completed system to work from, that of his native tongue. But in fact children do not develop in the way that I just described. The processes of activating the bioprogram grammar and modifying the bioprogram grammar to fit the native-tongue grammar are concurrent, not consecutive processes. It is as if the bioprogram handed a grammar to the child in prefabricated sections: 'Here's the punctual-nonpunctual distinction'; 'Here's your question rule'; 'Here's how to embed sentences'. And on getting each new section, the child does not merely wait for the next section but begins the task of modifying the first section to fit its nearest equivalent in the target language. Indeed, it may be the case that many bioprogram instructions are suppressed altogether, because by the time they are handed out they no longer fit into the modified structure.[14]

Something like this sequential, handing-out-sections process is of course what is attempted by practically all second-language teaching texts, and for the very natural reason that piecemeal acquisition (starting with the 'simplest' pieces first) seems obviously easier than plunging head-first into an entire, and entirely new, system. Ignore what you already know, these texts seem to be saying, turn yourself into a blank slate and then gradually build up the new system a bit at a time. But it is not practically possible to ignore what one knows. Learning is moving from the known to the unknown, not diving off a plank while blindfolded. No matter how small and digestible the second-language tidbits which the texts offer him, the learner cannot of his very nature refrain from making guesses as to how these bits link up with those still unknown to him — i.e. guessing about the target system in ways that are at least in part determined by the system(s) already known. Thus, again, there is a sense in which primary acquisition is simpler than nonprimary acquisition.

6.   *Can the bioprogram influence secondary acquisition?*

The question that we must now consider, and that is most relevant to the field of second-language acquisition, is whether any of the guesses a nonprimary acquirer makes are guided by the bioprogram. This, as I suggested earlier, is an empirical question. On the basis of the little we know about brain structure and brain activity, we cannot hope, as yet, to test this or perhaps any other aspect of the hypothesis. We must look at the ways in which people actually acquire second languages — preferably, cases free from pedagogical intervention — and see to what extent, if at all, those ways conform to what the bioprogram would predict: i.e. rapid and errorless acquisition of those features acquired rapidly and errorlessly in primary acquisition (Bickerton 1981,

Chapter 3) or other evidence that the categories laid down in the bioprogram were being utilized by second-language learners alongside, if not in preference to, the categories used in the native and target languages. Note that the field of second-language acquisition can only provide a positive test for the language bioprogram hypothesis (unlike primary acquisition, which can provide both positive and negative tests). It cannot provide a negative test, because the finding that the bioprogram played no part in nonprimary acquisition would be as consonant with the supposition that the bioprogram decayed after primary acquisition as it would be with the supposition that there never was a bioprogram in the first place.

Even positive tests, however, may not be conclusive. Consider the following case. In English, the simple past tense refers to protracted and repeated actions as well as to single unitary ones; we say not only *He walked to school yesterday* but *The pilgrims walked from Jerusalem to Mecca* and *John walked five miles a day until he was 65*. In the bioprogram grammar, the first (punctual) case would have to be alloted a form different from that of the second or third (nonpunctual) cases. A similar (although not identical) difference exists between the preterite and imperfective forms in Spanish. Thus an English sentence such as *For many years he lived in Pennsylvania but he studied French in Montreal* would be rendered as *Vivía en Pennsylvania durante muchos años pero estudiaba el francés en Montreal* rather than **Vivió en Pennsylvania durante muchos años pero estudió el francés en Montreal*. If a Spanish-speaking learner of English then produces **For many years he was living in Pennsylvania but he was studying French in Montreal*, are we to assume that this is due to first-language interference or to continuing influence from the bioprogram, or to a mixture of the two?

These are some general and theoretical considerations which any studies of possible effects of the bioprogram on nonprimary acquisition must take into account. However, when we turn from these general considerations to a consideration of the empirical evidence, we find that the latter appears to be both limited in quantity and equivocal in nature.

The secondary acquisition of English, for example, yields two cases which appear contradictory; one involving Hindi speakers in which the bioprogram seems no longer operative, and one involving Spanish speakers in which it still seems to be influential. In the course of nonprimary acquisition of English, native speakers of Hindi frequently make mistakes such as **I am liking it* or **He is wanting to see you* (Gordon Fairbanks, p.c.). Use of nonpunctuals with statives is a bioprogram as well as an English violation; Hindi speakers apparently commit it because in Hindi imperfective marking can be used with statives. (Unlike some other supposed universals, the injunctions of the bioprogram are not immune to cultural evolution.) Thus in this case mother-tongue influence clearly overrides the bioprogram in nonprimary acquisition.

However, recent research by James Lantolf (p.c.) suggests that in their acquisition of English articles, native speakers of Spanish are influenced by the specific-nonspecific distinction, one of the linchpins of the bioproram. Lantolf's study is not complete, and it would not be fair to prejudge its results, but it seems to point in a direction diametrically opposed to that in which the Hindi evidence points. The question that arises is whether such apparently contradictory evidence can be accounted for.

I believe that it can, and that in doing so we can derive fruitful insights into the way in which second languages are acquired. The study by Huebner (1979, 1982) of longitudinal acquisition of English by an untaught Hmong refugee examines nonprimary acquisition in greater detail and with more sophisticated techniques than any previous study has done. Huebner's final analysis suggests how the bioprogram and mother-tongue influence may mesh in determining the highly variable behavior which nonprimary learners exhibit.

Huebner (1982, Chapter 5) describes acquisition of the English definite article by Ge, the Hmong subject. In the bioprogram the distribution of articles is determined by the interaction of two semantic oppositions, specific/non-specific and known/unknown to hearer (henceforth S/NS and K/NK, respectively). In creoles, definite articles are restricted to S, K. In English, definite articles extend to all K; i.e. they can be applied to generic NP, which is impossible in creoles. In the earliest stage of Ge's development, almost all articles fall within S, K, but they do not (unlike creoles) fill that domain. What Ge appears to be doing is using *the* to mark all known-to-hearer NP which fall within the comment domain of his predominantly topic-comment sentences. In other words, his analysis of *the*, althouh possibly influenced by the bioprogram, is also strongly influenced by the topic-comment[15] grammar of his mother-tongue, which leads him to mark off the topic domain of his sentences by intonational and morphological means; he does not use *the* within this topical domain, perhaps because he thinks that within that domain topicality is already sufficiently marked, viz. by sentence-initial positioning.

Shortly thereafter, Ge generalizes *the* to all NP. From other parts of Huebner's study, this 'flooding' technique would seem to be a clear 'nonprimary' strategy — perhaps a primary one also — which leads to those previously inexplicable regressions in correct production which have been observed by all students of language learning. It is as if the speaker, having made an incorrect hypothesis about the role of a grammatical feature, cannot simply microadjust that hypothesis; instead of increasing production in the appropriate category, the speaker generalizes maximally and then prunes down his generalization, so to speak, until he achieves the appropriate fit.

Certainly, after a period in which NP are marked with *the* regardless of semantic factors, Ge begins the pruning operation by eliminating *the* from the NS, NK category, that which is furthest from the bioprogram domain of definiteness (and which includes such things as NP objects of desideratives, NP in the scope of negation, etc.). Subsequently he eliminates *the* from the S, NK category and thus arrives at approximately the English distribution of *the*. In other words, he uses the bioprogram features, but not in the way that a child would use them; children have few problems in acquiring English articles (except for an over-distribution of zero marking for nonspecifics) since English articles, which seem to have followed the bioprogram pattern when they emerged, have not deviated from it all that much in subsequent centuries.

Obviously it would be absurd to lean too heavily on a single study of a single learner. However, that study does strongly suggest that in nonprimary acquisition the promptings of the bioprogram are by no means extinguished but rather overlaid by subsequent learning, and that future study of the interaction of the bioprogram, mother-tongue interference, and perhaps other factors may be able to show us how the nonprimary acquisition process really works at a psychological level.

There is, however, at least one further way in which the bioprogram hypothesis may affect the theoretical study of second-language acquisition, although we are still so far from being able to gauge this effect that I shall say very little about it. Hitherto, second language acquisition — along with some other fields, such as the study of linguistic change processes — has suffered from the lack of any typology of language that went beyond mere taxonomic groupings based on fairly superficial features such as word order. This lack was in turn a direct consequence of the belief in the equality of all contemporary languages discussed at the beginning of the present paper (see fn.1); for if this held, there could be no possible ranking of languages in terms of their development levels.

However, according to the bioprogram hypothesis, it should be possible to rank all synchronic languages along a developmental hierarchy in terms of their closeness to, or distance from, the bioprogram grammar (which of course, in historical or rather prehistorical terms was also the grammar of the species' first fully human language). This should provide us with accurate measures of the distance (in terms of grammatical development) between given languages as well as, for any given pair of languages, L_j, L_k, an objective measure of which should prove the more complex task: learning of L_k by L_j speakers or learning of L_j by L_k speakers.[16] Comparison of results of the latter measure with the results of real-world acquisition processes may then, in turn, shed light on whether nonprimary language acquisition is still fully within the domain of the *faculté de langage* or whether, and if so to what extent, it is a task in which more general cognitive faculties play a part.

Thus, while the language bioprogram hypothesis cannot provide ready-made solutions to the problems facing the study of second language acquisition, and still less can provide direct assistance in second-language pedagogy, it can still furnish a novel perspective on those problems and help to specify and define them more precisely, thus making them hopefully easier to handle. This is probably as much as any applied field can reasonably ask of a theory; and it is certainly as much as any theory of universals can offer. For if any natural universal process were definitively in charge of second language acquisition, then all second-language teachers would be out of a job, and so would the body of distinguished theoreticians who have come to this conference.

NOTES

1) As discussed in Bickerton 1981, 300, this belief is mainly ideological in origin. The only argument in its favor known to me is really an argument against the claim that there *are* developmental differences; a claim thought to be refuted by the fact that there is no relation between the grammatical complexity of a language and the cultural level attained by speakers of that language. True, but irrelevant: that language must develop in tandem with culture, if it developed at all, was simply another groundless assumption.

2) These of course were not the only factors involved. Take the origin of creoles. It is quite simply scandalous that the study of first-language acquisition, for example, should so long have ignored a situation in which the children know the language better than their parents, while making such pronouncements as 'Mothers teach their children to speak' (Bruner 1979) or 'all children...receive a simplified, well-formed and redundant corpus' (Snow 1979 — see discussion in Bickerton 1981:136-40). But creoles are spoken by people who are poor, usually illiterate, non-white, and in the Third World, and their avoidance by the academic establishment is merely a symptom of the institutional racism shared by that body despite its painfully frequent liberal protestations.

3) At the Pacific Conference on Contrastive Linguistics and Language Universals held at the University of Hawaii. January 14-16, 1971.

4) For fuller discussion of this point, see Bickerton 1981: 208-9.

5) 'Learning a language (including, of course, a first language) involves learning what the predicates of the language mean. Learning what the predicates of a language mean involves learning a determination of the extension of these predicates. Learning a determination of the extension of the predicates involves learning that they fall under certain rules (i.e., truth rules). But one cannot learn that P(redicate) falls under R(ule) unless one has a language in which P and R can be represented. So one cannot learn a language unless one has a language' (Fodor 1975, 63-4).

6) See discussion in section 3.1.

7) This change is so abrupt and so sharply timed that where a pair of fledglings, hatched a couple of days apart, occupy the same nest, the elder can be observed already trying to widen the entrance while the younger is still engaged in trying to narrow it.

8) For example, the punctual-nonpunctual distinction, which may have its origin in a phenomenon known as *habituation* which may be observed in organisms as lowly as sea-slugs (for discussion, see Bickerton 1981, 282-3).

9) This rule is discussed in more detail in Bickerton (1979:12-13 and 1981:33-7).

10) The phenomenon generally described as 'language death' may be relevant here. It sometimes happens that when an individual has no occasion to use a language for a period of many years, that language may come to be 'forgotten', in part or even in whole. It is hard to see what could underlie this phenomenon if not the physical decay of the set of neural connections which served as the infrastructure of competence in that language, and hard to see what could cause that precise and limited decay if not failure to keep the network in use. Since the bioprogram grammar is never actually used (except, if the theory is correct, by creole speakers), it may be that it decays more rapidly than acquired grammars, but this suggestion must remain purely speculative, for the present at least.

11) This approach, pioneered for first-language studies in Brown (1973), has been followed by a number of scholars in the field of second-language acquisition. For critical discussion see Bickerton (1981:142-3), Huebner (1982, Chapter 1).

12) This particular example is taken from Table 8 of Schumann (1981) (incidentally, perhaps the soundest account yet of the relationship between pidginization and second-language acquisition). The interlanguage expression is a calque on *es mejor ahora* — Spanish doesn't require dummy subjects.

13) By the plural, I wish to remind the reader that the bioprogram grammar is not a static system but one which is continually changing and developing throughout the one-to-four period, yet changing quite independently from the input the child receives during that period.

14) Anterior tense is a case in point. This emerges in all creole systems (for the most complete discussion of its role in such a system, see Bickerton 1975, Chapter 2). However, it seems to play little part in primary acquisition. This may be because it emerges quite late in the development of the bioprogram (for reasons why this should be so, see Bickerton 1981:281-6) at a time when the development of the child's auxiliary-verb system has already been sharply tilted in the direction of the primary-target grammar. To be more specific, evidence (see Bickerton 1981:163ff) from the acquisition of French and Italian as well as English suggests that the 'punctual tense' of the bioprogram gets converted into a true past by the strong salience of the past-nonpast distinction in those languages. True past and true anterior cannot co-exist in the same auxiliary system, since their domains overlap (see Bickerton 1975, loc. cit.).

160   DEREK BICKERTON

15) In the sense of Li and Thompson (1976).

16) There has long been anecdotal evidence that some languages are 'easier' or 'harder' for speakers of a given native language, but no systematic way in which such evidence could be evaluated. One by-product of the bioprogram hypothesis just might be a revival of contrastive linguistics.

REFERENCES

Andersen, R.W. (ed.). 1981. *New Dimensions in Second Language Acquisition Research.* Rowley, Mass.: Newbury House.

Bever, T.G., 1970. The cognitive basis for linguistic structure. In J.R. Hayes (ed.), *Cognition and the Development of Language.* New York: Wiley.

Bickerton, D. 1975. *Dynamics of a Creole System.* Cambridge: Cambridge University Press.

Bickerton, D. 1979. Beginnings. In K.C. Hill (ed.), *The Genesis of Language.* Ann Arbor: Karoma.

Bickerton, D. 1981. *Roots of Language.* Ann Arbor: Karoma.

Brown, R. 1973. *A First Language,* Cambridge, Mass.: Harvard University Press.

Bruner, J.S. 1979. Learning how to do things with words. In D. Aaronson and L.W. Rieber (eds.), *Psycholinguistic Research: Implications and Applications.* Hillside, N.J.: Erlbaum Associates.

Chomsky, N. 1962. Explanatory models in linguistics. In E. Nagel et al., *Logic, Methodology and the Philosophy of Science.* Stanford: Stanford University Press.

Chomsky, N. 1965. *Aspects of the Theory of Syntax.* Cambridge, Mass.: M.I.T. Press.

Chomsky, N. 1968. *Language and Mind.* New York: Harcourt, Brace & World.

Chomsky, N. 1979. *Language and Responsibility.* Cambridge, Mass.: M.I.T. Press.

Fodor, J.A. 1975. *The Language of Thought.* New York: Crowell.

Givón, T. 1979. *On Understanding Grammar.* New York: Academic Press.

Goldin-Meadow, S. 1979. Structure in a manual communication system developed without a conversational language model. In H. Whitaker and H.A. Whitaker (eds.), *Studies in Neurolinguistics, Vol. 4.* New York: Academic Press.

Howard, I. 1971. On several conceptions of universals. *Working Papers in Linguistics* (University of Hawaii), 3.4:243-8.

Howell, R.A. 1976. Comparative reflections of sociocultural differences in the pidgins of Japan and Hawaii. In K. Kozu and R. Mathur, *Proceedings of the Language, Thought and Culture Symposium, 1976*. Japan: K.U.F.S.

Huebner, T. 1979. Order of acquisition versus dynamic paradigm. *TESOL Quarterly 13*:21-29.

Huebner, T. 1982. *From Topic to Subject Dominance in the Interlanguage of a Hmong Speaker*. Doctoral dissertation, University of Hawaii.

Klima, E., and U. Bellugi. 1966. Syntactic regularities in the speech of children. In J. Lyons and R.J. Wales (eds.), *Psycholinguistics Papers*. Edinburgh: Edinburgh University Press.

Lamendella, J. 1976. Relations between the ontogeny and phylogeny of language: a neo-recapitulationist view. In S.R. Harnard, et al. (eds.), *Origins and Evolution of Language and Speech*. Annals of the New York Academy of Science, Vol. 280.

Lamendella, J. 1977. General principles of neurofunctional organization and their manifestation in primary and nonprimary language acquisition. *Language Learning 27*:155-96.

Li, C.N., and S.A. Thompson. 1976. Subject and topic — a new typology of language. In C.N. Li (ed.), *Subject and Topic*. New York: Academic Press.

Schumann, J.S. 1981. Simplification, transfer and relexification as aspects of pidginization and early second language acquisition. Presented at the 1981 TESOL Convention, Detroit.

Scovel, T. 1981. The effects of neurological age on nonprimary language acquisition. In Andersen (ed.) 1981.

Selinger, H.W. 1981. Exceptions to critical period predictions. In Andersen (ed.) 1981.

Snow, C. 1979. Conversations with children. In P. Fletcher and M. Garman (eds.), *Language Acquisition*. Cambridge: Cambridge University Press.

Taylor, D. 1971. Grammatical and lexical affinities of creoles. In D. Hymes (ed.), *Pidginization and Creolization of Languages*. Cambridge: Cambridge University Press.

COMMENTS ON THE PAPER BY BICKERTON

CHARLES A. FERGUSON
Stanford University

Derek Bickerton's paper is, as we might expect, full of ideas, brilliant, and provocative, but it is also in many respects wrong. In the time allotted for discussants I cannot do justice to the rich contents of the paper let alone offer general comments on the fuller statement of his position in *Roots of Language*, which incidentally I would advise all of you to buy and read. Let me comment on several points where I agree strongly with Derek's position where he is taking issue with widely held views of linguists. Then I will turn to several points where I either misunderstand him or cannot agree with his position.

First, I am happy to see him question the linguistic myth that 'all languages are developmentally equal.' The notion that all languages are somehow exactly equal in complexity and expressiveness is often taught as scientific truth in linguistics courses — indeed the other day I heard it pronounced authoritatively by a distinguished linguist speaking on the radio. But as far as I know there is no evidence at all that this is the case. A slogan of this kind is useful in combatting racist, ethnocentric, and otherwise misguided stereotypes about human languages, but as a scientific hypothesis it deserves careful formulation and empirical testing. I have given my views on this elsewhere and this is not the time or place to repeat them. Incidentally, I note that Derek himself slips back into this myth when he refers (p. 153) to non-primary acquisition as being 'movement between two systems of equal but differing complexity.'

Second, I applaud his concern — one shared by many creolists, but not enough non-creolists — that linguistic theory should offer an explanation for the striking similarities among all creoles. Of course, he exaggerates in saying they are all nearly identical except for the lexical stock. Translations between different creoles are not always all that easy, but he is surely right in suggesting that linguists should attend to the similarities and compare them with the phenomena of language acquisition and connect them with serious speculation about the origin of human language.

This brings me to a third point of agreement. Linguists should be concerned with the evolution of human language and should draw on all the available linguistic, psychological, anthropological, and biological information that may be helpful. Just as synchronic descriptions of languages and synchronic language universals can often be understood better by studying what diachronic predecessor states they could have come from and what successor states they could lead to, so our characterization of the unique phenomenon of human language may be informed by attempts to understand how it could have come into being and perhaps where it might be going in some fundamental biological and social senses. Even here though, Derek gets himself into some trouble for the sake of showmanship. Can he really take seriously the position that 'one must already know a language in order to learn a language' (p. 144)? If that is so, then language could never have evolved. There must have been a time in the history of the species when individuals were somewhere between knowing a language and not knowing a language. The linguistic preference for all-or-none positions may have its virtues, but it also gives us trouble.

There are other bits of exaggeration for effect, or overstatements of a good case, that I will not comment on. I accept them happily both for their attention-getting qualities and their entertainment value. But at a conference on language universals I don't think we should permit him to erect a straw man about the work on language universals. He says it has all been based on the assumption that 'a language universal is something that is found in all languages' (p. 141). No one at this meeting has taken that position. I have heard mention of implicational universals, universal tendencies, universal hierarchies, universal continua, and other kinds of claims about general characteristics of human language. The Bickerton claims are interesting enough in their own right. They don't need this straw man.

But what are some points in the paper that seem to be seriously wrong? One thing that bothers me is typified by his position that pidgins are 'too variable to be learned' (p. 145). Here, Derek, surprisingly for the variationist and innatist that he is, underestimates the variability of human languages and underestimates the abilities of human children. Language inputs to children can be highly variable even in a relatively homogeneous speech community. Members of the immediate family and of the social networks in which the child's communication takes place may speak very different dialects and show a great range of stylistic or registral shifting. The child makes his way among all these variant forms of language, sometimes mastering two dialects simultaneously, sometimes constructing his own intermediate variety, but in any case acquiring his own patterns of variability. The child has no way of knowing that some of what he hears would be called by linguists a pidgin, a standard, a regional dialect, or a restricted register. He copes with variability as part of his human bioprogrammed (if you will) capability. The language learning situation of a highly multilingual community with lots of code-switching and style-shifting in the household is not a rare phenomenon in the world.

I am just as mystified by Derek's insistence that the Hawaiian adult pidgin speaker cannot learn a creole. He says there is a rule of fronting and copying which he says the pidgin speakers cannot acquire. Why should they? Among the myriad forms of language they hear, how do they know that they should take as their target only the particular set of varieties characterized by the Bickerton grammar of an ideal creole? Part of the problem here is that Derek has not rebelled enough against another linguistic myth. During the period of American structuralism a myth became well established that the native speaker cannot make a mistake, that there is a mother tongue which is acquired early on and any other language that is acquired is learned imperfectly. Also the Saussurian myth — very useful in its day and still an excellent heuristic notion — that a language is a completely unified system where everything fits together, was attached to the native speaker/mother tongue myth. Language behavior is not so neatly compartmentalized and neatly defined. There is not a dichotomy native speaker/non-native speaker, but a multidimensional continuum of behaviors. It is not always possible to determine whether an individual is a native speaker or not, whether the person is speaking a pidgin or a creole.

The issue of what happens when a child grows up in a pidgin-speaking environment or in a creole continuum environment can be settled only by having L1 acquisition research carried out in such settings. Just as Elinor Ochs and Shirley Heath yesterday called for L1 research in different sociocultural contexts, I would plead for L1 research in settings of high linguistic variability. How does a child learn to shift up and down the creole continuum in accordance with the norms of the speech community? This is an L2 question also. How does an American learn to shift up and down the scale of Classical and Colloquial Arabic in the highly variable way that Arabs do? Such questions are of more than passing interest for linguistic theorists.

I have very little more time, so let me deal with the most important point: the 'language' we are born with, the bioprogram of our species. First off, I wish Derek would stop calling it a 'grammar' or a 'language'. Too many things are called grammars or languages already. After all, a bioprogram for nest-building is not a nest. The bioprogram consists apparently of the ability to conceptualize and to give names to referents, and in addition the ability to make certain abstract distinctions, including those between state and non-state, causative and non-causatives, punctual and non-punctual actions, specific and non-specific referents. The bioprogram is also constructed to operate in successive stages, as triggered by appropriate external and internal events. This is a challenging list of characteristics, and with further thought and empirical investigations on the part of Bickerton and other creolists, could readily be expanded, I believe, to a fuller list. It sounds to me like the kind of list that many people might accept as part of what they call a 'predisposition' for acquiring language or the 'linguistic prepotentiation' of human beings. In any case, my first questions are of the evolutionary sort: To what extent are these characteristics part of the more general cognitive, socially adaptive bioprograms of human beings and not specifically linguistic in nature? To what extent do these abstract distinctions have counterparts in primate and general mammalian behavior? My next questions are about all the rest of language acquisition: How does this bioprogram help with the acquisition of the incredibly complex facts of human languages and the incredibly complex patterns of the uses of language? Does the bioprogram still need a component of knowing how to learn a language?

I don't have the time to express the many reservations I have about the Language Bioprogram Hypothesis, but it certainly provides a new agenda for L1 and L2 acquisition research, and I think we should be grateful to Derek Bickerton for pointing us to important issues and in some instances making very concrete claims about language acquisition which we can investigate.

A UNIVERSAL INPUT CONDITION*

JACQUELYN SCHACHTER
University of Southern California

1. *Introduction*

   1.1. In recent years the study of language learning has to a large extent focused on the capabilities of the language learner. A good deal of attention has been directed toward determining the nature of the learner's innate predispositions, which play such a critical role in determining the linguistic knowledge that results when a learner interacts with a given body of linguistic experience. Chomsky (1981) and others (cf. Hornstein and Lightfoot 1981, Baker 1979) use the term *universal grammar* to characterize this field of inquiry.

   Chomsky notes that in the learner's transition from lack of knowledge of a specific language to mature knowledge of that same language both universal grammar (UG)[1] and experience make a contribution (Chomsky 1981:38). He also claims that the explanation of how linguistic knowledge develops offered by an explanatorily adequate theory of universal grammar is 'illuminating to the extent that properties of UG, rather than properties of the course of experience, determine the elements' of the resulting mature linguistic knowledge (ibid.).

   1.2. Given this focus by Chomsky and others on the properties of the learner's innate predispositions, it is not surprising to note a corresponding lack of focus on the properties of the linguistic experience[2] (i.e., the input and the learner's interaction with it), which also contributes to the resulting state of mature linguistic knowledge. Yet we must not forget the critical role of this experience. Knowledge of the properties of the input available to the language learner is crucial,[3] since one's assumptions about this input partially determine one's view of the properties that a model of UG must have. If a model were proposed, for example, which required for its successful operation some kind of input known to be unavailable to the learner (i.e., that each syntactic phrase presented to the learner be identified as a phrase, to take an outlandish example), it would have to be abandoned on empirical grounds alone. Conversely, if a model were developed which did not make use of certain kinds of linguistic input clearly available to the learner (intonation cues, for example), one would certainly want to know what characteristics of the learner made that input irrelevant and why the learner should exhibit those characteristics. Answers to these two kinds of questions will clearly influence the development of an explanatorily adequate model of universal grammar.

One might go a step further in the advocacy of the study of input and ask if there are necessary and sufficient characteristics of input such that if one is missing language learning will not take place. We might coin the term *universal input conditions* to characterize this field of inquiry whose object is to discover the nature of the learner's input requirements.

2. *Negative input: its nature and relevance*
    2.1.   One candidate[4] for a universal input condition is what may be termed *negative input*. Negative input can be roughly characterized as information provided to the learner that her utterance was in some way deviant or unacceptable to the native speaker, i.e. that it wasn't understandable, wasn't grammatically correct, wasn't situationally appropriate, etc.[5] Corrections come to mind as an obvious source of negative input, but it is on this point that many researchers balk (see, for example, Brown and Hanlon 1970), for two reasons: (1) it is not obvious that corrections are available to learners in any quantity (i.e., a language acquisition model requiring negative input for its successful operation would be suspect), and (2) it has been argued that even when they are available learners do not make use of them (see Braine 1971, McNeil 1966). I want to take up these two reservations in turn, but before doing so I will establish a conceptual framework within which the importance of the negative input question becomes much clearer.
    2.2.   The relevance of negative input in the learning of the syntax of a language is closely related to the framework of a model of language learning that we know as the hypothesis testing model. Katz (1966) in his characterization of Chomsky's concept of such a model says that language acquisition is viewed as a process of implicit theory construction similar in character to theory construction in science but without the explicit intellectual operations of the latter. According to Chomsky's conception, the child 'formulates hypotheses about the rules of the linguistic description of the language whose sentences he is hearing, derives predictions from such hypotheses about the

linguistic structures of sentences he will hear in the future, checks these predictions against the new sentences he encounters, eliminates those hypotheses that are contrary to the evidence, and evaluates those that are not eliminated by a simplicity principle which selects the best hypothesis concerning the rules underlying the sentences he has heard and will hear' (Katz 1966:274-5). Similar claims have been made for child second language acquisition by Dulay and Burt (1974), who coined the phrase *creative construction* to label the process, and for adult second language acquisition by Corder (1974), who argues in essence that there is no difference in the processes learners make use of, whether first or second language learners, although there are differences in the previous knowledge that they bring to bear on the subject.[6]

This concept of the way in which learners process input has been with us for some time now, and is generally, but not universally, accepted. A language learner's hypothesis is said to be a prediction that a certain aspect of the language is organized in a certain way. It is contingent upon feedback and therein lies the difficulty.

2.3. In his interesting (1971) article, 'Two models of the internalization of grammars,' Martin Braine presented a critique of hypothesis testing models of language acquisition that has yet to be dealt with, to my knowledge, by defenders of such models. And the criticism deals with the question of negative input (which he calls *negative data*). He points out that in studies of concept formation and problem solving, the areas in which hypothesis testing models have been most successful, subjects typically receive feedback — viz. *Right* or *Wrong* after every trial — and that subjects are heavily dependent on feedback since that is what alerts them to whether or not they are on the right track. If the experimenter gives the wrong feedback, the effect on learning is, he claims, disastrous. In short, he says, it follows from the logic of the hypothesis testing model that for hypothesis testing to be an efficient model of learning appropriate feedback has to be always available to the learner (Braine 1971:155).

The typical experimental situation is the optimal one — the learner always receives both positive and negative information and the information is always right. It is clear that these optimal conditions do not hold in the language learning situation. And Braine further claims that it is doubtful that anything remotely resembling these conditions holds.

Braine then asks if a hypothesis testing model for language learning can dispense with such information, and claims that it cannot. His argument is that negative data are necessary to reject over-inclusive grammars, grammars that will generate all grammatical sentences of the language but also some ungrammatical sentences. An example is in order here and what I will do is substitute an attested adult-learner data problem for the hypothetical data Braine uses. Suppose the learner is in the process of dealing with uninflected verb complements in which the subject of the complement differs from the subject of the matrix sentence. She hears utterances like *I want him to go, John expects me to go, They told the men to leave*, etc., as well as utterances like *I made him go, We had him polish the floors, They let the children cross the street*. And in addition, she also hears a few unexceptionable utterances like *I helped him wash the dishes*, and *We helped her to find a new place*. Suppose the learner, being a rational human being, infers that there is one pattern in question, V+NP+V, with an optional element *to* between NP and the second verb. The learner then, in addition to producing *want him to go, made him go*, etc., would also produce the anomalous structures *want him go and made him to go*. How is the learner to know that the latter two are ungrammatical unless the input contains data about non-sentences, i.e., negative data? If the input contained no negative data, the learner would face the dilemma of trying to figure out which *non*occurring sentences *could not* occur.

In general, Braine argues, for any correct natural language grammar, it would be possible, by merely eliminating details in the correct grammar, to construct a grammar which generated all of the grammatical sentences of the correct grammar plus, unfortunately, a set of sentences which are *not* generated by the correct grammar. Not only would this be possible, it seems quite plausible that a learner faced with the input just described would construct a general rule (viz. V+NP+ (*to*) V) to account for both structures, and in fact, there is evidence that learners do just this at certain stages in their development (cf. Schachter and Hart 1979, Reilly 1978). Braine's argument is a convincing one. It appears very clearly that a hypothesis testing model is, in fact, crucially dependent on negative input. Acceptance of this argument, however, puts us in an uncomfortable position. We must either provide evidence that learners have available and also make use of negative input, or we must abandon hypothesis testing models for language learning.

Braine's approach is to abandon hypothesis testing models since he believes that learners do not have sufficient negative input available and are not generally capable of making use of it. He brings up three kinds of evidence to support his beliefs. Now Braine is concerned with first language acquisition, not second, but his arguments are ones that must be considered by proponents of a hypothesis testing model for both first and second language learning. I will present them first as first language claims and then convert them into their corresponding second language claims.

Braine first points out the universality of first language acquisition despite vast differences of cultures and child-rearing practices, implying by this, I assume, that among these differences would be different emphases on correction of child speech. It is clear that such differences exist. Brice Heath (1981) and Ochs (1982) provide interesting descriptions of different cultural assumptions about appropriate ways of interacting with children as language learners. These differences, however, do not lead one to conclude that negative input could be totally lacking in a certain culture and that this could be beneficial for language learning. What they may show, rather, is that preferences for how negative input is provided could vary from culture to culture. Much the same can be said about second language learning. Although we cannot speak of its universality, we can point to its pervasiveness across cultures and thus also to differing focuses on the various types of input. Yet again, there is no evidence whatsoever to show that in a certain culture one type of input is missing and that this is beneficial.

Braine next reiterates the well-known claim (based on the Brown and Hanlon study) that parents often conspicuously miss opportunities to correct their children's speech, focusing rather on communicative intent than on structural form. Transcripts of second language learners interacting with mature native speakers show this as well. Day et al. (1981) show that in their data 90% of all occurring learner errors are not corrected.

Braine's third and last argument, a restatement of McNeill (1966), is that children are incapable of accepting corrections, (i.e., the 'nobody don't love me' phenomenon, or Braine's daughter's 'Want other one spoon daddy'). In these cases it is not claimed, of course, that learners are incapable of accepting directions, but rather that as they attempt the requested imitation they are incapable of producing the correct grammatical form. This is claimed to be true of second language learners also, both child and adult, by those who assert the validity of elicited imitation tasks as tools for collecting samples based on the learner's current grammar (cf. Swain, Dumas, and Naiman 1974).

Summarizing and rephrasing these last two arguments then, we have the following claims to concern ourselves with: (1) that there is a deficiency in the primary data learners receive in that on the whole mature speakers do not correct learners when they utter something ungrammatical and (2) that the learners themselves are generally incapable of incorporating those corrections they do receive.

3. *The availability of negative input*

3.1.   The major weakness in both of these arguments, however, is that negative input is viewed from a peculiarly narrow perspective. Of all the possible sources of negative input, Braine and many others have considered only one: explicit correction of error.[7] What he failed to consider, and what I view as equally important as sources of negative input, is a whole set of response types, ranging from explicit corrections at one end of a continuum, through confirmation checks and clarification requests, to at least two kinds of failures to understand at the other end. Each of these response types has as its underlying motive the intelligibility factor, which is what provides the continuum over which these responses range. All of these are indications to the learner that something has gone wrong in the transmission of a message. All of them identify the learner's utterance as anomalous in some way, and thus qualify as negative input. Let us consider each response type in turn, beginning with the least serious in terms of intelligibility failure, and progressing to the most serious.

3.1.1.   Clearly the most obvious source of negative data, explicit correction, is also the least serious in terms of the intelligibility factor and thus, one might argue, is the least efficacious as a source of negative input. The *explicit correction* is, according to Bolinger (1953), the border beyond which we say 'no' to an expression. It is meant to convey the message that the conversational partner knows exactly what message was transmitted by the learner but is unwilling to accept it in the form in which it was transmitted. Whether the learner picks up this message is a question to be discussed later, but at least when an explicit correction is offered the message is available to the learner. Some examples follow (where the arrows serve as indicators of the exact location within the dialog of the phenomenon under discussion):

Explicit Corrections

      child: Want other one spoon, Daddy.
→ adult: You mean, you want the other spoon.
      child: Yes, I want other one spoon, please, Daddy. (Braine 1971)
      NNS: Yes, left eye is wink.
→ NS: Left eye is winking.
      NNS: *Left eye is winking.* (Day et al., 1981 transcripts)
      NNS: Last year was monkey's year.
→ NS: Year of the monkey, yeah.
      NNS: *Then this year was chicken.* (Day et al., 1981 transcripts)

3.1.2. *Confirmation checks*, according to Long, are expressions by the native speaker which are designed to elicit confirmation that the utterance has been correctly understood or correctly heard. They are always formed by rising intonation questions, with or without a tag. They always involve repetition of all or part of the interlocutor's (i.e., the nonnative speaker's) preceding utterance. They are answerable by a simple confirmation (*Yes*, *MmHm*) in the event that the preceding utterance was correctly understood or heard, and require no new information from the interlocutor (Long 1981:81-2). As Chenoweth (1981) points out, confirmation checks may carry a double function — either to confirm understanding of the nonnative speaker or to provide a correction in a nonthreatening manner, or both. Note in the following examples that although confirmation checks can in one sense be viewed as repetitions of the learner's utterances, they are not exact repetitions by any means. In fact, they typically provide correct grammatical structures in contrast to the learner's incorrect forms.

Confirmation Checks

	child (1;?):	fei	(child is looking at electric fan)
	adult:	Hm?	
	child:	fæ	
→	adult:	Bathroom?	
	child:	fani	
		fai	
	adult:	Fan! yeah.	(Scollon 1976)

- - - - - - - - - - - - - - - -

	NNS:	All the people think the Buddha is the people same.
→	NS:	Same as the people?
	NNS:	Yeah.

(Day et al., 1981 transcripts)

- -

3.1.3. *Clarification requests*, unlike confirmation checks, request that the interlocutor either furnish new information or recode information previously given (Long 1981:80). They consist, for the most part, of Wh or Yes/no questions but can be expressed by other forms as well.

Clarification Requests

	child (2;2):	Read to me a book.
→	adult:	What?
	child:	Read a book to me.

(Reilly 1978)

- - - - - - - - - - - - - - - -

child (6;10): I figured something you might like out.
→ adult: What did you say?
child: I figured out something you might like.   (Reilly 1978)

- -

NNS: Ernest Hemingway is, doesn't believe in God, in a way, so.
→ NS: Isn't he dead?
NNS: Dead?
NS: He must know by now.   (Day et al., 1981 transcripts)

- -

NNS: And and when we go there we play too much.
NS: Too much?
NNS: Yeah.
NS: Or a lot? Do you play too much, really?
NNS: Too much.
→ NS: You don't like to play too much?
NNS: Every day.   (Schumann 1975 transcripts)

- -

3.1.4.   The last two response types can be labeled *failures to understand*.
It is not clear to me which of the two is more serious in terms of the intelligibility factor, since both provide immediate evidence to the learner that message
transmisson failure has occurred. It is clear, however, that each qualifies as
negative input. In the one case, the conversational partner fails to understand
and does not realize it, responding instead to what she perceives the message
to be: what may be called *unrecognized failure to understand* (or *misunderstanding*).

Unrecognized Failures

adult: ...long skirt you know and the pattern it was a check just like
                a blanket — Charlotte's blanket and she (the child) said,
                'Lady, blanket, blanket.' She thought the lady was wearing
                a blanket.
child: (1;?)   Brenda. Sleeping.
→ adult: Hm? Yeah, you thought the lady was wearing a blanket
                didn't you?
child: Bus. Bus.
adult: Yeah, on the bus, hm?
'What is interesting about this story is that Brenda is talking about sleeping on the bus, which is more or less not understood by the mother. Later

after making the transcription of the tape I asked the Mother how they
went to the doctor's office and if Brenda had slept in the office or on the
bus. The Mother reported what Brenda had told me. She always falls
asleep when they ride on the bus.'   (Scollon 1976:121)

- -

NS: What's the movie tonight? (referring to TV)
NNS: I don't know.
NS: What was it last week?
NNS: Yesterday?
NS: Yeah.
NNS: Em, ah, no, me no, no looked, no?
NNS: You didn't look at it?
NNS: No. Eh, eh, I look play.
→   NS: You play?
NNS: No, I look play hockey. The game.
→   NS: You play hockey? You play the game?
NNS: No! In the television.
NS: Uh, huh?
NNS: I'm looking one game.
NS: At a game, you looked at a game on television.
          What kind of a game?
NNS: Hockey.   (Schumann 1975 transcripts)

- -

In the other case the conversational partner fails to understand and
realizes it, often producing a 'What?' or 'Huh?' in response. This may be called
the *recognized failure to understand* and can be viewed as the opposite side
of the coin from the explicit correction. (It is what Schegloff et al. (1977)
would call other-initiated self-repair).

Recognized Failures

"Christine is a 4-year-old girl, Steven is an adult male. They are riding in
the back seat of a car. Christine is acting rowdy. Steven tells Christine she
'must behave' if she wants Steven to read her a book. He is, however, paying
more attention to a cassette tape which is playing music than he is to Christine.
A couple of minutes later:
C: Steven I am /heyv/.
S: What? You hate? What do you hate?
C: /heyv/. I am /heyv/.

S: You hate? You hate me? The music? What?
C: No, I am /heyv/. /heyv/.
→ S: I don't know what you are talking about.
Silence. A bit later:
C: I /heyv/.
S: You hate me?
C: (shakes her head no)
S: Who do you hate?
Silence. A bit later:
C: I am behaving.　　　(Peters 1982, observed by Steven Schoen)
- -
NNS: Um in Harvard, what you study?
→ NS: What?
NNS: What you es study?
NS: What am I studying?
NNS: Yeah.　　　　　　　　　　　　(Schumann 1975 transcripts)
- -

In both cases the learner is clearly faced with the failure to transmit the intended message and thus is provided with negative input. In the first case, the unrecognized failure, the learner has the option of attempting to repair the failure or accepting the topic shift and going along with it. In the second case, the recognized failure, the learner must either respond with a new attempt to transmit or indicate that no further attempt will be made.

3.2. I do not wish to be understood as claiming that confirmation checks, clarification requests and failures to understand function solely as negative input sources. They can and do serve as requests to speak louder, to reaffirm one's facts, etc. (although that too might reasonably be viewed as negative input). Nevertheless, what these examples show clearly is that they are available to learners as sources of negative input and, I suspect, rather widely available. Thus, with this expanded concept of negative input, the widely accepted claim of the lack of availability of negative input is severely weakened, and may well be untenable.

Schegloff, Jefferson, and Sacks (1977) assert that among adult native speakers there is a preponderance of self-corrections over other-corrections (and for them other-corrections include confirmation checks and clarification requests), due to the understanding between participants that if the hearer understands the message well enough to correct it, she also understands it well enough to produce the next turn, not the correction. And in our culture, at least, this is what is done. They point out an apparent exception to the constraints on other-correction — viz. the domain of adult/child interaction (and I shall add here another domain, that of adult/second language learner interaction) — and they note that the relaxation of the constraints 'may well be more generally relevant to the not-yet-competent in some domain without respect to age'. 'Thus,' they say, 'other-correction is not so much an alternative to self-correction in conversation in general, but rather a device for dealing with those who are still learning or being taught a system which requires, for its routine operation, that they be adequate self-monitors or self-correctors as a condition of competence' (Schegloff, Jefferson, and Sacks 1977:381).

Schegloff, Jefferson, and Sacks note that on the basis of a limited amount of data it appeared that other-correction was not as infrequent in adult/child interaction as it was in adult/adult interaction. The Day et al. (1981) study on adult native and adult nonnative interaction appears also to confirm the relative frequency of other-corrections in such interactions, as compared with their infrequent appearance in native/native interactions. This interpretation of other-correction as a training device for language learners seems an eminently reasonable one to me.

4.   *Learner response to negative input*

At this point the question of the availability of negative input to the language learner can be put to rest. If one accepts the expanded definition of negative input proposed herein, it is clear that learners have available to them a substantial amount of negative input. What remains to be addressed is the claim that learners are often incapable of making use of the negative input they receive. This is a difficult claim to evaluate, given presently available data, but various phenomena suggest themselves as evidence that learners can and in fact do make use of negative input also.

4.1.   In transcripts of conversations between mature native speakers and language learners (first and second) there can be found spontaneous learner imitations of native speech beyond their current productive competence indicating that sometimes, if not always, learners do take advantage of explicit corrections and confirmation checks, perceiving that the original form was inappropriate. That they do not take advantage of all such opportunities is not surprising. In general, every learner has a double agenda in an interaction sequence: (1) to get the message across and understand it (the communicative function) and, (2) to use the interaction as an opportunity to observe and produce features of the language they are concerned with (the learning function). It should not be surprising that often, in particular interactional sequences, message conveyance should take priority over the observation and production of form — particularly in those instances where the native speaker indicates the correct message has been received. Since spontaneous imitations of form do occur commonly, they indicated to me at least that the learner recognizes the value of negative input and is at times willing to put message conveyance temporarily aside. Furthermore, in the same transcripts, one finds that in situations in which the conversational partner indicates a failure to understand, learners will often spontaneously switch to alternate syntactic forms in their attempts to convey the original message. This too can be an indication that the learner perceives that the original form was inappropriate for the conveyance of a particular message.

4.2. The two phenomena just described — learner imitation of correct structures and learner switches to alternate forms — suggestive though they may be, do not, however, provide conclusive evidence that learners take advantage of negative input. Such evidence may never be possible with the kinds of information on language learning presently available. Nevertheless, there are, in addition, some phenomena available to us in the concept learning literature on hypothesis testing that add further weight to the claim that learners take advantage of negative input.

One phenomenon, observed by Levine (1975), is what he labeled the *Blank Trials Law*, and it involves learner interpretation of different types of input. This phenomenon emerges during what are called *nonoutcome problems*, in which the subjects receive neither confirmation nor disconfirmation of their guesses. What Levine found was that 'during a nonoutcome problem the subject behaved each time as though the experimenter were saying "Right."' (Levine 1975:173). To quote Levine, 'the finding has been consistently confirmed in four differently structured experiments that the behavior of subjects during trials when no outcomes **are given** is the same as the behavior of subjects when the experimenter **says** 'Right' following each response' (Levine 1975:173). Levine's hypothesis-testing model predicts, and his experiments show, that both the experimenter's 'Rights' and the experimenter's failures to respond produce no changes in the subject's hypothesis and therefore no difference in the sequence of subject responses manifested. 'In contrast,' he claims, '"Wrong" causes the subject to alter or reject his hypothesis and, thereby, produce a very different response series' (Levine 1975:177). So too in language learning it could be that negative input, as relatively infrequent as it may be in contrast to nonnegative input, has a strong impact on the learner's behavior and furthermore that a conversational partner's failure to correct the learner's output (let us say in those cases in which the message has been understood) is interpreted by the learner as confirming information.

The second phenomenon discovered by researchers in concept learning that is relevant to our consideration of this issue — the phenomenon called *processing time* — was first pointed out for adults by Wason and Johnson-Laird (1972). In certain (and I might add rather difficult) concept learning experiments, it took some time for subjects to exhibit behavior indicating they had made use of negative input. In these experiments subjects were asked to stop their training when they believed they had arrived at the correct hypothesis and to state the hypothesis. Whenever they were wrong, they were told so[8] and training would continue. Wason and Johnson-Laird found that, over all subjects, 51.6% of the instances which were generated immediately after a rejected hypothesis were responses consistent with, rather than inconsistent with, the just rejected hypothesis. On more than half the possible occasions then, the hypothesis was not immediately relinquished, even when it was known to be wrong. Typically it took time — processing time — for a new hypothesis to be formulated — and subjects would operate with the old hypothesis even as they were formulating the new one. They claim that learner behavior in these cases was consistent with Kuhn's (1970) thesis that scientists only relinquish a theory when an alternative theory or hypothesis is available. In the context in which Wason and Johnson-Laird were operating, the thesis entails that the subject will abandon a hypothesis only when another one is conceived (Wason and Johnson-Laird 1972:207).

Karmiloff-Smith and Inhelder (1977) also discussed this phenomenon in their description of experiments with middle-aged children on block-balancing tasks. They make the interesting claim that negative responses are only effective *after* the child has established a hypothesis, not before, and that even then children hold on to their initial hypotheses for as long as they can, preferring to create new hypotheses to account for counter-examples before finally attempting to unify all events under a single broader hypothesis (Karmiloff-Smith and Inhelder 1974:305-6).

5. *Conclusion*

In sum, closer inspection of the negative input issue demonstrates that it encompasses considerably more than linguists have looked at seriously so far. It was shown that such phenomena as confirmation checks, clarification requests, and failures to understand (both recognized and unrecognized) qualify as negative input. Furthermore, it was pointed out that learner imitation and learner reformulation phenomena relate to the negative input issue since they indicate that learners are, at times, aware of negative input. And last, it was suggested that both learner processing time and learner interpretation of both input and lack of input indicate that the learner may be operating under constraints yet to be taken into account when considering the negative input issue. All of this demonstrates that the issue of negative input is far from settled and therefore that it is premature either to assume that language learning can take place without negative input or to abandon hypothesis testing models as possible processing models for language acquisition. What is clear is that further exploration of the issues raised herein will contribute to a better understanding of the kinds of models required to characterize the human language learning ability.

NOTES

* I have benefitted from the comments of many who have discussed the contents of this paper with me. I particularly want to thank Dick Day, Elizabeth Kimmell, Ann Peters, Judy Reilly, and John Schumann for their useful comments and contributions of valuable data.

1) The 'black box,' variously labeled UG, LAD, 'the initial state,' can be viewed as containing at least two components: pre-experiential knowledge of the target language (be it first or second) as one component and a complex and multifaceted processing mechanism as the second component. I will have more to say about one aspect of the processing mechanism in section 2.

2) For some exceptions to this generalization, see Snow and Ferguson (1977) for studies of child L1 input and Chaudron (1979), Freed (1981) for studies of L2 input.

3) Note that the focus herein is not on the linguistic content proper but rather on the presentation of the content and possibly metalinguistic kinds of information made available to the learner. One may ask, given a body of linguistic content that the learner needs to analyze, does the learner benefit from its presentation in certain ways and not in others? Alternatively, one might view this field of inquiry as the study of various methods of information presentation (cf. Gold 1967) with a view to determining the relative effectiveness of such methods.

4) Other possible candidates are: comprehensible input (i.e., utterances which are embedded in enough context so that the learner can grasp their meanings); simplified input (i.e., utterances the structure or vocabulary or length of which have been stripped down in some way to accommodate the learner); sufficient input (i.e., is there a critical mass of input such that below that mass language learning will not occur and above it language learning will occur?).

5) Negative input can, in fact, logically come from two sources: (1) anomalous utterances produced by native speakers and identified by them as anomalous (e.g., self-corrections) or (2) anomalous utterances produced by adult and child learners and identified by the native speaker as anomalous. Although it would be interesting to explore the possible effects on the learner of the

former source, the focus of this paper will be directed toward the latter, involving the native speaker's response to the learner's anomalous utterance. Furthermore, in the interest of brevity, only syntactic anomalies are taken up herein.

6) This claim is a hotly debated one among second language acquisition researchers. For the purpose of this paper nothing hinges on it. Although there may be differences in the processes adults and children use in learning languages, the hypothesis testing model has been proposed for each population (cf. the Dechert (1978) and Schachter (1981) claims for adult second language learners) and needs to be evaluated for each.

7) One exception is McCawley (1982), who mentions misunderstandings and failures to understand as sources of negative data. He also proposes self-corrections by adults and children's failures to place interpretations on utterances encountered as further sources of negative data.

8) The subject's hypothesis may be viewed as analogous to the language learner's utterance (which represents a hypothesis) and the experimenter's 'Wrong' in this case may be viewed as analogous to a confirmation check, clarification request, or failure to understand in the language learning situation.

REFERENCES

Baker, C.L. 1979. Syntactic theory and the projection problem. *Linguistic Inquiry 10*: 533-581.

Bolinger, Dwight. 1953. The life and death of words. *American Scholar* 22:323-35.

Braine, Martin D.S. 1971. On two types of models of the internalization of grammars. In Slobin, Dan (ed.), *The Ontogenesis of Grammar*. New York: Academic Press.

Brice-Heath, Shirley. 1982. *Ways with Words: Ethnography of Communication in Communities and Classrooms*. London: Cambridge University Press.

Brown, Roger, and Camille Hanlon. 1970. Derivational complexity and order of acquisition in child speech. In John R. Hayes (ed.), *Cognition and the Development of Language*. New York: John Wiley & Sons, Inc.

Cazden, C., H. Cancino, E. Rosansky, and J. Schumann. 1975. *Second Language Acquisition Sequences in Children, Adolescents and Adults*. U.S. Dept. of HEW Office of Research Grants. Final Report Project #730744, Grant #NE-6-00-300014.

Chenoweth, Ann. 1981. Corrective Feedback in NS/NSS Conversations. Unpublished M.A. Thesis, University of Hawaii at Manoa.

Chomsky, Noam. 1981. Principles and parameters in syntactic theory. In N. Hornstein and D. Lightfoot (eds.). *Explanation in Linguistics*. London: Longman.

Corder, S.P. 1974. The significance of learners' errors. In J. Schumann and N. Stenson (eds.), *New Frontiers in Second Language Learning*. Rowley, MA: Newbury House Publishers.

Day, R., A. Chenoweth, A. Chun, S. Luppescu. 1981. Native speaker feedback to ESL student errors. Paper presented in AAAL Symposium at the 1981 ACTFL annual conference.

Dechert, Hans W. 1978. Contextual hypothesis-testing procedures in speech production. Paper presented at the 5th International Congress of Applied Linguistics. Montreal.

Dulay, H., and M. Burt. 1974. Natural sequences in child second language acquisition. *Working Papers on Bilingualism 3*. Toronto: Ontario Institute for Studies in Education.

Freed, Barbara. 1978. Talking to foreigners versus talking to children: similarities and differences. In R. Scarcella & S. Krashen (eds.), *Research in Second Language Acquisition*. Rowley, MA: Newbury House.

Gold, E. Mark. 1967. Language identification in the limit. *Information and Control 10*:467-474.

Hornstein, N., and D. Lightfoot. 1981. *Explanation in Linguistics*. New York: Longman.

Karmiloff-Smith, Annette, and Barbel Inhelder. 1977. If you want to get ahead get a theory. In P.N. Johnson-Laird and P.C. Wason (eds.), *Thinking: Readings in Cognitive Science*. Cambridge: Cambridge University Press.

Katz, Jerrold. 1966. *The Philosophy of Language*. New York: Harper & Row.

Kuhn, T.S. 1970. *The Structure of Scientific Revolutions*. 2nd Edition. Chicago: University of Chicago Press.

Levine, Marvin. 1975. *A Cognitive Theory of Learning: Research in Hypothesis Testing*. Hillsdale, NJ: Lawrence Erlbaum Associates.

Long, Michael. 1981. Input, interaction and second language acquisition. In H. Winitz (ed.), *Native Language and Foreign Language Acquisition*. *Annals of the New York Academy of Sciences 379*:259-278.

McCawley, James D. 1983. Towards plausibility in theories of language acquisition. *Communication and Cognition 16*:169-183.

McNeill, David. 1966. Developmental psycholinguistics. In F. Smith and G. Miller (eds.), *The Genesis of Language*. Cambridge: The MIT Press.

Ochs, Elinor. 1982. Talking to children in Western Samoa. *Language and Society 11*:77-104.

Peters, Ann. 1983. The units of language acquisition. *Cambridge Monographs and Texts in Applied Psycholinguistics*. Cambridge: Cambridge University Press.

Reilly, Judy. 1978. Childrens's repairs. Unpublished manuscript. University of California, Los Angeles.

Schachter, Jacquelyn. 1981. Negative transfer. Paper presented at IXth Annual Applied Linguistics Conference: Language Transfer. Ann Arbor.

Schachter, Jacquelyn, and Beverly Hart. 1979. An analysis of learner production of English structures. *Georgetown University Papers on Language and Linguistics 15*:18-75.

Schegloff, E.A., G. Jefferson, and H. Sacks. 1977. The preference for self-correction in the organization of repair in conversation. *Language 53*: 361-382.

Schumann, John. 1975. Transcripts of the data used as the basis for Cazden, C., H. Cancino, E. Rosansky and J. Schumann, *Second Language Acquisition Sequences in Children, Adolescents and Adults*. Final Report. Project 730744, Grant NE-6-00-3-0014. U.S. Dept. of HEW, NIE Office of Research Grants.

Scollon, Ronald. 1976. *Conversations With a One-year Old*. Honolulu: The University of Hawaii Press.

Snow, Catherine, and Charles Ferguson. 1977. *Talking to Children: Language Input and Acquisition*. Cambridge: Cambridge University Press.

Swain, M., G. Dumas, and N. Naiman. 1974. Alternatives to spontaneous speech: Elicited translation and imitation as indicators of second language competence. *Working Papers on Bilingualism 3*.

Wason, P.C., and P.N. Johnson-Laird. 1972. *Psychology of Reasoning: Structure and Content*. London: Batsford.

UNIFORMITY AND SOURCE-LANGUAGE
VARIATION ACROSS DEVELOPMENTAL CONTINUA*

HELMUT ZOBL

Université de Moncton

1. Introduction

1.1. Uniformity and variation

What would constitute a strong hypothesis on developmental uniformity among learners of a second language (L2)? Bickerton (1980) proposes a *unilinear model* of the decreolization process, which he explicitly extends to L2 acquisition continua: '...there is a single series of sequent changes in any continuum (perhaps even in all continuums that share a common superstrate) which serve to link a basilect to its related acrolect...' (p.123). While Bickerton (personal intervention at this conference) maintains that the unilinear model speaks only to the continuum between particular pairings of target (TL) and source languages (SL), the hypothesis that there exists 'only a single possible sequence of linguistic developments between any pair of linguistic states' (p.125) can readily be extended. In such an extended version of the unilinear model the structure of the TL solely maps out the sequence of linguistic states leading to it.[1]

A unilinear model essentially makes two claims about the developmental progression. First, it rules out the possibility of (>1) developmental paths to a TL system. Although an impressive body of L2 acquisition research thus far bears out this claim, I shall treat one case in some detail later on which disconfirms it.[2] Turkish and Romance speakers follow distinct routes in acquiring nominal possessives in German. This variation relates in a rather direct way to typological differences between Romance languages and Turkish.

According to the second claim, every learner would have to traverse the same number of sequent changes to arrive at a target feature. Zobl (1982) presents evidence which does not square with this claim. In that paper I compare the acquisition of the definite article form in English by a child learner whose L1 possesses this category (i.e. Spanish) with one whose L1 does not (i.e. Chinese). For the latter it can be shown that definiteness is first marked with a demonstrative pronoun. An examination of the production data of the Spanish learner (or Pienemann's (1980:61) data on Italian L1 - German L2) furnishes no evidence for such an initial approximation to the definite article; in fact, in both cases the definite article form appears earlier than the demonstrative pronoun as a segmental marker of definiteness.

This different selection of forms for marking definiteness implies as well a difference in the structural elaboration these speakers can implement in a single sequential change. The Italian and the Spanish learner move directly from zero representation to the target form. The Chinese speaker, on the other hand, follows the language evolutionary route, in which a deictic form is first employed to mark definiteness segmentally. This case of variation — a difference in the number of changes necessary to arrive at the target form — suggests that, depending on whether the SL and TL share a common category, the developmental continuum itself can vary in its extension.

Evidence thus exists which disconfirms both claims made by a unilinear model. However, as stated above, the empirical evidence available thus far compels one to recognize a significant degree of uniformity in developmental continua leading to a particular TL. How then can we begin to theoretically delimit the domain of potential SL variation? In the body of this paper I shall pursue this question in both an inductive and deductive manner. For the moment I wish merely to indicate the perspective from which this question will be approached.

As proposed in Chomsky (1965) and subsequently developed in Peters (1972), the acquisition faculty comes equipped with an evaluation procedure which permits selection of the most highly valued grammar for a set of input data. The evaluation procedure selects the formally simplest grammar and at the same time opts for that grammar which maximizes universal aspects of language (Peters 1972:181). Recently, the evaluation procedure has also been interpreted as a markedness metric for data intake (Grimshaw 1981:174ff). We can thus see the evaluation procedure as performing two tasks. Given a grammar Gn, it will prefer certain input data over other, available data for the construction of grammar Gn+1. Furthermore, the evaluation procedure will prefer a certain analysis over other, equally possible analyses. In this connection, it is a reasonable and empirically motivated assumption that an analysis which entails only a minimal adjustment to the current grammar will be more highly valued (cf. Bickerton 1973, Bever and Langendoen 1971). To illustrate the operation of the markedness evaluation on data intake, consider once again the case of category elaboration outlined above. For the Chinese child and the two Romance language children we can let Gn stand for the initial stage of zero representation of definiteness. We can be confident that all three learners were exposed to data which contained demonstrative forms and the definite article. For the construction of Gn+1 the evaluation metrics preferred different data. These can be contrasted along a number of dimensions, such as their semantic-functional transparence, morphological independence, and ability to carry stress. On each of these dimensions the definite article is located at the grammaticized end; in contradistinction to it, the deictic form combines properties that make it more highly valued for processing requirements (cf. Slobin 1977): it can bear stress; it can occur in isolation; and it retains, more transparently than the article, its pointing function to a referentially-given entity. It would seem then that prior linguistic knowledge is able to influence the evaluation procedure both with respect to what constitutes a minimal adjustment to the current grammar (cf. Zobl 1982) and the markedness evaluation placed on input data.

In the following sections I propose to examine the issue of uniformity and source language variation in a framework in which prior linguistic knowledge is one component of the non-primary acquisition faculty's evaluation metric. Before proceeding with an analysis of a number of TL continua, however, I would like first to introduce two types of change processes which, I propose, are constitutive of L2 acquisition continua. These are targeted and nativizing/optimalizing changes.

1.2. *Targeted and nativizing/optimalizing changes*

It is a reasonably accurate observation that SLA research has tended to concentrate on what, following Bickerton (1980), I shall refer to as targeted change. This focus can be readily identified in definitions of interlanguage continua: 'a dynamic goal-oriented language system of increasing complexity' (Corder 1977:13). Studies that seek to establish hierarchies of difficulty and/ or developmental sequences in the acquisition of mature L2 structures or systems fall within the compass of this focus.

As Corder's definition shows, targeted change entails complexification of the grammar. Formal marking replaces reliance on the discourse and/or situational context, new categories are introduced, and restrictions on the application of rules are added. Targeted change can thus be interpreted as entailing a movement towards more marked systems (cf. Bailey 1973). I shall examine this type of change process with reference to the development of negation in English.

Among the changes that can be termed targeted there is a subclass which merits separate consideration. I will refer to this subclass as *evolutive* changes, a term borrowed from Henning Anderson (1973). This designation seeks to underscore the fact that certain change processes in L2 continua replicate known sequences in historical language change. To illustrate the distinction I am drawing between a targeted and an evolutive change, let me refer you yet again to the difference between the Chinese speaker and the Romance language speakers in the acquisition of the definite article. Viewed from the perspective of the target language, the Chinese speaker's use of a demonstrative pronoun to mark definiteness constitutes a step toward the target, as does the use of the definite article form by the Spanish and the Italian child. Viewed from the perspective of the antecedent state — zero representation — only the Chinese speaker's innovation respects an historically attested diachronic constraint on the eventual elaboration of a definite article category by a language. Evolutive changes in acquisition then are a subclass of targeted changes which instantiate an invariant change sequence holding across historical and acquisition continua. However, what significance can we attach to this constraint if, as we have seen, it can be violated? At this point it may be useful to conceptualize the notions of core grammar and departures from core grammar (Chomsky and Lasnik 1977; Koster 1978, 1981) in dynamic terms. Just as the theory of grammar allows marked exceptions from the idealization represented by core grammar, so a theory of dynamic linguistics should enable us to scale the changes that can be effected in a single sequence as more or less marked. The Chinese learner's innovation is relatively unmarked inasmuch as it draws on a universal option for definitizing. Every language, regardless of the systemic means it has available for definitizing an NP (e.g. word order, definite article), provides to its speakers the latent option of definitizing by means of a deictic. Languages which evolve a definite article category from a deictic have gone the route of specialization. The fact that the Spanish and the Italian child are able to effect a marked change is thus best viewed as a dynamic parallel to marked exceptions in grammar.

The evolutive change I shall be concerned with in this paper bears on developmental continua leading to L2 targets with SVO word order and grammaticized subjects; that is, L2 targets with characteristics as set forth by Thompson (1978). More specifically, I shall be concerned with subject pronoun deletion, and the interpretation given to this by Jürgen Meisel (1977,

1980) and Manfred Pienemann (1980).

Meisel and his co-workers, Pienemann and Clahsen, note that in the German L2 speech of Romance language speakers, subject pronoun deletion does not begin to occur to any marked degree until sentence constituents begin to be preposed. Now the verb-second constraint in German requires subject-verb inversion at this point; what happens is that the pronoun either remains in pre-verb position or is deleted. Meisel (1980) proposes that this deletion represents a purposeful cognitive easification and he refers to this type of phenomenon as 'elaborative simplification'. It permits the integration of a new feature — preposing of constituents — into the learner's grammar while at the same time it prepares the next step, the acquisition of inversion. In Meisel's words, elaborative simplification 'helps to complexify the grammatical system' and 'represents an extension of the earlier system and a step toward the target variety' (p.37).

In the body of this paper I shall attempt to demonstrate that what Meisel, in connection with subject pronoun deletion, terms elaborative simplification is the product of an evolutive change. Languages do not evolve an SVO typology with grammaticized subjects overnight; nor, apparently, do learners. The phenomenon on which Meisel builds his case for elaborative simplification has a straightforward historical parallel in Old French. The identical deletion phenomena in Old French can scarcely be attributed to an avoidance of cognitive complexity. Moreover, as I shall show with reference to English L2 continua, subject pronoun deletion is not related to the inversion which German requires. In fact, I will argue that subject pronoun deletion in environments in which more than one sentence constituent competes for preverbal position is universally predictable in the acquisition of SVO languages with grammaticized subjects. In both the historical and the acquisition continuum the deletion phenomenon is the result of an incomplete analysis of SVO structure.

The third type of change that I shall examine are nativizing changes (Andersen 1980), which I will henceforth term optimalizing changes. Optimalization refers to a systems-internal norm which induces spontaneous changes in the interlanguage system, thus leading the system away from the target norm. For a better understanding of the conceptual content of optimalization, it should be pointed out that I do not take it to mean failure on the part of the learner to acquire a particular target feature, e.g. missing copulas. A learner who does not possess a target feature has failed to make progress toward the target; he has not been led away from the target. Since optimalization involves change processes with systems-internal motivation, they are 'natural' change processes in the sense of Bailey (1977)[3]; that is to say, their net effect is to bring about a demarking of forms and structures that are opaque and irregular. Optimalization will be examined with reference to the structural generalization of the preposition FOR.

2. Targeted change: negation

In a survey of the acquisition of L1 negation across a variety of languages, Wode (1977a) concludes that development toward the mature system will involve a progression from the use of a free negative morpheme — most commonly the anaphoric negator of the adult language — to a bound negative morpheme. The former occurs external to a verbal nucleus whereas the bound form will occur in intra-sentential negation.

Yet another aspect of the development of negation concerns the position of the negator relative to the verb. Recent evidence from the acquisition of negation in languages with post-verb negation in main clauses suggests that there is variable placement of the negator initially, with there being 'no discrete developmental stage in which NEG is placed exclusively before the verb' (Clahsen n.d.). While Clahsen (1981) reports similar variability in the acquisition of German by adult Romance speakers, Hyltenstam's (1977) findings on the acquisition of Swedish by speakers from a variety of languages do show a developmental progression from pre- to post-verbal negation in main clause.

The variable positioning of the negator in the L1 acquisition of languages with post-main verb negation has a parallel in historical change. If we consider English and French, two languages that have moved from pre-verb to post-verb negation in their historical development, we will note that the latter was innovated as a negative emphasizer, presumably in response to a semantic bleaching of the pre-verbal form; i.e. English: *ne ... nought*; French: *ne ... pas*. This positional cycle, first remarked on by Jesperson (1917) and dealt with in detail by Horn (1978), suggests that post-verbal negation arises out of bracketing negation. (Catalan Spanish is currently innovating such a device.) Thus, post-verbal negation must go through a period of co-existence with pre-verbal negation. The transition from the one to the other is continuous. Stated differently, both in diachrony, acquisition and, I believe, in synchrony post-verbal negation implies pre-verbal. I am not aware of a converse restriction on pre-verbal negation. These historical and acquisitional regularities furnish us with two measures of markedness:

1. NEGATOR SPELLING - the bound negative morpheme is more marked than the free, anaphoric form

2. NEGATOR POSITIONING - post-verbal negation is more marked than pre-verbal

The development of negation in English L2 continua conforms to the above two measures, regardless of the learner's L1. Below this macro-level, we find L1-related variation.

Let us begin with negator positioning. Spanish speakers acquire post-verbal negation later. They proceed from NO to mono-morphemic DON'T before acquiring post-verbal negation in modal contexts. Other language groups (e.g. Norwegian, German, Chinese and French) proceed from NO to NOT and acquire DON'T last. While the generalization of DON'T to pre-modal contexts follows right upon NO - Verb structures with Spanish speakers, other language groups do not arrive at this generalization until after a period of post-verbal negation in modal contexts (see, e.g. Wode 1977b). I shall not dwell on the details of the overall developmental sequences here; suffice it to say that initially Spanish speakers' positioning of the negator is not sensitive to verbal subcategories.

Another difference between Spanish speakers and other language groups, one which has not been noted in the literature, has to do with distribu-

TABLE 1.   Preverbal Negative Spelling in Alberto (Schumann 1978) in Relation to Subject Deletion.*

Samples		1-4	5-8	9-12	13-16	17-20
NO	+ subject	26	56	29	30	19
	− subject	20	23	23	19	13
NOT	+ subject		1	1	1 (+1)	(1)
	− subject					

( ) = contracted negative

* The tabulation (raw numbers) is based on the corpus in the Appendix. Only spontaneous utterances and only negative declarative utterances were considered.

TABLE 2. Preverbal Negative Spelling in Enrique (Young 1974) in Relation to Subject Deletion*

Sample		Oct.	Nov.	Jan.	Feb.	April	May
NO	+ subject		8		11	2	6
	− subject	1	7		1		
NOT	+ subject		(1)	(1)		2 (+2)	1 (+6) 5 (+2)
	− subject		(1)	1 (+1)			

( ) = contracted negative

* The tabulation (raw numbers) is based on the corpus in the Appendix. As with Alberto only spontaneous, negative declarative utterances were tabulated. Enrique also used NA as a negator. Utterances employing NA were excluded because of its ambiguous status.

tional restrictions on negator spelling. Unlike other language groups, Spanish speakers' use of the anaphoric negator NO is not sensitive to the distinction between sentence-internal environment with subject NP present, and nucleus-external environment with subject deleted. Table 1 shows the distribution of NO in the speech of Alberto, an adult Spanish speaker studied by Schumann (1978), and Table 2 that of Enrique, a six-year-old Spanish speaker studied by Young (1974).

With both speakers, NO freely occurs in sentence-internal environments. This stands in marked contrast to the distributional restriction on NO one finds in the English speech of other language groups. An examination of Ravem's (1968) and Huang's (1971) data on, respectively, a Norwegian and Chinese learner reveals that in sentence-internal environments NO is not used as a preverbal negator.

> I not got it (Huang 1971)
> I not like that (Ravem 1968: Rune, Time I)
> I not looking for edge

Table 3 shows the distribution of NO ~ NOT in the speech of adult French-speaking learners.

TABLE 3.   Preverbal Negative Spelling in Francophone Learners in Relation to Subject Deletion (N = 9)*

Speakers	+ Subject → NOT/NO		− Subject → NO/NOT	
1	+	+	+	−
2	+	−	+	−
3	+	−	n.s.	n.s.
4	+	−	n.s.	n.s.
5	−	+	+	−
6	+	−	n.s.	n.s.
7	+	−	n.s.	n.s.
8	−	+	+	−
9	n.s.	n.s.	+	−
Total (absolute)	9	4	13	0

* Tabulation is based on oral interview transcripts of beginning ESL learners. Only 9 speakers of a population of 21 (cf. Table 4) had NO~NOT preverbally. Each interview is approximately 15-20 minutes in length.

Spanish speakers thus do not appear to have any distributional restrictions on NO spelling. The difference between Spanish speakers and the other language groups with respect to preverbal negative spelling requires us to assume different structural analyses, with negative spelling operating on the configuration inside the internal bracket.[4]

Spanish   Non-Spanish

[<X> [__ Vb...] ... Y]   [[<X> __ Vb ...] ... Y]

+ Main

In addition, one can formalize the difference by viewing negative spelling as being functionally related to subject deletion in non-Spanish speakers. For these speakers there is clear evidence that deletion and negative spelling are ordered with respect to each other:

Spanish	Non-Spanish	
1. negative lowering[5]	1. Negative lowering	
2. spelling→NO	2a. + deletion	2b. − deletion
	↓	↓
	3a. Spelling→NO	3b. Spelling→NOT

With respect to the two markedness measures we identified — negator positioning and negator spelling — we can see that Spanish speakers operate with a less marked system. There are no derivational or rule ordering constraints on negator spelling; furthermore, there are no verb subcategorizational restrictions on negator positioning: an invariant form has an invariant distribution. Note that this system of negation does represent the initial stage of negation for acquirers of English. However, it also represents the mature system of negation in Spanish. In Zobl (1980a) and (1982) I propose that progress beyond this initial stage in the negation continuum requires the Spanish speaker to advance to a system of negation that is more marked (in the sense outlined above) than that of his L1. The protracted use of the initial form of negation by Spanish speakers reflects this difference in markedness. When unanalyzed DON'T is added to the negator repertoire, the evaluation metric opts for that solution which requires the least readjustment since DON'T is invariably preverbal in the input. Hence, both with regard to data intake and its analysis the Spanish system of negation appears to bias the evaluation metric in favour of solutions involving minimal increments in markedness on it and a maximal degree of compatibility with it.

To sum up, while the development of negation in English L2 is uniform with respect to the two markedness measures we identified at the outset, there is clear evidence that preverbal negation in Spanish speakers operates with a less marked system, there being no derivational constraints on negative spelling.

3. *Evolutive change: subject deletion and fledgling SVO languages*

In his discussion of word order in the L1 acquisition of German, Clahsen (1980:66-67;70) observes that the gradual predominance of SVO word order can be traced to two factors: 1) perception of the difference between finite and non-finite verbs, with finite verbs occurring in second position, and 2) topicalization of the subject.

In their study of the Dutch of Turkish and Moroccan immigrant workers, Jansen, Lalleman, and Muysken (1981) arrive at essentially the same two factors: verbs occur in second position when they are finite and when there is a sentence subject. Hence, languages whose acquisition exhibits more word order variability than English point to the crucial role played by the second position of the verb when all three sentence constituents, S, V, and O, are present. By virtue of its second position the verb separates the subject from the object perceptually while at the same time word order becomes available for the marking of grammatical relations.

For acquisition continua of SVO languages it has also been noted that the preverbal subject position generally admits only one constituent, a pronoun or an unexpanded noun. (For L1 acquisition, see Bowerman 1973:138 and Brown, Cazden, and Bellugi-Klima 1969:43; for L2 acquisition, see Butterworth 1972, Hernandez-Chavez 1977, and Felix 1978.) When constituents other than the subject compete for pre-verbal position, subjects, but especially pronoun subjects, take a back seat. Initial negation almost categorically leads to subject deletion. With WH-fronting, subject (pronoun) deletion is frequent:

(1) How feeling? (Clyne 1975: immigrant worker)
(2) Where find it? (Ravem 1974: Reidun, 4th month)
(3) Where's going? (three-year-old French L1 learner)
(4) Why driving in the motorcycle? (adult French L1 learner)

With noun subjects a kind of WH-subject flip can occasionally be observed:

(5) Where goes wheel? (Menyuk 1969: L1 English)
(6) What call that man? (Ravem 1974: Reidun, 6th month)

In the L2 speech of Spanish and Italian speakers one finds two phenomena which to the best of my knowledge are not documented for acquisition continua of other language groups. First, negation can lead to the same kind of flip that we noted above with respect to WH-constituents:

(7) Kein verheiratet meine Schwester (Clahsen 1981)
     'My sister is not married'.

Also, only in the L2 speech of Spanish and Italian speakers do we find negation leading to subject pronoun deletion with retention of the copular verb; other language groups delete the copula:

(8) No is mine. (Schumann 1978)
(9) Nee is libanesa. (Clahsen 1981)
     'She is not Lebanese'.

Thus, while SVO acquisition continua furnish evidence for a pre-verbal one-constituent constraint, this constraint seems to be somewhat more severe in L2 continua of these two Romance language groups.

What is one to make of this pre-verbal one-constituent constraint? Vennemann (1974) has proposed that before a fledgling SVO language acquires such properties as grammaticized word order and obligatory subjects, it will first pass through a pseudo-SVO stage, which he terms TVX. Since discourse constraints conspire to make subjects the topic, TVX has the appearance of an SVO word order language. What distinguishes a TVX from a true SVO language is a constraint on the position of the verb: it is the second sentence constituent, in SVO.

For example, French, which now is an SVO language with grammaticized word order and obligatory subjects, was a TVX language throughout the medieval period up to the 16th century (approximately). In main clauses object topicalization, adverbial preposing, sentence adverbs and preceding subordinate clauses all triggered subject-verb inversion; e.g.

(10) Dont dist le dus au chevalier... (*La Chastelaine de Vergi*, p.217)

When the subject was a pronoun, deletion was the rule (Foulet 1966:313). (I shall not go into the question of how inversion and deletion were ordered with respect to each other, although it seems counter-intuitive to order deletion after inversion.) A perspective on the growing obligatory nature of subject pronouns can be gained by examining the debates of prescriptive grammarians. Brunot (1933:383-384) presents the following documentary evidence:

16th Century: grammarians insist on expression of subject pronouns
17th Century: discussion over whether a pronoun was necessary when it had an antecedent. Zero anaphora in these cases was not tied to identical syntactic function, e.g.,
               Vous m'avez bien conseillé, et Ø vous croirai une autre fois.
               'You have advised me well and Ø will believe you another time.' (je/I → Ø)
               It was still acceptable to omit impersonal *il* as in *il pleut* and *il faut* ('it is raining; it is necessary').

These historical aspects of French during its TVX stage show some striking similarities to the pre-verbal one-constituent constraint discussed above in connection with SVO acquisition continua. In fact I would like to claim that acquirers of SVO languages having grammaticized word order and obligatory subjects will pass first through a pseudo-SVO stage. Whenever a constituent other than the subject competes for pre-verbal position, subject pronoun deletion is favoured. I would also suggest that Meisel's interpretation of pronoun deletion in these environments is misguided. Meisel's perspective on pronoun deletion is targeted. To him it represents an avoidance of cognitive complexity, while at the same time it 'prepares the next step,' the acquisition of inversion. First, it should be pointed out that the identical deletion phenomenon in Old French in no way admits of an interpretation as 'elaborative simplification'. Old French definitely did possess inversion, so that one can scarcely speak of deletion being the result of an inability to carry out inversion. Second, as we shall see below, highly similar deletion phenomena occur in English L2 continua. Modern English, for all intents and purposes, has no verb-second constraint requiring inversion of the subject and verb after topicalization and adverbial preposing (except with negative adverbs *hardly*, *never*, etc.).

Given the perceptually grounded preverbal one-constituent constraint, and given the historical aspects of pronoun deletion in Old French during its TVX stage, we can make the following predictions concerning subject pronoun deletion:

1. In second language SVO continua the pronoun deletion rate will be higher in contexts in which a constituent competes with the subject for pre-verbal position than it will be in contexts in which the subject is sentence-initial.
2. Impersonal pronouns will be the preferred input form for deletion.

Below we proceed to an examination of subject pronoun deletion in Alberto's English speech and compare this with deletion in the English speech of Francophone learners. While I was not able to control for level of development, I am confident that this does not invalidate the findings.

Since we predict that the one-constituent constraint promotes deletion, we establish two separate contexts: (a) subject-initial contexts (#S-Vb) and (b) constituent-other-than-subject-initial contexts (C-S-Vb). Type (b) contexts include preposed prepositional phrases, adverbs (including sentence adverbs like *maybe*), sentence connectors, and sentence embedding. In sentence embedding, either the complementizer or the matrix sentence was considered the C-context, i.e.

(11)   Matrix $-\frac{}{s}$ [(Comp.)$_s$ [Pro. ...]

Tables 4 and 5 present the findings from an analysis of oral interviews with 21 Francophones in type (a) and type (b) contexts, respectively.

TABLE 4.   Subject Pronoun Deletion in #__Verb Contexts in Francophone Learners (N=21)*

$$\frac{\text{Total Deletions}}{\text{Total Contexts}} \quad \frac{23}{281} = \text{Deletion rate .08}$$

$$\frac{\text{Deletion in #__IS Contexts}}{\text{Total #__IS Contexts}} \quad \frac{22}{136} = \text{Deletion rate .16}$$

$$\frac{\text{Deletion in #__IS Contexts}}{\text{Total Deletions}} \quad \frac{22}{23} = \text{Deletion rate .96}$$

Deletions with Input Form IT .83

*Tabulations in Tables 4-7 are based on declarative affirmative utterances only.

TABLE 5.   Subject Pronoun Deletion in Const.-Subj.-Verb Contexts (C__Vb) in Francophone Learners

$$\frac{\text{Total Deletions}}{\text{Total Contexts}} \quad \frac{15}{101} = .15$$

$$\frac{\text{Deletion in C__IS Contexts}}{\text{Total Deletions}} \quad \frac{4\,(+2)^*}{15} = .27/.40$$

$$\frac{\text{Deletion with Input IT}}{\text{Total Deletions}} \quad \frac{5}{15} = .33$$

* ( ) = copula Ø

Scanning Table 4 we find a total deletion rate of .08. Of these .96 occur in #__IS contexts and the pronoun *it* is the input form in .83 of the cases. Table 5 reveals .15 deletions in type (b) contexts. Here, however, C__IS contexts only account for .27/.40 deletions and *it* is the input in .33 of the cases. Thus (b) contexts are the heavy environment for deletion.

When we examine the type (a) contexts more closely, we find that *it* deletion occurs predominantly in three types of environments:

1. Ø *is* NOUN (8)
2. Ø *is* (expressions of temperature and weather) (6)
3. Ø *is* (expressions of time) (5)

Thus, in the majority of these *it* deletions, the pronoun has the non-referential, dummy place-holder function. The function of *it* in environments (2) and (3) corresponds to impersonal *il* in French. As we had occasion to observe earlier, it was in this function that pronoun deletion persisted longest in French, historically.

The examples below illustrate subject pronoun deletion in (b) contexts:

(12)   He say Ø is getting late. (*it*)
(13)   The man thinks outside Ø is raining. (*it*)
(14)   Here Ø have man. (impersonal *we* or *you*)
(15)   After the game or practice Ø study. (*I*)
(16)   Because Ø put your (= his) letter in mailbox. (*he*)

The type (b) contexts should be differentiated further. Some of the cases of pronoun deletion involve the same kind of extended zero anaphora which 17th century French grammarians could not agree on. The missing pronoun in (17) has an antecedent in the conjoined sentence, but this antecedent bears a different grammatical relation to its verb than the omitted pronoun.

(17)   Here we have two boys and Ø have a conversation. (*they*)
(18)   He can't because Ø too big. (*he*)

Let us now turn to Schumann's Spanish-speaking informant, Alberto. Tables 6 and 7 present the findings on subject pronoun deletion in type (a) and type (b) contexts, respectively. Beginning with Table 6 we see that, as with the Francophone speakers, #__IS contexts represent the heavy environment for pronoun subject deletion. Unlike the Francophones, Alberto's overall frequency of deletion is higher (.08 vs. .28-.47), as is the rate of deletion in #__IS contexts (.16 vs. .45-.62). Also, Alberto shows a slight tendency to delete a greater variety of subject pronouns (.17 vs. .02-.30).

TABLE 6. Subject Pronoun Deletion in #__Verb Contexts in Alberto

Tapes	Total Contexts	Total Delet.	Total #__IS	Delet. in #__IS	Input IT
1-4	72 (+1)	20	43 (+1)	20	19
5-8	177 (+4)	63	121 (+4)	63	62
9-12	206 (+1)	91	166 (+1)	90 (+1)	64
13-16	152	70	112	69	55
17-20	120 (+1)	40	86 (+1)	39	33

( ) = verb not supplied

	Range
$\dfrac{\text{Total Deletions}}{\text{Total Contexts}}$	.28 - .47
$\dfrac{\text{Deletions in \#\_\_IS}}{\text{Total \#\_\_IS}}$	.45 - .62
$\dfrac{\text{Deletion in \#\_\_IS}}{\text{Total Deletions}}$	approx. 1.0
Deletions involving IT	.70 - .98

TABLE 7. Subject Pronoun Deletion in Const.-Subj.-Verb Contexts in Alberto

Tapes	Total Contexts	Total Deletions	Delet. in C__IS	Input IT
1-4	9	6	5	5
5-8	13	9	8	5
9-12	28	22	19	13
13-16	24	18	18	11
17-20	12	7	5	4

	Range
$\dfrac{\text{Total Deletions}}{\text{Total Contexts}}$	.58 - .80
$\dfrac{\text{Deletions in C\_\_IS}}{\text{Total Deletions}}$	.71 - 1.0
Input IT	.55 - .83

Turning to the (b) contexts we find a striking parallel: as in the speech of the Francophones, the deletion rate doubles (.08 → .15 vs. .28/.47 → .58/.80). In C__IS contexts, Alberto's pronoun deletion rate is close to being categorial (.71-1.0).

In addition to the quantitative difference, there are two other differences between theFrancophones and Alberto that are worth noting. In tapes 1-20, Alberto supplies 12 occurrences of *it* as a subject pronoun in #__IS contexts. His repertoire contains a number of alternate pronoun forms that can serve as a 3rd person neuter pronoun. Compare their frequencies in his speech to their frequencies in the Francophone group:

TABLE 8. Frequencies of Alternate 3rd Person Neuter Subject Pronoun Forms

Alberto		Francophones	
this	(98)	it's	(58)
it's	(75)	it	(25)
that's	(33)	this	(8)
it	(12)	that's	(4)
that	(2)		

Alberto relies heavily on emphatic, free forms and contracted *it's*. This difference suggests that Alberto — in attempting to conform to the target language — is following a strategy that says: emphatic free forms and contracted *it's* cannot constitute input to deletion; therefore, rely on them. The statistical preference for the emphatic free form *this* brings to mind the use, initially, of a demonstrative by the Chinese speaker for marking definiteness. Just as in Chinese definiteness would only be marked segmentally when it needs to be emphasized, so in Spanish subject pronouns may occur for emphasis. In both cases the speaker's L1 lacks a grammaticized counterpart to the TL category; and in both cases we find that from the possibilities provided in the input the evaluation metric prefers stress-bearing free forms in elaborating the obligatory TL category.

A second, and not merely quantitative, difference between Alberto and the Francophones concerns noun subject postposing in the C-contexts. It is only attested in Alberto's speech, e.g.,

> In England is more big the problem.
> For me is better the beer.
> In this country is crazy the weather, no?

We have seen that irrespective of whether the learner's L1 possesses grammaticized subjects subject pronoun deletion is promoted when the pronoun is non-referential and/or when it is not in sentence-initial position. Since reference-bearing pronouns are as a rule not deleted in sentence-initial position, we are justified in assuming that two independent processes underlie deletion in these environments. For non-referential pronoun subjects we adopt a variable deletion rule:[6]

$$\left\{ \begin{array}{c} \text{it} \\ \text{there} \end{array} \right\} \rightarrow \emptyset \; / \; \#\_\_IS^{\beta}$$

$$[-\text{reference}]^{\alpha}$$

For C__Vb contexts, which manifest the verb-second constraint, a different process must be postulated, for here reference-bearing pronouns are deleted.

One should note, first of all, that deletion cannot be attributed to some putative restriction on the number of elements that can be programmed in preverb position. If this were the case, we would expect the deletion frequency to be lower in utterance like (19) and (20) and higher in utterances like (21); this is not the case, however.

> (19) Here Ø have man
> (20) Because Ø put your ...
> (21) After the game or practice Ø study

We can conclude, therefore, that deletion is not related to some limitation on programming longer strings. In those cases in which a reference-bearing pronoun is involved, deletion permits the verb to fill the position of second *syn-*

tactic constituent, and where the first constituent itself can be a sentence, a prepositional phrase, a conjunction, an adverbial, etc. At the very least this suggests that the subject is defined as the first syntactic constituent of SEN-TENCE in surface structure and not in terms of an abstract dominance relationship to SENTENCE.[7]

Given such an incomplete analysis of S by acquirers of SVO languages with grammaticized subjects, we can readily explain the higher rate of deletion in Alberto's speech. As I have argued elsewhere (Zobl 1980 a and b; see also Andersen 1980 and 1981), the occurrence of SL influence on a TL continuum is a matter of whether the structural property of the SL is compatible with the learner's current grammar of the relevant TL domain. In the case we are considering, subject pronoun deletion in Spanish supports those interlanguage-specific factors we have identified. Furthermore, VS word order in Spanish — which is pragmatically motivated (Contreras 1976) but may also be a reflection of a typological drift to VS word order (Green 1976; Schwartz 1975) — provides a means of resolving the positional conflict when a constituent other than the subject competes with it for the preverbal position.

The acquisition of grammaticized subjects by L2 learners recapitulates a number of salient structural phenomena that can be observed in the diachronic development of languages towards grammaticized SVO word order. Regardless of whether the learner's L1 possesses grammaticized subjects, the initial analysis performed on subjects is influenced by their distribution; i.e., they are commonly the first syntactic constituent. Much the same kind of distributional analysis must be assumed to have operated historically in English when dative NPs (as in *me likes it not*) came to be reanalyzed as the subject NP. Other aspects of the invariance of the developmental process pertain to the omission of non-reference-bearing subjects and zero anaphora in embedded or conjoined clauses under co-referentiality with a subject or object NP in the matrix or preceding clause. Berman (1980), who discusses these and similar features in connection with Modern Hebrew, advances them as diagnostics for non-subject-prominent languages. In conclusion then, the phenomena surrounding subject pronoun omission in the speech of the L2 learners appear to be integral to a universal process in the elaboration of an SVO word order with grammaticized subjects. Assuming subject to be a universal syntactic function, we can see that subject prominence represents a language-typological specialization of the universal. Once again, as with the article, the inter-learner variation shows up in the pace with which the specialized property is acquired.

4. *Optimalization processes: the syntax and semantics of FOR*

As we have seen with reference to subject pronoun omission, the description of developmental continua in isolation from historical continua misses significant invariant constraints which hold for change processes. Moreover, in failing to take these constraints into account, explanations of developmental phenomena become biased in favour of specifics of the target language. This is the case with Meisel's interpretation of pronoun omission.

Andersen's Nativization Hypothesis represents the recognition of further processes of change in interlanguage whose origins can be said to reside in the relationship between linguistic universals and linguistic specialization. Whereas our discussion of targeted and evolutive changes focused on developmental aspects of the route to specialization, in this section I shall examine change processes whose net effect is to bring about a leveling of formal differentiation, a movement away from the linguistic specialization implicated in marking changes. Very little work has been done on the nature of this counter-force, although both Andersen (1981, 1982) and Schumann (1978) see its analogue in pidginization. It is my opinion that calling this counter-force pidginization has, at the present state of knowledge, mainly metaphoric value.

Andersen (1980) does, however, single out one process as a candidate for the nativization process: '... the creation of form-meaning relationships in the L2 by making previously learned forms take on the functions for which the learner has not acquired the target language forms' (p.275). The interesting question, of course, is what are the linguistic motivations behind the reinterpretation of form-meaning relationships?

I would contend that nativization optimalizes linguistic resources for performability, rendering them more regular and transparent in response to processing and storage requirements. The essence of optimalization is demarking, the operation of which involves

1. the selection and reinterpretation of semantically transparent, morphologically independent forms to serve functions for which the TL input provides grammaticized and semantically opaque forms;
2. the regularization of form-meaning relationships by exploiting language-universal semantic and functional affinities; and
3. the regularization of the phrase structure along analogic lines.

To illustrate these effects of demarking, I would like to turn to an examination of the structural uses of prepositional FOR in the English speech of Francophone learners. I intend also to put the analysis on a broader linguistic footing by pointing out parallels to other contact varieties of English. The examples in Table 9 below illustrate the uses to be considered.

TABLE 9.   Structural Uses of FOR in Speech of Francophone Learners

---

Infinitive Complementizer

1. He needed money for to get a clean shirt.
2. He goes to library for buy his book.
3. How many oranges d'you want for buy?
4. He ask for do (= go) the movie.
5. Phil decide on the street for speak again with the girl.
6. My father encourage me for play hockey.
7. He suggest for to shoot.
8. He go for to meet the girl.

Sentential Complementizer

9. And (they) is very happy for when he (= they) see the visitor.
10. Phil come back for you (= Phil) give her the bill.
11. He ask for his parents come to see him.
12. The policeman stop the car for the people can cross the street.
13. The young boy is not crying for because they have not good temperature outside?

Directional Locative

14. She want to go for the disco.
15. I would buy a trip for Florida.
16. We went for Chicoutimi.

FOR as a Dative and Genitive Case Marker

17. What is colour for taxi?
18. What is name for capital Saskatchewan?
19. Equilibrium for the nature is disturb.
20. habits for the animals
21. mood for man
22. center for the note   (middle of the class; average)
23. The next test for me Monday   (my next test...)
24. no car for me   (I don't have a car)
25. It's a very beautiful performance for Minnesota North Stars
26. become a friend for her   (become her friend)
27. parents for she   (her parents)

4.1.   FOR with infinitival and sentential complements

Andersen (1980) and Zobl (1980c) have remarked on the pervasive use of FOR as an infinitive marker in the English speech of, respectively, Spanish and French learners. These papers present a number of structural facts about English which would account for the appearance of FOR, irrespective of the L1; however, we each further propose that Spanish *para* + infinitive and French *pour* + infinitive promote this analysis of the input. Examples (1) - (13) illustrate the complement-introducing function of FOR.

In Zobl (1980c) I point out that prepositional FOR has once before occurred with infinitives in English, namely from the end of the 12th Century to the end of the 16th Century (approximately). In its earliest attested occurrences it introduces a purpose infinitive (Mossé 1952:101). Jesperson (1961:154-57) maintains that the introduction of FOR was in response to a semantic depletion of prepositional *to*, which had lost its directional meaning and become a sandhi form. By the end of the 13th Century, distributional restrictions on FOR have disappeared; it occurs even in aspectual environments, e.g. *Bigynneth ... for to go* (Mossé, p. 101). In Zobl (1980c) I argue that the generalization of FOR in infinitival environments follows the same course. It occurs first with infinitives of purpose (e.g. Table 9, no. 2) (which take *pour* in French), spreads to other environments (e.g. nos. 3 and 7), and again persists longest with infinitives of purpose in the replacement process with *to*. As in Middle English, the spread of FOR is an instance of rule generalization with system-internal motivation. It is a straightforward demarking process in which the original environmental constraints favouring its occurrence are dropped.

Jesperson's observation that all Germanic dialects availed themselves of a directional preposition with infinitives points us to yet another parallel in the use of FOR between Middle English and the English speech of the French learners. During the period when FOR occurred with infinitives, it also functioned as a directional preposition:

For England Cose, goe. (Shakespeare, *King John*, 111, iii, 71)

A similar reinterpretation of FOR as a directional preposition is attested, though not abundantly, in the speech corpus of the Francophones (e.g. Table 9, nos. 14-16).

Jesperson's account of the directional preposition plus infinitive construction is a genetic one. The genetic explanation comes up short, however, once we include in our purview data from English-derived Creole languages.

In these languages (see Washabaugh 1975) we also find a preposition, *fo~fi*, with a directional meaning functioning as an infinitival and a sentential complementizer:

im drap bred skrumz fi dey fala di trak
'He dropped bread crumbs so that they would follow the track'

im kom fi gi im...
'He came to give him...'

(Providence Island Creole,
Washabaugh 1975:117,118)

Washabaugh (p. 122) proposes that the complementizing function of FOR evolved out of the locative preposition. This language-universal, localist account fits the Middle English data, as well as our own acquisitional data. Jesperson's genetic account focuses on linguistic continuity. Another perspective is provided by linguists (Bailey and Maroldt 1977; Dominigue 1977) who focus on the possible creolizing influences English underwent subsequent to the Norman French conquest. In such a perspective, natural semantactic processes gave unique expression to the directional locative sense shared by infinitive complements of purpose and locative NPs.

In Middle English as well as in our acquisitional data the infinitive of purpose spearheads the generalization of FOR in infinitival environments. Semantically, the infinitive of purpose functions as a deep case argument to its matrix verb, its relation being that of GOAL. The semantic parallel between infinitives of purpose and NPs functioning as GOAL to their verb motivates the use of a formally identical segment. As to the syntactic status of FOR with infinitival and sentential complements (e.g. Table 9, nos. 4, 11, and 13), it seems entirely plausible to treat it as a preposition. These complements would then have the following structural analysis.

[for]]...] s] np]pp

4.2.   FOR as a dative/genitive case preposition

Examples 17-27 in Table 9 illustrate yet another reanalysis of FOR: it is used as a dative/genitive case preposition to mark possessive and part-whole relationships. The signaling of possessive relationships by marking the possessor for dative or benefactive object is one of the commonest devices cross-linguistically (Ultan 1978). At this time it may no longer come as a surprise that *fi* occurs in identical function in English-derived creoles. In Providence Island Creole we find

Wan a di granson fi di daata ...
'One of the grandsons of the daughter'   (Washabaugh 1975: 116)

and in Jamaican Creole English

a fi-mi book dat
'That is my book'   (Todd 1975: 64)

FOR in the English speech of the Francophones and *fi* in English-derived creoles thus occurs in three identical functions:

 (i) as a directional locative preposition
 (ii) as an infinitival and sentential complementizer
(iii) as a dative/benefactive case preposition to mark possessive relationships.

The semantic affinity between possessive and locative relationships is well established (Lyons 1967), as is the functional affinity between prepositions and complementizers (Washabaugh 1975; Mühlhaüser 1980:42-43). These semantic and functional affinities motivate the selection of one form, FOR. Note that what is thereby achieved is a maximal regularization of form-meaning relationship. This regularization maximizes the iconic tendency in language whereby 'semantic sameness is also reflected by formal sameness' (Anttila 1972:89).

While the maximizing of the iconic tendency in language represents one aspect of the demarking process, the use of FOR for the expression of possessive relationships illustrates yet another side of the demarking process, one which we have encountered at several points in the course of this paper: degrammaticization. As a genitive/dative case preposition, FOR gives analytic expression to the TL inflectional genitive; it permits the bound possessive determiner to be expressed by a morphologically independent NP, and it formally relates the semantically transparent GOAL/BENEFACTIVE sense of FOR in expressions like *a book for you* to possessive and part-whole relationships.

4.3.   *Analogizing of the phrase structure*
Finally, let us turn to a consideration of how the demarking process affects the phrase structure. French speakers initially use possessive determiners in their standard pre-head position (e.g. *my friend*). Since this is not the case with nominal possessive determiners — which are categorically realized as prepositional phrases in post-head position (e.g. *friend of the man*) — this initial acquisition seems, therefore, to be faciliated by the shared surface structure position. Yet in spite of the initial acquisition in pre-head position, this seems to represent a marked order relative to the rules of the base. Exam-

ples such as *parents for she* and *friend for her* are clear cases of analogic regularization. Pronominal possessive determiners are aligned with nominal determiners so that both can be generated as prepositional phrases in post-head position.

If we survey examples 1-27 of Table 9, we can discern a pervasive HEAD-COMPLEMENT pattern. This pattern can be identified in the NP (e.g., *colour for taxi, friend for her*) and in the VP (*go for Quebec, go for to meet the girl, stop the car for the people can cross the street*). The symmetry of this pattern in the NP and the VP derives from the status of noun and verb: both function as the HEAD of their respective phrases and both HEAD categories can be followed by the category COMPLEMENT, which is preferentially realized as $(FOR (...)_{NP})_{PP}$. The symmetry of the NP and the VP argues that demarking in the phrase structure promotes cross-category generalizations, not unlike those captured by X-Bar Theory (Chomsky 1970; Jackendoff 1977) and Hawkin's (1982) Principle of Cross-Category Harmony.

In the NP the class of specifiers is reduced in that possessive determiners are generated as N^2 complements, the level corresponding to that of restrictive modifiers.[8] In the VP the complements corresponding to this bar projection are the infinitival and sentential complements of purpose. Other complements of the VP strictly subcategorize the verb, which makes them V^1 complements. Taking prepositional phrases as our third phrasal category and P (Preposition) as its HEAD, the symmetry across all three phrasal categories reduces to the following rules:

$$(22) \quad P^1 \rightarrow P - \left\{ \begin{array}{c} NP \\ N\widehat{P}S \end{array} \right\}$$

e.g., go *for Quebec*, ask *for his parents come to see him*

$$(23) \quad V^1 \rightarrow V - (NP) \ (P^1)$$

e.g., *stop the car, want for buy, ask for his parents come to see him*

$$(24) \quad \left\{ \begin{array}{c} N \\ V \end{array} \right\}^2 \rightarrow \left\{ \begin{array}{c} N \\ V \end{array} \right\}^1 P^1$$

e.g., *colour for taxi, needed* money *for to get a shirt*

The structural motivation for this pervasive HEAD-COMPLEMENT pattern has more than one source. It could be argued that this pattern is optimal for acquisition. The universal categories NOUN and VERB are seized on first, and specifications are added after them. On a typological level, the HEAD - COMPLEMENT order across phrasal categories mirrors directly the predominant directionality of branching in two SVO languages like French and English. As we have seen, the directionality of branching in the NP is made more consistent with other phrasal categories. Nonetheless, I would contend that the more regular HEAD-COMPLEMENT structure of French in the NP contributes to the analogizing we can witness in examples like *friend for her*. We can gauge this influence in a number of ways. First, I know of no evidence from English L1 acquisition that children produce pronominal possessive determiners in post-head position (e.g. *cup my*); however, in French L1 acquisition *livre à/de moi* clearly precedes *moi/mon livre* developmentally (François et al. 1977). Second, all French-derived creoles have the definite article in postposition (Valdman 1978). This is not the case with English-derived creoles. These facts suggest that the pre-head position in French is a highly grammaticized position. Yet another, albeit indirect, way of gauging the influence from French is to compare our findings with those of Meyer-Ingwersen (1977) and Meisel (personal communication) on the acquisition of possessive determiners in German by, respectively, Turkish and Romance language speakers. Like English, German has pre-position for pronominal possessives although nominal possessives are more consistently in postposition. Turkish, an SOV language, places noun modifiers in pre-position. With regard to pronominal possessives, therefore, the order in German is congruent with Turkish, and Turkish speakers do in fact acquire these first. Nominal possessive constructions are avoided altogether at first. When they begin to be be attempted, Turkish speakers seize on a non-standard construction of German in which the possessor is topicalized, i.e. *my father, his car*. The topicalized-possessor construction allows them to retain the modifier-head order of Turkish. Initially, therefore, both Turkish and Romance language speakers have a grammar Gn which generates (pronominal) possessive determiners in pre-head position. Romance speakers have no difficulty in proceeding to the post-head position (Gn + 1) for nominal possessives. Their grammar's evaluation metric evidently judges this position to be compatible with Gn. In contrast, for Turkish speakers the evaluation metric clearly fixes a higher valuation on the topicalized-possessor construction, judging the standard German order to be incompatible with Gn. These different valuations of alternate forms in the input relate in a straightforward fashion to the order of head and modifier in Romance languages as opposed to Turkish.

5. Conclusion

In this paper I have proposed that L2 continua be studied with reference to three types of change: targeted, evolutive, and optimalizing changes.

The distinction between the first two types rests on their relationship to diachronic change. Evolutive changes reveal universal constraints on the transitional possibilities between two successive grammatical states; hence the apparent recapitulation of diachronic change. For example, it is not the case that all L2 learners of English will first mark definiteness with a deictic pronoun. On the other hand, it does seem to be the case that in the acquisition of SVO targets with grammaticized subjects learners will pass through a verb-second stage as a result of having analyzed subjects as the first syntactic constituent in surface structure.

The distinction between targeted and evolutive changes has clear implications for the study of diachronic change within a learnability framework. In Latin, there was neither a definite article nor an obligatory subject pronoun. By the Medieval French period the definite article had become a grammaticized category; not so the subject pronoun. The difference we have identified between targeted (the article) and evolutive (obligatory subject pronouns) change in L2 continua thus shows up as well in differences in the rate of grammaticization in historical change.

The need to recognize optimalizing changes in L2 continua is simply a consequence of subscribing to the axiom that interlanguages share the properties of natural language systems. As a result, they are subject to internally-motivated 'natural' changes, which are demarking (Bailey 1977). In interlanguage, demarking changes act to regularize the relationship between meaning and form and to regularize the form of the rules that generate phrasal categories.

Our examination of uniformity and variation focused on the interplay between prior linguistic knowledge and the markedness metric as components of the evaluation procedure. The existence of grammaticized (i.e. obligatory and morphologically dependent) categories in the learner's L1 promotes the acquisition of corresponding grammaticized TL categories. The evaluation metric does not appear to adjudge these grammaticized forms as highly marked as when the L1 lacks them.

Finally, we have also seen that the L1 can assign different markedness values to the change from Grammar G_n to $G_n + 1$. Although both Turkish and Romance language speakers initially produce pronominal possessive determiners in pre-position, the transition to postposition carried with it different markedness evaluations. The two groups prefer different data for the construction of $G_n + 1$. Moreover, there is strong evidence that the core rules of the L1 assign differently valued analyses to G_n. For the Turkish speakers the grammar generating possessive determiners in pre-head position is unmarked. For the Francophone speakers the pre-head position acquires a marked status relative to $G_n + 1$ once NP possessives become productive.

In conclusion, we can see that the unilinear model is too strong in its claim that there is but a single sequence of changes between any two grammatical states. It fails to allow for variation in the markedness increment represented by grammar $G_n + 1$ over G_n. Significantly, this variation surfaces in cases when $G_n + 1$ lies in the direction of what I have referred to as linguistic specialization on a language universal. I have also presented evidence pointing to variation in demarking changes whereby formal differentiations are leveled in favour of a greater degree of harmony between the NP and the VP. Clearly, in L2 acquisition, the optimal grammar at any particular point in the developmental continuum is not solely a function of the input data, as has been argued for L1 acquisition by White (1980). Instead, we must postulate formal constraints between two successive grammars. These are, partly, a function of prior linguistic experience which can place differential markedness valuations on the grammatical change that can be effected in one sequential step. Against this background, it appears that the study of L2 acquisition can make a valuable contribution to markedness theory if pursued in an attainability framework (Kean 1979); that is, in terms of the number of interim grammars necessary to arrive at a mature structure. In cases where all language groups pass through the identical number of stages — congruent L1 - L2 structures or typologies notwithstanding — we may have succeeded in isolating universal parameters of markedness from language-contrastive differences in markedness.

NOTES

* I am grateful for valuable comments on an earlier version of this chapter from Roger Andersen.

1) Krashen's Natural Order Hypothesis (1981: Chapter 4) embodies such a view.

2) There is a certain measure of imprecision to this statement since many of the structures studied have not been examined in enough detail. For some findings, see Rutherford 1982.

3) Bailey (1977:8) defines a 'natural' change as a change from more to less marked. I assume that this principle of change can only apply to change processes with interlanguage-internal motivation since targeted changes proceed in the opposite direction.

4) Angled brackets indicate variable output of X, which here represents the subject NP. Note that for non-Spanish speakers the verb is further specified through the feature [+ Main] since these speakers do not have preverbal negation with copular verbs, nor, at the stage we are considering, with modal verbs.

5) I assume the logical form NEG (PROPOSITION). Lowering inserts the NEG operator into the proposition.

6) The deletion process probably obeys a different weighting of constraints in Alberto's Speech. Alberto does have deletion of 3rd person human pronouns (see Appendix, pp. 141, 149, 152, 168), so that for him IS represents the α constraint and [− reference] the β constraint.

7) The competition between pronouns and other preverbal constituents argues that the latter attach to S as the first branching node. This, however, is also the analysis for the subject NP. Development towards a more abstract analysis would involve the creation of higher-level Ss to which topicalized constituents attach.

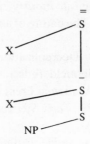

8) I here follow Jackendoff, Chapter 4.

REFERENCES

Andersen, Roger. 1979. Two perspectives on pidginization as second language acquisition. In R. Andersen (ed.) 1981, *New Dimensions in Research on the Acquisition and Use of a Second Language*. Rowley, Mass.: Newbury House, pp.165-195.

Andersen, Roger. 1980. Creolization as the acquisition of a second language as a first language. In A. Valdman and A. Highfield (eds.), *Theoretical Orientations in Creole Studies*. New York: Academic Press.

Andersen, Roger. 1981. Transfer to somewhere. Paper presented at the Conference on Language Transfer in Language Learning, Ann Arbor, March 1-2.

Anderson, Henning. 1973. Abductive and deductive change. *Language* 49:765-93.

Anttila, Raimo. 1972. *An Introduction to Historical and Comparative Linguistics*. New York: Macmillan.

Bailey, Charles-James. 1973. The patterning of language variation. In R. Bailey and J. Robinson (eds.), *Varieties of Present-Day English.* New York: Macmillan.

Bailey, Charles-James. 1977. Linguistic change, naturalness, mixture and structural principles. *Papiere zur Linguistik 26*:6-73.

Bailey, C.-J., and K. Maroldt. 1977. The French lineage of English. In J. Meisel (ed.), *Langues en contact-Pidgins-Creoles-Languages in Contact.* Tübingen: Gunter Narr.

Berman, Ruth. 1980. The case of an (S)VO language: subjectless constructions in Modern Hebrew. *Language 56*:759-76.

Bever, Thomas, and D.T. Langendoen. 1971. A dynamic model of the evolution of language. *Linguistic Inquiry 2*:433-63.

Bickerton, Derek. 1973. The nature of a creole continuum. *Language 49*:640-69.

Bickerton, Derek. 1980. Decreolization and the creole continuum. In A. Valdman and A. Highfield (eds.), *Theoretical Orientations in Creole Studies.* New York: Academic Press.

Bowerman, Melissa. 1973. *Early Syntactic Development.* Cambridge: Cambridge University Press.

Brown, Roger, C. Cazden, and U. Bullugi-Klima. 1969. The child's grammar from I to III. In J. Hill (ed.), *Minnesota Symposia on Child Psychology,* v.III. Minneapolis: University of Minneapolis Press.

Brunot, Fernand, and C. Bruneau. 1933. *Précis de grammaire historique de la langue française.* Paris: Masson.

Butterworth, Guy. 1972. A Spanish-speaking Adolescent's Acquisition of English Syntax. M.A. Thesis, U.C.L.A.

Chomsky, Noam. 1965. *Aspects of the Theory of Syntax.* Cambridge, Mass.: The MIT Press.

Chomsky, Noam. 1970. Remarks on nominalization. In R. Jacobs and P. Rosenbaum (eds.), *Readings in English Transformational Grammar.* Waltham, Mass.: Ginn.

Chomsky, Noam, and H. Lasnik. 1977. Filters and control. *Linguistic Inquiry 8*:425-504.

Clahsen, Harald. 1980. Variation in der frühkindlichen Sprachentwicklung. *Wuppertaler Arbeitspapiere zur Sprachwissenschaft 3*:55-83.

Clahsen, Harald. 1981. The acquisition of German word order: a test case for cognitive approaches to L2 development. Paper presented at the European - North American Workshop on SLA Research, Lake Arrowhead, Sept. 7-14.

Clahsen, Harald. n.d. Some more remarks on the acquisition of German negation. Dept. of Romance Languages, University of Hamburg.

Clyne, Michael. 1975. German and English working pidgins. Paper presented at the International Conference on Pidgins and Creoles, Honolulu, January 6-10.

Contreras, H. 1976. *A Theory of Word Order with Special Reference to Spanish*. Amsterdam: North-Holland.

Corder, S. Pit. 1977. Language continua and the interlanguage hypothesis. In S.P. Corder and E. Roulet (eds.), *The Notions of Simplification, Interlanguages and Pidgins and their Relation to Second Language Pedagogy*. Geneva: Librairie Droz.

Dominigue, Nicole. 1977. Middle English: another creole? *Journal of Creole Studies 1*:89-100.

Felix, Sascha. 1978. *Linguistische Untersuchungen zum natürlichen Zweitsprachenerwerb*. Münich: Wilhelm Fink.

Foulet, Lucien. 1966. *Petite syntaxe de l'ancien français* (3rd ed.). Paris: Librairie Honoré Champion.

François, F., et al. 1977. *La syntaxe de l'enfant avant cinq ans*. Paris: Librairie Larousse.

Green, J. 1976. How free is word order in Spanish? In M. Harris (ed.), *Romance Syntax: Synchronic and Diachronic Perspectives*. Salford: University of Salford.

Grimshaw, Jane. 1981. Form, function and the language acquisition device. In Carl Baker and J. McCarthy (eds.), *The Logical Basis of Language Acquisition*. Cambridge, Mass.: MIT Press.

Hawkins, John. 1982. Cross-category harmony, X-bar and the predictions of markedness. *Journal of Linguistics 18*:1-35.

Hernandez-Chavez, Edouardo. 1977a. *The Acquisition of Grammatical structures by a Mexican-American Child Learning English*. Ph.D. Thesis, University of California at Berkeley.

Hernandez-Chavez, Edouardo. 1977b. The development of semantic relations in child second language acquisition. In H. Dulay, M. Burt, and M. Finocchiaro (eds.). New York: Regents.

Horn, Lawrence. 1978. Some aspects of negation. In J. Greenberg (ed.), *Universals of Human Language, v. 4: Syntax*. Stanford: Stanford University Press.

Huang, Joseph. 1971. A Chinese Child's Acquisition of English Syntax. M.A. Thesis, U.C.L.A.

Hyltenstam, Kenneth. 1977. Implicational patterns in interlanguage syntax variation. *Language Learning 27*:383-411.

Jackendoff, Ray. 1977. *X̄ Syntax: A Study of Phrase Structure.* Cambridge, Mass.: The MIT Press.

Jansen, B., J. Lalleman, and P. Muysken. 1981. The alternation hypothesis: acquisition of Dutch word order by Turkish and Moroccan foreign workers. *Language Learning 31*:315-36.

Jesperson, Otto. 1917. *Negation in English and Other Languages.* London.

Jesperson, Otto. 1961. *A Modern English Grammar on Historical Principles, Part 5: Syntax, v. 4.* London: Allen and Unwin.

Kean, Mary-Louise. 1979. On a theory of markedness: some general considerations and a case in point. *Social Sciences Research Report 41.* University of California at Irvine.

Koster, Jan. 1978. Conditions, empty nodes and markedness. *Linguistic Inquiry 9*:551-94.

Koster, Jan. 1981. Configurational grammar. In Robert May and J. Koster (eds.), *Levels of Syntactic Representation.* Dordrecht: Foris.

Krashen, Stephen. 1981. *Second Language Acquisition and Second Language Learning.* Oxford: Pergamon Press.

Lyons, John. 1967. A note on possessive, existential and locative sentences. *Foundations of Language 3*:390-96.

Meisel, Jürgen. 1977. Linguistic simplification: a study of immigrant workers' speech and foreigner talk. In S.P. Corder and E. Roulet (eds.), *The Notions of Simplification, Interlanguages and Pidgins and their Relation to Second Language Pedagogy.* Geneva: Librairie Droz.

Meisel, Jürgen. 1980. Strategies of second language acquisition: more than one kind of simplification. *Wuppertaler Arbeitspapiere zur Sprachwissenschaft 3*:1-53.

Menyuk, Paula. 1969. *Sentences Children Use.* Cambridge, Mass.: MIT Press.

Meyer-Ingwersen, Johannes. 1977. *Zur Sprachentwickling türkischer Schüler in der Bundesrepublik,* 2 vls. Kronberg: Scriptor.

Mossé, Fernand. 1952. *A Handbook of Middle English.* Baltimore: John Hopkins Press.

Mülhäuser, Peter. 1980. Structural expansion and the process of creolization. In A. Valdman and A. Highfield (eds.), *Theoretical Orientations in Creole Studies.* New York: Academic Press.

Peters, Stanley. 1972. The projection problem: how is a grammar to be selected? In S. Peters (ed.), *Goals of Linguistic Theory*. Englewood Cliffs, N.J.: Prentice-Hall.

Pienemann, Manfred. 1980. The second language acquisition of immigrant children. In S. Felix (ed.), *Second Language Development: Trends and Issues*. Tübingen: Gunter Narr.

Ravem, Roar. 1968. Language acquisition in a second language environment. *IRAL 6*:175-85.

Ravem, Roar. 1974. *Second Language Acquisition*. Ph.D. Thesis, University of Essex.

Rutherford, William. 1982. Markedness in second language acquisition. *Language Learning 32*:85-108.

Schumann, John. 1978. *The Pidginization Process: A Model for Second Language Acquisition*. Rowley, Mass.: Newbury House.

Schwartz, Arthur. 1975. Verb anchoring and verb movement. In C. Li (ed.), *Word Order and Word Order Change*. Austin: University of Texas Press.

Slobin, Dan. 1977. Language change in childhood and in history. In J. Macnamara (ed.), *Language Learning and Thought*. New York: Academic Press.

Thompson, Sandra. 1978. Modern English from a typological point of view: some implications of the function of word order. *Linguistische Berichte 54*:19-35.

Todd, Loreto. 1974. *Pidgins and Creoles*. London: Routledge and Kegan Paul.

Ultan, Russell. 1978. Towards a typology of substantival possession. In J. Greenberg (ed.), *Universals of Human Language, v. 4: Syntax*. Stanford: Stanford University Press.

Valdman, Albert. 1978. *Le creole: Structure, statue et origine*. Paris: Editions Klincksieck.

Vennemann, Theo. 1974. Topics, subjects and word order: from SXV to SVX via TVX. In J. Anderson and C. Jones (eds.), *Historical Linguistics I*. Amsterdam: North-Holland.

Washabaugh, William. 1975. On the development of complementizers in creolization. *Working Papers on Language Universals, No. 17*:109-140.

White, Lydia. 1980. *Grammatical Theory and Language Acquisition*. Indiana University Linguistics Club.

Wode, Henning. 1977a. Four early stages in the development of L1 negation. *Journal of Child Language 4*:87-102.

Wode, Henning. 1977b. On the systematicity of L1 transfer in L2 acquisition. In C.A. Henning (ed.), *Proceedings of the First Los Angeles Second Language Research Forum*. Dept. of English, U.C.L.A.

Young, Denise. 1974. The Acquisition of English Syntax by Three Spanish-speaking Children. M.A. Thesis, U.C.L.A.

Zobl, Helmut. 1980a. Developmental and transfer errors: their common bases and (possibly) differential effects on subsequent learning. *TESOL Quarterly 14*:469-79.

Zobl, Helmut. 1980b. The formal and developmental selectivity of L1 influence on L2 acquisition. *Language Learning 30*:43-57.

Zobl, Helmut. 1980c. Contact-induced language change, learner-language and the potentials of a modified Contrastive Analysis. Paper presented at the Third Los Angeles Second Language Research Forum, U.C.L.A., Feb. 29-March 2.

Zobl, Helmut. 1982. A direction for Contrastive Analysis: the comparative study of developmental sequences. *TESOL Quarterly 16*:169-183.

COMMENTS ON THE PAPER BY ZOBL

CARMEN SILVA-CORVALÁN
University of Southern California

The questions raised by Helmut Zobl in his paper are well considered and penetrate to a wide range of issues not only in studies of first and second language acquisition but also in studies of language change in contact situations in stable bilingual communities.

Zobl raises the general question: Is there a single developmental path to a mature L2 system, as proposed by Bickerton's Unilinear Hypothesis? Or are there, rather, multiple paths? If the latter is true, what are the constraints on individual variation and what role does the L1 play in the shaping of these constraints? Quite correctly, in my view, Zobl proposes that L2 acquisition is broadly uniform across acquirers and languages but that there is some amount of variation determined by the typological characteristics of the L1. In order to support this proposal, he examines three types of data from case studies of L2 acquisition: 1. negation; 2. subject pronoun deletion and the development of SVO syntax; and 3. the use of *for* in English as a second language. These correspond, respectively, to three types of change process: targeted, evolutive, and nativizing/optimalizing.

Zobl contends that the differences in the acquisition of pre- or post-verbal negation in English L2 reported for speakers of Spanish — who acquire postverbal negation later as compared to Norwegian, German, Chinese, and French speakers — are related to L1 differences. But both Spanish and Chinese have preverbal negation, as the examples below show, so the unanswered question is why L1 should be relevant in the case of Spanish and not in the case of Chinese.

Spanish: El *no* me   gusta.
         he *not* to-me pleases
Chinese: Wǒ *bù* xihuan tā.
         I   *not* like   he
         'I don't like him'

Another difference that Zobl notices relates to the distribution of the form *no*, which Spanish speakers use both in sentence-external and sentence-internal environments. The supporting evidence is provided in Tables 1-3. An examination of this evidence, however, does not appear to support all the differences or Zobl's explanations for the ones that exist. My interpretation of Table 3 is that out of nine speakers of French six use *not* sentence-internally, one uses both *not* and *no*, and two use *no* in this position. On the other hand, Tables 1 and 2 seem to indicate that Alberto and Enrique are still in the process of acquiring the form *not*; but notice that when *not* occurs it is categorically used sentence-internally by Alberto and almost categorically by Enrique. There does not seem to be a major difference then between Spanish and French speakers and, assuming that Ravem's and Huang's learners are at the same stage of ESL acquisition as Alberto and Enrique, the proposed differences with the Norwegian and Chinese speakers may reflect different rates of acquisition of a lexical item (*not*), which is phonologically quite foreign to the Spanish system, rather than differences in syntactic facts.

Zobl draws interesting parallels between L2 acquisition processes and historical language change. In this context, however, many historical linguists would disagree with his statement that 'it is rather difficult to speak of historical change as being targeted and involving "increasing complexity", given the fairly widespread acceptance of what Anttila (1972:194) summarizes in the following words: 'In linguistic change, an observable tendency toward a goal is known as *drift*. As in biology, it takes a form of complex synchronization, for example, loss of inflection with increased use of prepositions and word order in English.'

If the notion of *drift* is accepted, the difference between *targeted* and *evolutive* L2 changes becomes opaque. Indeed, as Zobl himself notes for his example of targeted change, the acquisition of postverbal negation has a parallel in historical change. The historical and acquisitional regularities that he observes constitute the macro-level constraints below which there is L1-related variation. Similarly, with his example of evolutive change, the L2 acquisition of SVO syntax with obligatory subject expression parallels historical change but is also an example of L1 transfer, since transfer appears to be the most adequate explanation for the different rates of subject deletion between French and Spanish learners of ESL. No example, therefore, is clearly illustrative of a different type of change: the acquisition of postverbal negation as well as SVO word order with obligatory subject expression appear to respond to the definition of both targeted and evolutive changes.

Zobl proposes broad uniformity with strictly circumscribed L1-related variation. Other researchers have minimized the impact of the L1. Felix (1980:97), for example, has argued that in L2 acquisition in natural environments 'interference does not play any significant role'. He compares Spanish learners of ESL with English learners of German as a second language and observes that both groups delete subject pronouns. He concludes that even though deletion by English learners is less frequent, the omission of the subject is a general feature 'and does not demonstrably reflect ... the influence of the learner's L1' (p.100).

Transfer from L1 may be difficult to detect on the basis of isolated examples, especially so in cases of variable syntactic phenomena when transfer is reflected in higher versus lower percentages of use of the variants involved, and subject pronoun deletion is an example of one such variable phenomenon. Rigorous quantitative analyses are needed in cases like these in order to decide between alternative hypotheses. For example, in a study of Spanish-English contact in a stable bilingual community — viz. Puerto Ricans in New York — Klein (1980) quantifies the use of progressive versus nonprogressive present tense forms by monolingual and bilingual Puerto Ricans. She observes that the influence of English on bilinguals' Spanish manifests itself not in ungrammatical utterances but rather in a relatively higher frequency of use of the progressive present and a correspondingly lower frequency of use of the simple present, in reference to present activity.

It seems to me, therefore, that Zobl's claim that in L2 acquisition there is a certain amount of L1-related variation is well justified. He has shown that even though certain features occur in the interlanguage of L2 learners with different language backgrounds, they occur with different frequencies and these differences reflect the influence of the L1. Zobl does not explicitly evaluate the significance of the interference, but from the discussion we conclude that it at least correlates with different rates of acquisition of a given feature of the target language.

Zobl also argues convincingly that the uses of *for* in the interlanguage of Francophone learners is a nativizing/optimalizing process. Interestingly, this phenomenon also has parallels in historical change. Zobl refers to the history of English. In addition, I may refer the reader to García's (1982) study of *a/para* ('*to/for*') in U.S. Mexican Spanish, where she shows that *para* is taking over some of the functions of *a*.

To conclude, then, it seems to me that Zobl's proposals are thought-provoking and attractive, but some of the evidence presented to support the existence of three types of change seems inconclusive. As suggested by other writers in this volume, more research is needed that will focus on the acquisition of an L2 by speakers of typologically quite different languages before we can really evaluate which developmental phenomena may be due to macro-level constraints (and also the nature of these constraints) and which ones may be L1-related, or which ones are targeted, evolutive, or nativizing/optimalizing changes. And once an area of transfer has been identified, the almost unavoidable question to pursue would be 'why', i.e., what factors — structural, functional, or social — motivate the transfer of any one specific feature rather than another feature of the primary language.

REFERENCES

Anttila, Raimo. 1972. *An Introduction to Historical and Comparative Linguistics*. New York: MacMillan.

Felix, Sascha W. 1980. Interference, interlanguage, and related issues. In S.W. Felix (ed.), *Second Language Development: Trends and Issues*. Tübingen: Gunter Narr.

García, Maryellen. 1982. Syntactic variation in verb phrases of motion in U.S.-Mexican Spanish. In J. Amastae and L. Elias-Olivares (eds.), *Spanish in the United States: Sociolinguistic Aspects*. New York: Cambridge University Press.

Klein, Flora. 1980. A quantitative study of syntactic and pragmatic indications of change in the Spanish of bilinguals in the U.S. In W. Labov (ed.), *Locating Language in Time and Space*. New York: Academic Press.

IN WHAT WAYS ARE LANGUAGE UNIVERSALS
PSYCHOLOGICALLY REAL?*

KENJI HAKUTA
Yale University

1. *Introduction*

Any particular human language can be specified by its location within an n-dimensional space which defines the limits of variation of all human languages. As a psycholinguist, I understand the study of language typology and language universals to be an attempt to determine what the relevant dimensions are, and to determine how many meaningful dimensions exist. I assume as a working hypothesis that the n-dimensional space bears some relevance to the facts of human language learning. Perhaps there is some isomorphism between the n-dimensional space defined by language typologists and the hypothesis space of the language learner. Basically, I see the n-dimensional space as a linguistic characterization and the hypothesis space as a psychological one, the goals of our interdisciplinary endeavor being to understand how they map onto each other.

Not everyone would agree that the study of language typology and universals will yield a full understanding as to the nature of the constraints and biases with which humans are equipped to acquire and use language. Perhaps, as Chomsky (1965) claims, much of our present state of knowledge about language universals reflects unimportant surface characteristics of languages that are trivialized by the potentially revolutionary insights to be gained from a careful and disciplined rationalist approach. Yet, the currently rapidly accumulating knowledge base of language universals will yield statements that challenge those who yearn for an empirical handle on the problem. They yield a network of hypotheses that have a potential contribution to make to an inquiry into the language-potentiated mind. This view, I believe, constitutes one half of the spirit under which the present conference was conceived.

The other half of the spirit is that the psychological study of the language learner can help to discipline the definition of the n-dimensional space. Formulations of typologies and of language universals have been notably descriptive in nature. They can be seen as interesting empirical observations that are in need of some explanation (but see Comrie, 1981). While I am skeptical about the power of current psychological principles (if any exist) in accounting for the n-dimensional space, data from language learners can be informative in constraining its formulation. Aside from explicit psychological explanations with respect to principles of memory, attention, and so forth (e.g., Kuno, 1974), we can see how the n-dimensional space might be influenced by other psychologically relevant factors, such as age of the learner, and in the case of second language acquisition specifically, experience as reflected in the nature of the native language structure. The purpose of this paper is to make explicit the possible relationships between the study of language typology and universals on the one hand and the language learner on the other.

2.   *The determination of the n-dimensional space.*

One might draw an analogy between the language typologist's attempt at mapping the n-dimensional space of language with attempts that psychologists have made in formulating personality dimensions through the statistical technique of factor analysis. Factor analysis begins with a matrix of correlations between a large number of variables. From this matrix, factors are extracted, through various alternative mathematical specifications, that are correlated with subsets of the variables. This approach has a great advantage in reducing large numbers of variables into fewer, supposedly more abstract and underlying factors.

In the factor-analytic approach to personality, the investigator typically begins with a set of 'trait' words about personality in the language, such as 'adventurous' versus 'shy'. Independent raters are asked to rate a large number of people with respect to each of these trait words. Then the ratings are factor analyzed. Cattell (1965), for example, derived roughly 15 or so factors of personality using this approach. He argued that these factors, rather than the trait words themselves, reflect true personality dimensions that are uncluttered by everyday colloquial nuances of trait words. While it would be unfair to label Cattell's approach to personality as atheoretical, Cattell was essentially at the mercy of the empirically derived factors. Often, he labeled the factors with words of his own invention, such as *H. Parmia* versus *Threctia*. Factor analysis was seen as the cornerstone of scientific research in personality: 'Factor analysis...believes that there are natural, unitary structures in personality and that it is these traits, rather than the endless labels in the dictionary, on which we should concentrate. In other words, if there are natural elements in the form of functional unities, logically equivalent to an element in the physical world, then it would be far better to begin our studies...our comparisons and developmental understandings...on measures of such traits' (p. 55-56). He had, in short, great faith in inductively straining the building blocks of personality through factor analysis. These factors constitute the primitives of human personality which demand explanation.

On a conceptual level, the goal of language typologists can be seen as similar to the factor-analytic personality psychologist, with languages being used instead of people as random variables. Unlike psychologists, however, linguists do not go around asking raters to rate a large number of languages along various linguistic dimensions (although I wouldn't put it past simple-minded psychologists to try, and it might even be a worthwhile endeavor when we have a better idea of our variables). In addition, the types of data, or scales of measurement, used in language typology are different. The linguistic dimensions are commonly considered categorical (Greenberg, 1978), while personality dimensions are interval scale data, and assumed to be continuous. But these differences constitute differences in statistical treatment. Recent advances in statistics which enable the analysis of complex, n-way contingency tables opens the way for sophisticated analysis of the linguist's type of data, if such were desirable (Fienberg, 1980). The working assumption seems to be that once enough typological dimensions have been formulated and investigated with respect to a large number of languages, these variables can be reduced through statistical techniques to a smaller number of underlying dimensions by analyzing commonly co-occurring features. As Greenberg recently put it, 'a theoretical analysis of basic typological concepts helps us to broaden our conception of cross-linguistic generalizations, while its application provides a useful methodology for discovering such generalizations at the lower empirical levels and thus providing the materials for broader and deeper conclusions about the nature of human language' (p. 58).

I get the impression that linguists can be explanation-shy, and they have sometimes avoided hypothesizing as to the reasons for the existence of cross-linguistic generalizations (see, however, Kuno (1974), Givón (1979), and other papers in this volume). For example, Downing (1978), in formulating universal characteristics of relative clause structures, writes: 'In their present form they may serve as a summary of observations on the nature of relative clauses across languages, with which the data of additional languages may be compared. As such generalizations are refined, they afford an increasingly solid empirical basis for the formulation of explanatory principles in functional and psychological terms' (p. 411). Along similar lines, Steele (1978) formulates constraints to account for word order variation, such as the following: 'A variation on basic word order in which the object precedes and the subject follows the verb is to be avoided' (p. 604). While such constraints serve to explain at one level the observed data on word order variation, she writes in a footnote that 'I am not offering explanations for the constraints' (p. 604, footnote 15). It appears to me that the best people to theorize about the causes of typological facts are the people who formulate the statements, and I am puzzled by the lack of their speculative efforts on this front.

Given this tendency, the developed product of language-typological research will be essentially a set of factors with loadings on different linguistic variables (e.g., direction of branching, order of verb and object, etc.). These n factors will constitute the n-dimensional space of human languages. My understanding of language typological research in its present state is that it is not yet at this stage, but it is perhaps not too early to discuss at the abstract level the psychological question, which is basically the title of this paper, 'in what ways is the n-dimensional space psychologically real, and how can we understand changes in the relationship between the n-dimensional space and the learner's hypothesis space under different psychological conditions of language acquisition?' I will use the term *psychological correspondence* to refer to an empirical correspondence between the linguist's dimensions and psychological data obtained from studies of language learners.

For the sake of discussion (and I realize that the crudeness of the units of analysis may offend some), consider the following variables along which languages are known to be distributed:

(1) POSITION (postposition/preposition)
(2) BRANCHING DIRECTION (left-branching/right-branching)
(3) WORD ORDER VARIABILITY (rigid word order/free word order)
(4) DUMMY SUBJECT (has no dummy subjects/has dummy subjects)
(5) OBJECT-VERB ORDER (verb-object/object-verb)
(6) AGREEMENT (has no subject-verb agreement/has agreement)
(7) PASSIVIZATION (has no passives/has passives)

LANGUAGE VARIABLES

LANGUAGE	POSITION	BRANCHING	WORD ORDER	DUMMY SUBJECT	OBJECT VERB	AGREEMENT	PASSIVE
1	0	1	1	0	0	0	0
2	1	1	1	0	0	0	0
3	0	1	1	1	0	1	1
4	0	1	0	1	0	1	0
5	1	1	0	0	0	0	0
6	0	1	0	0	0	0	1
7	1	1	0	1	0	1	1
8	0	0	1	0	1	1	1
9	0	0	1	1	1	0	0
10	0	0	1	0	1	0	0
11	1	1	1	1	0	1	1
12	0	0	1	0	1	0	1
13	1	1	1	1	0	1	0
14	1	1	0	1	1	1	1
15	1	1	0	0	0	0	1
16	0	0	1	0	0	0	1
17	1	1	1	1	0	1	1
18	1	0	1	0	1	0	0
19	0	0	1	0	1	1	1
20	0	0	0	1	1	0	1

Variable labels:
POSITION (0=postposition; 1=preposition)
BRANCHING (0=left-branching; 1=right-branching)
WORD ORDER (0=rigid word order; 1=free word order)
DUMMY SUBJECT (0=has no dummy subject; 1=has dummy subject)
OBJECT-VERB (0=verb-object order; 1=object-verb order)
AGREEMENT (0=has no subj-verb agrmnt; 1=has subj-verb agrmnt)
PASSIVE (0=has no passives; 1=has passives)

TABLE 2

Correlation matrix of language variables across 20 fabricated languages.

	POSITION	BRANCH	WORD ORDER	DUMMY SUBJECT	OBJECT VERB	AGREEMENT	PASSIVE
POSITION	1.00	0.66	-0.17	0.19	-0.66	0.50	.32
BRANCHING	0.66	1.00	-0.31	0.24	-1.00	0.52	.25
WORD ORDER	-0.17	-0.31	1.00	-0.38	0.31	-0.10	-.38
DUMMY SUBJECT	0.19	0.24	-0.38	1.00	-0.24	0.70	.53
OBJECT-VERB	-0.66	-1.00	0.31	-0.24	1.00	-0.52	-.25
AGREEMENT	0.50	0.52	-0.10	0.70	-0.52	1.00	.61
PASSIVE	0.32	0.25	-0.38	0.53	-0.25	0.61	1.00

TABLE 3

Factor analysis solution with varimax rotation for 20 fabricated languages.

	FACTOR 1	FACTOR 2
POSITION	0.63	0.26
BRANCHING	0.98	0.19
WORD ORDER	−0.21	−0.33
DUMMY SUBJECT	0.07	0.84
OBJECT-VERB	−0.98	−0.19
AGREEMENT	0.38	0.74
PASSIVE	0.15	0.70

Table 1 presents raw data for 20 hypothetical languages (fabricated from my imagination with a little help from the intuition of several colleagues about some real languages) with values on each of the variables. A value of '0' is entered where the language exhibits properties of the first level of the variable (e.g., for the variable position, if the language has postposition), and '1' is entered where the second level (e.g., if the language has preposition) is exhibited. The relationship between the variables across languages can be expressed in a correlation matrix, which appears in Table 2. A casual inspection of Table 2 reveals that there are many variables that are well correlated. For example, OBJECT-VERB and BRANCHINGNESS are correlated −1.00, a perfect negative relationship revealing that all OV languages are left-branching, and all VO languages are right-branching. AGREEMENT is correlated .70 with DUMMY SUBJECT, indicating that languages with subject-verb agreement also tend to have dummy subjects. An underlying structure of the intercorrelations between the variables can be revealed strikingly through factor analysis, the results of which appear in Table 3. Factor 1 is 'saturated' with the variables of branchingness, object-verb, and position. This may be interpreted as follows: languages that are left-branching tend to be object-verb and have postpositions, while right-branching languages tend to be verb-object and have prepositions. Factor 2 is 'saturated' with the variables dummy subject, agreement, and passive. The interpretation is that languages with dummy subjects also tend to have subject-verb agreement and passivization. When I fabricated the data for Table 1, I had in mind two clusters of variables that have been suggested in the literature, one related to the order of elements in sentences (e.g., Greenberg, 1963; Lehmann, 1973) and the other related to the subject-topic typological dimension suggested by Li and Thompson (1976). The factor structures in Table 3 reflect these dimensions, although I should point out that, for purposes of the present paper, the actual variables that load on the factors are irrelevant. What is important is simply the fact that this is the kind of way in which the ultimate outcome of the current thrust of language typology might be represented. In subsequent discussion of the factor structure of language, I will simply label the factors as Factor A and B, and the individual variables that load on the factors as Variables 1, 2, and so forth, so that our discussion will be uncluttered by the truth value of linguistic statements and concentrate on the logic of inquiry.

3. *In search of psychological correspondence.*

As Stephen Jay Gould points out in his elegantly written book on intelligence testing (Gould, 1981), we human consumers of statistics have an inherent bias towards reifying factors derived through factor analysis. This is a higher order bias similar to the bias of inferring causality from correlation, against which we are warned repeatedly in elementary statistics classes. Language factors are no more than statements about the distribution of the world's languages. We should be wary of using observed language factors as explanations for psychological data. Rather, the questions should be 'What are the principles that determine the observed factor structure?'

One would like to be able to write a play which says here: 'Enter the psychologists with their principles that explain on independent grounds the language factors observed.' Life is, however, not so sweet. Aside from the span of apprehension, short-term memory span, and a handful of other trophies on the empirical shelf of psychologists, there is indeed very little that psychology can at present directly offer in explanation of the results of language typologists. A glance through any contemporary book on cognitive psychology (e.g., Dodd and White, 1980) should confirm this impression. Cognitive explanations for language factors are not forthcoming.

Data from the language learner can, however, constrain the psychological plausibility of the n-dimensional space. We can look for the preservation or fragmentation of the factor structure (the n-dimensional space) in the language learner, under different circumstances. If it can be observed in some circumstances, but not others, then we might be able to formulate hypotheses about its governing principles. If we consider the n-dimensional space defined by language factors to be a good candidate as a psychologically real hypothesis about the target language on the part of the language learner, we expect there to be some correspondence between the language factor and data obtained from language learners. In this section, I will sketch out some considerations that must go into the search for psychological correspondence.

The task for the learner can be defined as a process of determination of the factor score for the particular target language. Having determined the factor score, the learner can be guided in the search for the particular realizations of the individual variables that go with the factor. Consider the situation in Table 4. A language with a high positive score on Factor A will have a value of

TABLE 4

Distribution of values on variables for three hypothetical languages.

	VAR1	VAR2	VAR3	VAR4	VAR5	VAR6
Loading on Factor A	+	+	+	−	−	0
LANGUAGE X	1	1	1	0	0	1
LANGUAGE Y	1	1	0	0	0	1
LANGUAGE Z	0	0	0	1	1	1

'1' on Variables 1 through 3 and a value of '0' on Variables 4 and 5, as in LANGUAGE X. A language with a high negative score on Factor A will have values of '0' on Variables 1-3 and values of '1' on Variables 4 and 5, a situation reflected in LANGUAGE Z. The two hypothetical languages, X and Z, are mirror images of each other with respect to Factor A. If all languages were of the types X and Z above, although this would be a highly interesting fact, it would be difficult to test for psychological correspondence, since there would be no variance across languages. However, such a situation is unlikely and is certainly inconsistent with current knowledge about cross-linguistic variation. Then, variations across languages with respect to their language factor scores, i.e., the extent to which they reflect the ideal factor structure, can be used to test the psychological coherence of the factor. Take for example LANGUAGE Y in Table 4, conveniently created for our purpose. The values on the variables mostly reflect a high positive loading on Factor A, with the exception of Variable 3. The structure of Variable 3 for LANGUAGE Y in fact matches that for LANGUAGE Z, which is the ideal language with negative loading on Factor A. There are several predictions that can be made, and empirically tested, given such a situation. One would expect that the learner of LANGUAGE Y would have fewer cues than the learner of LANGUAGE X, due to the mismatch on Variable 3. If the determination of the factor score is a psychologically real process, then one can predict differences in the ease of acquisition of structures that reflect variables with the same values for both languages, assuming that other sources of differences, such as frequency, can be controlled. Thus, for Variables 1, 2, 4, and 5, the learner of LANGUAGE X is at an advantage over the learner of LANGUAGE Y. In Table 4, I have also inserted Variable 6, which has no loading on Factor A. This might be considered a control variable, for which no difference would be predicted between the two languages.

If we had LANGUAGE Z for comparison, we could make further predictions, since the values on Variable 3 are similar for both LANGUAGES Y and Z. Since the value for LANGUAGE Z is consonant with the factor structure, while it is not for LANGUAGE Y, we would predict that the structure for Variable 3 would be easier for the learner of LANGUAGE Z than for the learner of LANGUAGE Y. Furthermore, we can make predictions about the frequency and kinds of errors that might be expected in the course of learning. Learners of LANGUAGE X will be likely to make errors on structures reflecting Variable 3 that deviate towards the value of '1'. This can be compared to the likelihood of such errors for learners of LANGUAGE Z.

Whether the psychological correspondence can be determined or not is an empirical question. Ideally, one should be able to iterate the above process across each of the variables, finding strategically located languages. If we find that certain variables consistently do not affect the acquisition of its *related variables* (i.e., variables with which it is related through the factor structure), we can weed them out from our mapping of psychological correspondence. The end result would be a psychologically real hypothesis space of language learners, which can be used in the further, and necessary, investigations into the nature of the task-specificity and species-specificity of language.

Aside from the gross determination of the hypothesis space, one would also like to make claims about the deductive process, i.e. how the learner goes about choosing between alternative structures for the target language. Each variable within a factor might be seen as having a particular weight value in the learner's deduction of the target language factor score. This might be empirically determined by computing, say, some transformation of the rate of acquisition of related variables in the absence of the variable in question.

There are, of course, an infinite number of ways in which the deductive process could take place. There are three alternatives, however, schematized in Figure 1, that might yield to empirical tests. Panel A represents an additive model, where the weights for the values on relevant variables observed are summed, and the sum is directly related to the deduction of the factor score for the target language. Panel B represents a threshold model, where the sum of the weights needs to attain a certain critical value before the determination is made. Panel C represents a 'triggering' model, where a single variable, or a set of variables, are necessary and sufficient conditions for the learner to conclude that the target language has a particular factor score. I must admit that at this highly abstract level of discussion, I find it difficult to specify exactly how one might go about distinguishing between these possibilities independently of the determination of psychological correspondence discussed earlier. The most important point, with respect to the goals of the present paper, is that the psychologically real hypothesis space available to the language learner should, in principle, be distinguishable from the deductive process based on the hypothesis space. One implication would be that child and adult learners may have similar hypotheses about language but may appear different because of differences in their deductive processes.

4.   *Implications for second language acquisition research.*

Consideration of the problem of language acquisition with respect to the hypothesis space and the deductive process has the potential contribution of clarifying some questions that have been traditionally asked in second language acquisition research.

One recurring question is whether the processes of first and second language acquisition are similar or different. The route towards answering this question has been to look at errors produced by L1 and L2 learners, and to classify them with respect to their possible sources. Similar errors were considered to be evidence for the L1=L2 hypothesis, while dissimilar errors, such as native language transfer errors, were seen as evidence for the L1/L2 hypothesis. Alternatively, studies have concentrated on the acquisition order

FIGURE 1

Three possible models for how the learner establishes the factor score for the target language. In the additive model (Model A) the weights for all the variables in Factor A are summed, and related additively to the certainty with which the learner establishes that the target language has a particular value on Factor A. In the threshold model (Model B) there is a critical value for the sum of weights. In the triggering model (Model C) any number of variables serve as sufficient condition for the certainty.

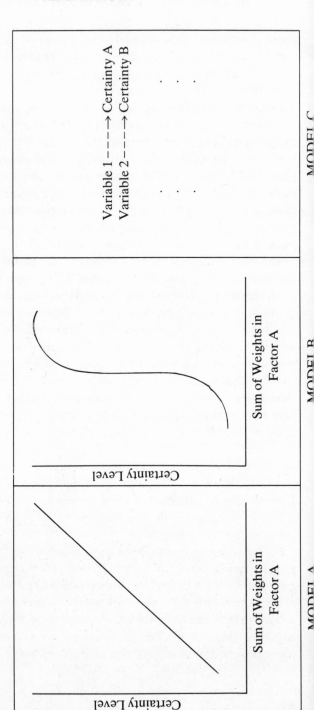

of grammatical morphemes in English, and results that second language learners show similar acquisition orders regardless of their native language background was seen as evidence for the L1=L2 hypothesis.

It appears that these studies take us no further than deciding between two alternative hypotheses. Consideration of language acquisition in terms of the hypothesis space and the deductive process sharpens the question: is the hypothesis space similar for L1 and L2 learners, and is the deductive process similar?

Naturally, if we found similar correspondences in L1 and L2 learners, the best conclusion would be that both the hypothesis space and the deductive process are similar. On the other hand, if we found differences between L1 and L2 learners, we would not simply conclude that they are different but ask in what ways they may be different. For example, it may be the case that the hypothesis spaces are different between the two types of learners but the deductive process remains unchanged. This might be revealed in differences in the psychological correspondence to the language factors between L1 and L2 learners, yet with similar weighting processes. Alternatively, it may be the case that second language learners construct their hypothesis space with respect to the factor weight of their native language, or it may be the case that the hypothesis space is similar across second language learners from different language backgrounds.

If the hypothesis space differs as a function of whether the situation is L1 or L2 acquisition, this tells us something about the nature of the hypothesis space. Perhaps certain parameters are unavailable to the learner due to the constraints of nonlinguistic, cognitive development. For example, the tense-aspect dimension of language may not be included in the young child's hypothesis space, while it would be readily available for the adult second language learner. On the other hand, the linguistic experience of acquiring the native language may profoundly affect the hypothesis space available to the learner in second language acquisition. In this case, there should be predictable changes in the hypothesis space of the second language learner, depending on the factor score of the native language. Observation of which particular variables show shift, and which do not, will bear heavily in the formulation of additional hypotheses about the nature of language acquisition. Particularly interesting would be if different shifts are observed for child and adult second language learners.

If the deductive process is different, the question is whether the differences in the deductive process are particular to the hypothesis space of language or are more true generally of the cognitive system. For example, are there similar changes with respect to age in other cognitive abilities, such as problem solving and decision-making?

Finally, an intriguing possibility would be where differences are observed between L1 and L2 learners on some factors but not others. For example, we may find no influence of the native language factor structure on Factor A, but a strong influence on Factor B. This is essentially a situation hypothesized by Rutherford (1983), who claimed that syntactically-based word-order related structures do not transfer, whereas discourse-based word-order does (but see Schachter, 1974; Kleinmann, 1976). Such findings would be of particular value in beginning to understand the functional underpinnings of language, by justifying language typological characteristics on functional/psychological grounds. Under these conditions, we can fully appreciate the complexity of the interaction between native language structure, target language structure, and age of the learner in the process of second language acquisition.

5. *Conclusion.*

In this paper, I have simplistically reduced the study of language typology and universals to factor analysis, and glossed over many of the technical difficulties that the researcher would encounter in searching for psychological correspondence for language factors. I undertook this exercise because I wanted to emphasize the viewpoint towards first and second language acquisition that is implicit in an approach that incorporates language typology and universals, a viewpoint that I believe at present to be potentially the most productive.

Recently, there was an article in the *American Scientist* that reviewed some recent research in developmental biology (Tickle, 1981). In particular, the article was concerned with similarities and differences between the growth of limbs during ontogeny on the one hand, and the regeneration of severed limbs (in certain species) on the other. Essentially, the problems faced by the cells in these two processes are similar: how does a growing cell know what part of the limb it is ultimately to become? To make a long story short, there are marked differences between the two, which can be characterized by the degree to which developing cells are sensitive to, and interact with, positional specifications of neighboring cells. In development, the positional specifications are developed in cell generation, while in limb regeneration the positional specifications of the new growth interacts with the already established positional specifications of its neighbors. This is an interesting statement about the relationship between the two processes that could not have been possible without a system for specifying position. (It turns out that position can be specified by three dimensions: anterior/posterior, dorsal/ventral, and proximal/distal, and some promising mechanisms for how this information is signaled have been proposed.)

The relationship between first and second language acquisition and language typology might be regarded in a similar way. The n-dimensional space hypothesized by language typologists, whose psychological correspondence is verified, can become a tool similar to the positional specification of the developmental biologist concerned with limb growth. It defines the problem, and the problem for the language acquisition researcher then becomes to observe and explain the role that this n-dimensional space might play in the different conditions under which language is learned. While we are still uncertain as to the nature of this n-dimensional space, I submit that it is not too early to begin speculating and formulating our research questions with respect to its manifestations under different psychological contexts.

* Preparation of the paper was supported by the Biomedical Research Support Grant 5-S07-RR07015 from the National Institutes of Health to Yale University. The manuscript for publication was completed while the author was a Fellow at the Center for Advanced Study in the Behavioral Sciences, Stanford, CA 94305.

REFERENCES

Cattell, R. 1965. *The Scientific Analysis of Personality*. Chicago: Aldine.

Chomsky, N. 1965. *Aspects of the Theory of Syntax*. Cambridge, Mass.: M.I.T. Press.

Comrie, B. 1981. *Language Universals and Linguistic Typology*. Chicago: University of Chicago Press.

Dodd, D., and R. White. 1980. *Cognition*. Boston: Allyn and Bacon.

Downing, B. 1978. Some universals of relative clause structure. In J.H. Greenberg (ed.), *Universals of Human Language, Volume 4, Syntax*. Stanford, Calif.: Stanford University Press.

Fienberg, S. 1980. *The Analysis of Cross-Classified Categorical Data*. Cambridge, Mass.: M.I.T. Press.

Givón, T. 1980. *On Understanding Grammar*. New York: Academic Press.

Gould, S.J. 1981. *The Mismeasure of Man*. New York: Norton.

Greenberg, J.H. 1963. Some universals of grammar with particular reference to the order of meaningful elements. In J.H. Greenberg (ed.), *Universals of Language*. Cambridge, Mass.: M.I.T. Press.

Greenberg, J.H. 1978. *Typology and cross-linguistic generalizations. In J.H. Greenberg (ed.), Universals of Human Language, Volume 1, Method and Theory*. Stanford, Calif.: Stanford University Press.

Kleinmann, H. 1976. Avoidance behavior in adult second language acquisition. Unpublished doctoral dissertation, University of Pittsburgh.

Kuno, S. 1974. The position of relative clauses and conjunction. *Linguistic Inquiry 5*:117-136.

Lehmann, W. 1973. A structural principle of language and its implications. *Language 49*:47-66.

Li, C. and S. Thompson. 1976. Subject and topic: a new typology of language. In C. Li (ed.), *Subject and Topic*. New York: Academic Press.

Rutherford, W. 1983. Language typology and language transfer. In S. Gass and L. Selinker (eds.), *Language Transfer in Language Learning*. Rowley, Mass.: Newbury House Publishers.

Schachter, J. 1974. An error in error analysis. *Language Learning 24*:205-214.

Steele, S. 1978. Word order variation: a typological study. In J.H. Greenberg (ed.), *Universals of Human Language, Volume 4, Syntax*. Stanford, Calif.: Stanford University Press.

Tickle, C. 1981. Limb regeneration. *American Scientist 69*:634-646.

COMMENTS ON THE PAPER BY HAKUTA

EVELYN HATCH

University of California, Los Angeles

Hakuta has presented two major points in this paper, both of which I will contest. His first point is that since the facts of language can be represented as distributed in an n-dimensional space, factor analysis is a useful way of *discovering* the dimensions which define or limit that space. Hakuta's second point is that language learners must also discover the dimensions of language along some lines and that therefore data on language acquisition could serve as a testing ground for the psychological reality of whatever dimensions factor analysis revealed. In this reply, I will argue that factor analysis does not work as a discovery procedure for language dimensions nor is it a helpful metaphor for language acquisition. While factor analysis could be useful as a validation procedure, other statistical procedures can more successfully link research on language universals and language acquisition.

Hakuta has pointed out that when factor analysis is used as a discovery procedure, a large number of facts (variables) are fed into the analysis kettle. The computer is then instructed to sift through all the correlations to find — to discover — those constructs around which groups of facts cluster. Factor analysis can reduce large numbers of variables to a few underlying factors. When the computer printout is received, the researcher must look at the variables which make up each factor cluster and, after considering how much each variable contributes to that factor cluster, label the factor. That's where the artistry comes in.

We very seldom throw all the facts we know about something into an analysis pot, unless we are running a fishing expedition (more affectionately called 'garbage can analysis'). You can imagine what might happen if we threw *all* the facts the learner or linguist needs to discover about a language into such an analysis. Instead, facts are selected by the researcher on some theoretical basis. As in Hakuta's example, these might be a set of facts which have been discussed in papers on language typology. The variables can be subjected to factor analysis to see if, indeed, typologies have construct validity. Factor analysis might then serve as a useful validation procedure — not a *discovery* procedure but a *validation* procedure for the claims made in early discussions of language typology.

Let's assume for the moment that the analysis in Hakuta's hypothetical example is run. Factor A turns out to be an underlying SVO dimension. According to the example, the Factor A score for any language would depend primarily on three facts — VO order, right branching, and prepositions (and, to a lesser extent, subject-verb agreement). Languages with high Factor A scores would be SVO languages; those with low Factor A scores would be SOV.

Dummy subject, subject-verb agreement, and passivization weight Factor B, the subject-topic dimension. High Factor B scores would be earned by languages with these three descriptors; low Factor B scores would indicate topic-prominent languages. This analysis gives the researcher statistical evidence for the validity of proposed typologies. In this example analysis, English would receive high Factor A and Factor B scores.

This review shows that, as described above, factor analysis can capture the rough outlines of the work that linguists have accomplished in language typology and universals research. I am not certain why Hakuta has chosen to represent language facts as dichotomous (+/− or 0 vs 1) for the example analysis. Most languages are not strictly plus or minus passive, or plus or minus right branching. Rather, some languages allow for more passive formation in more places than do others, have agreement for more persons than do others, allow right branching in more places than others, and so forth. It's seldom an all or nothing fact (as learners soon discover). Linguists, too, have expanded their statements about language universals and language typologies to cover 'more or less' scales rather than plus or minus dichotomies. Entering scaled data in the analysis might allow us to use factor analysis to refine some language typology claims in useful ways. Certainly, it would give more accurate factor scores for languages entered in the analysis.

Since the facts of language are not just present or absent, linguists have proposed sets of hierarchies for various facts of language — 'if X, then Y' types of statements. As we can see from the papers at this conference, hierarchies have been expanded in many cases to 'if Z, then Y, then X, then W, then V, and maybe even U'. Factor analysis is not a model that fits *these* kinds of proposals or one that would allow us to test claims with learner data. Implicational scaling is probably the model that comes to mind first as a possible alternative. It should be quite simple to mathematically validate hierarchies proposed by Comrie, Keenan, and others. The hierarchies can also be tested against learner data with the same procedure.

However, most of us would like to be able to make *causal* claims rather than just say that we can scale variables. Implicational scaling can only tell us whether there is a scale in the data that shows that fact A is more often present in languages than fact B, and that A and B are more often present in languages than fact C, and so forth. It doesn't allow us to say that a language (or learner) has to have A before it can get to B, or that we must have A and B before C. Much of the work in language universals is moving in the direction of such hypotheses. Implicational scaling can't be used to test claims such as those made by Bickerton for language change or language acquisition. For those kinds of hypotheses, a causal model is required. Path analysis is one such model. It allows one to say that a language (or learner) can't get to B without first going through A, or to C without A and B (or more complex interlinked pathways). Perhaps Path Analysis would be the best kind of model for the kinds of hypotheses and claims presented in recent years and here at this conference on language universals. (My own preference, however, would be the use of multidimensional scaling and/or computer graphics as a way of seeing how the facts of languages are distributed in space rather than any of the linear models.)

Now let's turn to a few objections that I want to raise regarding factor analysis as a link between the study of language universals and language typology and the study of second language acquisition. To do this, consider again Hakuta's hypothetical example. Assume that the learner in Table 4 is attempting to learn English (language X), a language with a high Factor A score. The learner's first language may be one with a similar Factor A score (language Y) or a very different Factor A score (language Z).

The first question to be considered is whether a learner (unconsciously) seeks out dimensions which do not occur in the first language — that is, if there are zeros or minuses for all the variables which weight heavily on that dimension. (Those which contribute little to the dimension probably show up in other factor dimensions and may not be especially useful in defining Factor A.) This would be the case of a learner from language Z in Table 4 if we assume that variables 1, 2, and 3 are heavily weighted in Factor A and that 4 and 5 (and control variable 6) contribute little to the Factor. What would lead the learner to search for this dimension? For example, how long does it take the English learner of Chinese to realize (unconsciously) that one is a possible dimension in the phonology of language? All dimensions will not be equally transparent and, of course, they won't all be important in the learning task.

When a dimension does exist in both languages, is it the ideal form of the dimension which shapes the predictions the learner will make? That is, the learner should, on discovering that English (language X) has a strong Factor A score for VO typology, be able to predict left branching, and the use of prepositions. He should also be able to predict possible subject-verb agreement. The speaker of language Y learning English should easily acquire variable 3 if this were the case. (We could also predict language change in that direction for Language Y.)

The problem with Table 4 is that for some reason the relative importance of the variables to the ideal Factor has been lost. It doesn't show that the learner's predictions should become weaker and weaker as variables contribute less and less to the dimension. The learner should not make equal predictions about the presence or absence of any variable in the dimension. Rather, as Hakuta says, the predictions should be based on the weighting of the variable in the Factor dimension.

However, the basic problem is that no matter how we play with the variables that make up the dimension — changing plus or minus to weights or whatever — we have moved away from what factor analysis does. Factor analysis reduces large numbers of variables to a limited number of underlying factors. When we move away from the factor back to the variables that contribute to that factor, the model hasn't helped us gain much ground. True, we consider the variables as part of a dimension but it is still the variables that are the focus of our attention (not the dimension).

Since we want to work with variables and their place in some dimension (rather than the dimension), then some other statistical model would seem more appropriate. The work that has been done linking universals and second language acquisition has used other statistical procedures. Consider a few examples testing phonological universals against second language data.

Hakuta claims that second language studies do *not* consider possible explanations for the data in investigating the L1=L2 hypothesis. This is far from the case, since *developmental* claims (particularly in phonology) have long been associated with language universals. Very simple procedures were used by Mulford and Hecht to analyze the phonology of an Icelandic child learning English. Comparing predictions of L1 transfer and developmental factors (a combination of universals of phonology and naturalness rules), they were able to show where L1 transfer or developmental factors would predict errors and where each would predict the substitutions used. Amastae and Eckmann both considered the weight of universals in phonology in their work with second language learners. Amastae, investigating naturalness theory (partially based on universals), used implicational scaling to test his predictions. Eckmann developed his markedness differential hypothesis from comparisons of predictions from natural phonology and first language transfer or interference. The procedures used in these studies included implicational scaling. It proved a useful method for checking the psychological reality of universals with second language data. Multidimensional scaling has also been effectively used as a statistical procedure to test the dimensions along which meanings are distributed (cf. Kellerman 1978). These studies and others like them show that other procedures can be used effectively to discover dimensions and to test the psychological reality of language universal claims.

As Hakuta has pointed out and as the above studies exemplify, second language data offer linguists a valuable testing ground for their proposals regarding language universals and language typology. No one claims that one statistical procedure will serve best to test these hypotheses. That must be determined by the hypotheses and the questions the researcher has in mind. However, as a model for a procedure to group languages into language typologies, I believe factor analysis leaves much to be desired. As a metaphor for second language acquisition, factor analysis raises many interesting questions. These questions, however, can be better investigated using other procedures.

REFERENCES

Amastae, J. 1978. The acquisition of English vowels. *Papers in Linguistics 11*:423-458.

Amastae, J. 1981. On markedness and sociolinguistic variation. In E.L. Blansitt and R.V. Teschner (eds.), *A Festschrift for Jacob Ornstein*. Rowley, Mass.: Newbury House Publishers.

Eckman, F. 1977. Markedness and the contrastive analysis hypothesis. *Language Learning 27*:315-330.

Kellerman, E. 1978. Giving learners a break: Native language intuition as a source of predictions about transferability. *Working Papers in Bilingualism 15*:59-92.

Mulford, R., and B. Hecht. 1980. Learning to speak without an accent: acquisition of a second language phonology. *PRCLD 18*, Stanford University.

REPLY TO HATCH'S COMMENTS

KENJI HAKUTA
Yale University

Statistical procedures are often good metaphors for thinking about complex problems, but they should not be taken literally. I chose the particular metaphor used in this paper for two reasons. First, it emphasizes the idea that linguistic variables can be related to each other. To me, at least, clusterings of variables are far more interesting as psycholinguistic phenomena than are isolated variables. And second, I wanted to emphasize the importance of explaining these clusterings, for the existence of clustering itself is only a descriptive statement. Any statistical procedure would have served as my metaphor, but I chose factor analysis. Regardless of what people might think about factor analysis, it is the most familiar statistical procedure, at least for psychologists. In addition, although I found this out after the paper was written, Joseph Greenberg (personal communication) tells me that it was his initial metaphor in thinking about language universals.

Hatch's criticism of the paper is primarily leveled at a literal interpretation of my metaphor. If I did imply in my paper that factor analysis is the best available *discovery procedure* for language typological dimensions, Hatch is correct in pointing out its shortcomings. But it should be apparent that it is not the specific procedure that is important. (If one were to use a statistical technique as an exploratory procedure, I would agree with Hatch that multidimensional scaling might be better suited, although it is curious that she suggests path analysis as an alternative, because it is from the same family of procedures as factor analysis). Rather, what is important is the realization that between linguistic structure and psychological structure there must be a mediator, and at this stage of the game we need a useful metaphor as a midwife. The usefulness of a metaphor can be judged on a variety of criteria. The one I subscribe to is the extent to which a particular metaphor allows understanding across disciplines. Hatch's seems to be primarily based on measurement criteria and the particular assumptions underlying interpretation of the statistical procedure. Although I do not fully advocate sophistry, I think that on some occasions, debating the usefulness of metaphors is itself a valuable tool for real progress.

REPERTOIRE UNIVERSALS, MARKEDNESS, AND SECOND LANGUAGE ACQUISITION*

CHARLES A. FERGUSON
Stanford University

The acquisition of a second language must be constrained in important ways by the very nature of human language. This is an obviously true statement, almost a tautology, and it loses only a little of its obviousness if rephrased as 'language universals help to explain second language acquisition'. The purpose of this paper is to spell out selected aspects of the obviousness of the second wording, utilizing two concepts, 'repertoire universals' and 'markedness', and providing three examples, one each in phonology, syntax, and discourse. Other concepts could be selected and other kinds of examples chosen, but these may suffice to reassure us of the obviousness when we are confronted with the difficulties of producing convincing research findings in such a promising field.

1. *Concepts*
    1.1. *Repertoire universals.*
    The term 'universal' has come to be used — fortunately or unfortunately — to refer to what might better be called 'cross-linguistic generalizations' (Greenberg 1978). Starting from the idea that cross-linguistic research may reveal important similarities among languages, Greenberg and other linguists have produced a large number of generalizations of various types such as absolute universals, implicational universals, universal tendencies; synchronic vs. diachronic universals; universals of existence, universals of process. The particular type to be discussed here is one of the simplest: generalizations based on the presence or absence of comparable elements or units across numbers of languages.
    Languages differ greatly in the size and composition of their repertoires of structural units at many levels, and the kinds of cross-linguistic generaliza-

tions that can be made are correspondingly numerous. If a language has lexical tone it is much more likely to have a two-level system than one of three or more levels (Maddieson 1978). All languages have at least one construction which changes declarative sentences into interrogatives (Ultan 1978). If a language has an established 'talking to animals' register it also has an established 'baby talk' register (Levin and Hunter 1983).

Repertoire universals have at least two possible uses for research in second language acquisition. One is to set a universal framework within which behaviors of language acquisition can be charted or predicted (whether L1, L2, or Ln); the other is to set a contrastive paradigm to chart or predict behaviors in the acquisition of a particular L2 (or L2 of certain properties) by speakers of a particular L1 (or L1 of certain properties). Using our sample universals we might predict that all learners of a language with lexical tone, other things being equal, will acquire a two-level distinction more rapidly than an n-level one (n > 2) and will make errors of the two-level sort when acquiring a more complex system. Similarly one might predict that all L2 learners will expect to find and will acquire some form of interrogative construction, in contrast with L2 learners faced with a language that has pervasive, overt marking of definiteness, a reported-observed distinction, or inflectional marking of politeness, which are not as universal as interrogative constructions. Speakers of a language such as Samoan or Kaluli, in which a baby talk register is relatively undeveloped, will presumably find it easier to acquire a baby talk register than an animal talk register in an L2. These are only loose indications of the relevance of repertoire universals in L2 acquisition; somewhat tighter indications will appear under the three main examples below.

1.2. *Markedness*.

It is generally assumed that the modern notion of markedness in linguistics began with the Prague School structuralist framework for phonology, in which one term of a privative opposition was held to have a phonetic characteristic (*Merkmal*) that the other one lacked (Trubetzkoy 1968). The conceptual framework included notions of frequency and neutralization, the unmarked term being typically more frequent in occurrence than its marked counterpart and more likely to appear in positions where the opposition is suspended or 'neutralized.' The notion of markedness was then extended to components of language other than phonology (cf. Greenberg 1966) and elaborated to allow for degrees of markedness in a series and different markedness states of the same opposition in different positions (cf. Waugh 1979). Jakobson (1941/1968) applied the notion of markedness explicitly to L1 acquisition, claiming that unmarked values occur more widely in the world's languages and are acquired earlier by children than the marked values (cf. also Jakobson and Halle 1956). Generative phonology adopted this framework, with some modifications, as a way of making its formalism agree with 'naturalness' in language (Chomsky and Halle 1968). The use of markedness in Chomsky and Halle has not found its way into many phonological descriptions and has not developed into a precise theory, but a related, vaguer concept of markedness has become common.

The terms 'less marked' and 'unmarked' are now commonly used to mean 'to be expected', 'normal', 'natural' in human languages, without the strict necessity to establish the 'mark' which the terms suggest. Although many instance of markedness in this sense are binary oppositions showing presence/absence of a phonetic or semantic feature, many more instances are series showing a scale of naturalness of some kind. In the sort of generalizations examined here, repertoire universals, the commonest form of markedness is probably an implicational series of the type:

(1) $A \supset B \supset C \supset D \supset E$

in which all languages are thought to have E in the repertoire, very few have A, and the others are in between, any point in the series implying the presence of the element(s) to the right of it. At some positions on such a scale there may be alternative possibilities or even branching chains. It is important to understand that no single causal explanation is proposed for the phenomenon of markedness. Perceptual, articulatory, cognitive, and other factors may be operative singly or in combination to result in the implicational series. From this perspective markedness is viewed as probabilistic, depending on the interaction of the factors involved. The value of the concept lies in the strong tendencies toward agreement among the various attributes of less or greater markedness (frequency, overtness, complexity, early acquisition, neutralization, etc.; cf. Brown and Witkowski 1980), and consequent possibilities of prediction. In the field of syntax a new interpretation of markedness has been proposed in relation to the notions of 'core grammar' and the 'fixing of parameters' (Chomsky 1981 and elsewhere); this has not been worked out in detail but lies in the same general realm of naturalness. Use of the concept of markedness in L2 research is relatively recent, but this work already has an excellent review (Rutherford 1982).

1.3.   *Second language acquisition.*
The concept of second language acquisition seems so clear and the field

of second language acquisition is thriving so well that a reminder is needed of how problematic the concept is and what a vast and difficult terrain L2 researchers have chosen to work in.

First, it is not clear when two language varieties constitute two different languages or two different dialects or registers of the same language. To the extent that this distinction is difficult or impossible to define, the difference between L1 and L2 acquisition vanishes, although a model of acquisition must be assumed that is complex enough to account for the acquisition of variation and the conditions for its occurrence.

Second, L2 acquisition may take place under an incredible array of different circumstances and outcomes; for example, at various ages, with and without formal instruction, in literate and non-literate communities, with varying social functions of the respective languages, and varying 'valorization' (Hamers and Blanc 1983) of the languages. Researchers have no assurance that the rates or paths of acquisition will be the same under these various conditions and indeed have much evidence to the contrary.

In spite of severe problems of definition and variability of circumstances, however, it seems likely that there is enough in common in L2 acquisition that cross-language generalizations of naturalness of repertoire based on other language phenomena may profitably be explored in similar ways across very different instances. With so many factors to consider and the relatively small populations typically available for L2 studies, researchers will often have to be contented with slight bits of evidence and tentative construction of small pieces of theory to match with other kinds of evidence and other language phenomena. Also, from the perspective adopted here, the relation between markedness and L2 acquisition phenomena is not to be interpreted as causal. Rather, any L2 evidence that is found constitutes part of the notion of markedness itself: the researcher is comparing one aspect of linguistic expectedness with another. Every finding, whether positive or negative, contributes, however, to greater understanding of L2 acquisition and ultimately to a comprehensive model of acquisition.

2. *Examples*.

2.1. *Stops*.

As a result of recent cross-language comparisons, a large number of generalizations can be made about the possible phonemic repertoires of human languages, going much beyond the generalizations of Chomsky and Halle 1968, Hockett 1955, and Trubetzkoy 1968 (cf. Greenberg et al. 1978

Vol. 2 and *UCLA Working Papers in Phonetics*), and most of these generalizations can be viewed in terms of markedness hierarchies. Here I will use as an example a stop hierarchy proposed by Gamkrelidze (1975, 1978), based in part on Melikishvili's dissertation (1972); see also Sherman 1976. I have discussed the hierarchy in connection with first language acquisition (Ferguson 1975, 1977), but to my knowledge it has not been discussed at any length in relation to second language acquisition. The hierarchy in question is the degree of naturalness of markedness of the six stops /p t k b d g/, i.e. voiceless and voiced stops at labial, dental/alveolar, and velar places of articulation. It may be stated in at least three ways. One is in terms of an implicational scale of least-to most-likely to be present in the repertoire of a human language:

(2) $g \supset p \supset d \supset b \supset k \supset t$.

If a language has obstruents at the three places of articulation and a voice distinction in the stops, then it is almost certain to have a /t/ (no known exception), and the most likely gap in the set is /g/, with the others strung along between, as listed.

The hierarchy can also be stated in terms of the place of articulation at which the voice distinction is most likely to be present in the repertoire: the /t d/ set is the most natural or 'umarked' contrasting pair (in the labial set /p/ may be missing; in the velar set /g/). This implication may be represented informally:

(3) $\begin{Bmatrix} p{:}b \\ \\ k{:}g \end{Bmatrix} \supset t{:}d$.

The hierarchy may also be stated in terms of occurrence of distinctive features: [+voice] is most likely to occur with [+labial] and least likely to occur with [+velar]; or conversely [−voice] is most likely with [+velar], least likely with [+labial]:

(4a) $g \supset d \supset b$, and
(4b) $p \supset t \supset k$.

Gamkrelidze uses the diagram:

(4c) $\uparrow\begin{matrix} b & p \\ d & t \\ g & k \end{matrix}\downarrow$

These formulations ignore differences of markedness depending on position in the word, nature of clusters, and a host of other differences that can be treated in the same framework. Also, they do not include the markedness relations of these stops with corresponding non-sibilant fricatives, emphasized in Gamkrelidze's formulations. Yet even in this very limited form, the hierarchy has strong implications for first language acquisition. It makes such predictions as the following:

a. Children will tend to acquire /p/ and /g/ later than the other stops.
b. Children will tend to acquire the voice contrast first in the dental/alveolar stops.

In spite of the complications of input characteristics, simplifying processes, different phonetic specifications for the voice contrast in different languages, and the small number of case studies providing detailed, reliable longitudinal data, there is rich evidence from child phonology for the validity of the hierarchy and its predictions. One kind of evidence is the phonemic repertoire of a child at one point in his development. A typical example is Jacob, studied by Menn (1976), who at one point had perceptual mastery of all six stops in initial position (i.e. he could regularly distinguish p- from b-, etc.) but in his productive repertoire had only /b t d k/. For other kinds of evidence cf. Ferguson (1975, 1977).

A phonological universal of repertoire of demonstrated validity in L1 acquisition is likely to be valid in L2 acquisition; i.e. evidence for the hierarchy should also be findable in the behavior of L2 learners. In some respects the evidence may even be clearer, since certain processes attested for L1 acquisition in early childhood will not be applicable — processes such as labial preference, consonant harmony, and fronting (the preference for front consonants near the beginning of the word and báck consonants toward the end). Thus it should be possible to find L2 evidence for the late or troubled acquisition of /p/ and /g/ and the early or easy acquisition of the voicing contrast in /t d/. More specific predictions can be made and tested. Examples:

c. L2 learners will tend to acquire the full phonetic details of pronouncing /p/ and /g/ later than, or with more difficulties than, the pronunciation of /b t d k/.
d. L2 learners who are speakers of an L1 without a voicing opposition in the stops will tend to acquire the t-d before, or more easily than, the p-b, k-g contrasts in L2.
e. L2 learners who are speakers of an L1 with a voicing opposition and are learning an L2 with final devoicing neutralization will tend to

master the devoicing first or most easily in velars, last or with most difficulty in labials.

Many other such predictions could be made. Unfortunately for the researcher, the evidence is likely to be convincing only if based on very large numbers of L2 learners. The observations required to obtain the relevant data from such subjects may be relatively straightforward, but the differences in timing, frequency, incidence of errors, etc. that are critical may be very slight, and the stop hierarchy can readily be overlaid or outweighed by other factors. In the case of some predictions (e.g. (d)) it may be very difficult to locate appropriate subjects (few languages lack a voice contrast of some kind in stops). The effort involved in a research project designed to test the validity of this hierarchy in L2 acquisition would, however, certainly be worth the investment if it resulted in decisive findings.

2.2. *Negation.*

Cross-linguistic syntactic generalizations that can be viewed in terms of naturalness are accumulating (cf. Greenberg et al. 1978 Vol. 3) and some of these, notably the noun phrase accessibility hierarchy in relativization (Keenan and Comrie 1977, Comrie 1981 Ch. 7), have been used as a starting point for research in L2 acquisition (e.g. Gass 1979). Here I will use as an example the repertoire universals of negation presented by Dahl (1979). The phenomena of clause negation have been a favorite topic of linguistic and psycholinguistic research in recent years, and a substantial literature on various aspects of negation in L1 acquisition exists. The literature on L2 acquisition is less extensive (but cf. Hyltenstam 1978, Schumann 1979, Wode 1981).

Dahl examined the principal means of effecting sentence negation in about 240 languages, concentrating on simple indicative sentences with a verbal predicate. He found two common mechanisms — an inflectional affix on the verb and an uninflected negative particle (108 and 99 languages respectively); another mechanism was less common: negative auxiliary, i.e. a negative word inflected in categories typical of verbs (49 languages). Other means (e.g. the English 'dummy auxiliary' construction) are rare. This hierarchy may be represented as follows:

(5) $\left\{\begin{array}{l}\text{dummy auxiliary}\\\text{main predicate}\\\text{etc.}\end{array}\right\} \supset \text{auxiliary} \supset \left\{\begin{array}{l}\text{affix}\\\text{particle}\end{array}\right\}$

This representation omits subtypes in that, for example, 'affix' includes tone change and 'particle' includes double particles such as French *ne...pas*. Also, it takes no account of two or more means being used in the same language in different tenses, kinds of clauses, registers, etc. It is, however, a finding which proposes a markedness hierarchy worth investigating in L1 and L2 acquisition. Unlike the implicational scale of (1) above, (4) does not refer to co-occurrence within the same language but to the likelihood of occurrence as the principal means of clause negation in any language selected at random.

2.3. *Respect register.*

Repertoire universals and markedness scales are not often sought in discourse analysis, but it is reasonable to assume that these characteristics of human language can be found in such varied aspects of discourse as the exchange of greetings, types of narration, or the expression of politeness. Cross-linguistic study of forms of discourse ('genres') and situational variation ('registers') should be especially promising, and the patterns discovered would presumably have direct relevance to L2 acquisition and foreign language teaching. The example I will use here is the phenomenon variously referred to as respect grading, the expression of social distance, or signals of power and solidarity.

All speech communities may be assumed to have linguistic means of signaling status and intimacy relations between speaker and addressee, but the means vary (Hudson 1980:122-128). On the basis of published studies it seems likely that the following markedness hierarchy will hold up:

(6)   special   special   special   special
       language   ⊃   register   ⊃   morphology   ⊃   names.

This implicational statement represents the claim that all speech communities use special forms of names, kin terms, and titles that express respect grading (addressee higher or lower status than speaker, more or less social distance, etc.) and that only a minority of the world's languages shift to a wholly different language for this purpose. The two intermediate types are more interesting. Register variation expressing social distance is universal if the analyst is willing to count such details as variation in names, but the term 'special register' is intended to refer to pervasive shifts in language form such as the 'brother-in-law talk' of Australian languages (Haviland 1979) or the six 'style levels' of speech in Javanese (Geertz 1960).

'Special morphology' refers to special forms of personal pronouns or (more marked) verbs. The literature on respect grading in pronouns is now very extensive, most of it deriving from Brown and Gilman (1960), and it is possible to find significant universals within this limited area. For example, all languages seem to have a pronoun or pronoun-like expression as the un-marked designation of addressee; many languages in addition use a second person plural pronoun to refer to a single addressee to express greater respect or social distance; and a much smaller number of languages use a third person pronoun for this purpose. B.F. Head includes this implicational universal among the many generalizations in his study examining pronominal respect grading in about 100 languages (Head 1978:191); it could be represented as

(7)   3rd pl ⊃ 3rd sg ⊃ 2nd pl ⊃ 2nd sg.

These two sketchy universals (6) and (7), even in this form, have implications for L2 acquisition. Societies differ greatly on what situations call for respect or social distance — and this kind of cultural difference is a recognized problem in L2 acquisition — but it is clear that some linguistic means of signaling respect are more natural, less marked than others, and this has not been the focus of much L2 research.

From these universals of repertoire one could hazard predictions such as: (other things being equal) L2 learners will acquire naming patterns as indices of respect more easily than special pronouns or verb forms; or L2 learners will acquire a second plural pronoun more easily than a third singular as a polite pronoun for second singular. Unfortunately for the researcher, other things are usually quite *un*equal, and psycholinguistic experiments correspondingly difficult. Also, the causal factors are even less clear here than in the phonological and syntactic examples given.

3.   *Comment*

As noted at the beginning of the paper, the intent here is to give reassurance of the obviousness of the relation between universals and L2 acquisition in spite of problems of research design and ambiguity of some experimental findings. The points made are essentially a set of assumptions that I hope I share with other researchers. They can be presented in an ordered list:

1. Of the many possible sources of hypotheses or research topics in the area of L2 acquisition, one that merits exploration is that of cross-linguistic generalizations of language structure ('language universals').
2. Of the many possible language universals, one type that merits exploration is that of simple presence vs. absence of particular structural elements ('repertoire universals').
3. 'Widespread presence' among many languages is one of a family of similar phenomena, including frequency of occurrence in texts, appearance in neu-

tralization, and ease of L1 acquisition, which characterize 'naturalness' in human language (lack of 'markedness').

4. Since markedness is not a unified concept, its ultimate causes are complex; the conditions affecting its operation in L2 acquisition are largely unexplored and experimental investigation is very demanding. 'Crucial experiments' are rare; cumulation of data and analyses is the rule.

5. Investigation of repertoire universals, markedness, and L2 acquisition will result in increased understanding of the nature of human language and the processes of L2 acquisition.

6. Findings from such research can be expected to provide small 'pieces' that can fit into larger theories of markedness and of language acquisition.

NOTE

* I found the Conference on Language Universals and Second Language Acquisition an exciting event. The papers and discussions revealed differences in theoretical perspectives and in preferred research strategies, but they all showed a conviction at some level that the basic characteristics of human language ('universals') are significant in special ways in second language acquisition and that research to explore this significance is desirable and feasible. It would have been difficult to locate willing participants for such a conference even a few years ago, but in 1982 it proved possible to mount a conference that included both theoretical considerations and empirical data. I was grateful to Rutherford and Scarcella as organizers for the opportunity to take part and again grateful to them as editors for the chance to add some thoughts of mine to the volume. Unfortunately I had no occasion to show the paper to others, so I cannot acknowledge assistance; my acceptance of responsibility for errors and other evils is fuller than usual.

REFERENCES

Brown, C.H., and S.R. Witkowski. 1980. Language universals. In D. Levinson et al. (eds.), *Toward Explaining Human Culture*. New Haven, CT: HRAF Press.

Chomsky, N. 1981. *Lectures on Government and Binding*. Dordrecht: Foris.

Chomsky, N. and M. Halle. 1968. *The Sound Pattern of English*. New York: Harper & Row.

Comrie, B. 1981. *Language Universals and Linguistic Typology*. Chicago: University of Chicago Press.

Dahl, O. 1979. Typology of sentence negation. *Linguistics* 17:79-106.

Ferguson, C.A. 1975. Sound patterns in language acquisition. *Georgetown University Round Table on Languages and Linguistics 1975*:1-16.

Ferguson, C.A. 1977. New directions in phonological theory: language acquisition and universals. In R.W. Cole (ed.), *Current Issues in Linguistic Theory*. Bloomington, IN: Indiana University Press.

Gamkrelidze, T.V. 1975. On the correlation of stops and fricatives in a phonological system. *Lingua 35*:231-161.

Gamkrelidze, T.V. 1978. On the correlation of stops and fricatives in a phonological system. In J.H. Greenberg et al. (eds.), *Universals of Human Language*. Vol. 2. Stanford, CA: Stanford University Press.

Gass, S. 1979. Language transfer and universal grammatical relations. *Language Learning 29*:326-344.

Geertz, C. 1960. *The Religion of Java*. Glencoe: Free Press.

Greenberg, J.H. 1966. *Language Universals with Special Reference to Feature Hierarchies*. The Hague: Mouton.

Greenberg, J.H. 1976. Typology and cross-linguistic generalizations. In J.H. Greenberg et al. (eds.), *Universals of Human Language*. Vol. 1. Stanford, CA: Stanford University Press.

Greenberg, J.H., C.A. Ferguson, and E.A. Moravcsik. 1978. *Universals of Human Language*. 4 vols. Stanford, CA: Stanford University Press.

Hamers, J.F. and M. Blanc. 1983. Towards a social-psychological model of bilingual development. *Journal of Language and Social Psychology 1*:29-49.

Haviland, J.B. 1979. Guugu Yimidhirr brother-in-law language. *Language in Society 8*:365-393.

Head, B.F. 1978. Respect degrees in pronominal reference. In J.H. Greenberg et al. (eds.), *Universals of Human Language*. Stanford, CA: Stanford University Press.

Hockett, C.F. 1955. *Manual of Phonology. International Journal of American Linguistics Memoir 11*.

Hudson, R.A. 1980. *Sociolinguistics*. Cambridge: Cambridge University Press.

Hyltenstam, K. 1977. Implicational patterns in interlanguage syntax variation. *Language Learning 27*:383-411.

Jakobson, R. 1968. *Child Language, Aphasia, and Phonological Universals*. Translated by A. Keiler. The Hague: Mouton.

Jakobson, R. and M. Halle. 1956. *Fundamentals of Language*. The Hague: Mouton.

Keenan, E.L. and B. Comrie. 1977. Noun phrase accessibility and universal grammar. *Linguistic Inquiry 8*:63-99.

Levin, H. and W.A. Hunter. 1983. Children's use of a social speech register: age and sex differences. *Journal of Language and Social Psychology 1*:63-72.

Maddieson, I. 1978. Universals of tone. In J.H. Greenberg et al. (eds.), *Universals of Human Language*. Stanford, CA: Stanford University Press.

Melikishvili, I. 1972. *Otnoshenie Markirovannosti v Fonologii*. Aftoreferat dissertatsii, Tbilisi.

Rutherford, W. 1982. Markedness in second language acquisition. *Language Learning 32*:85-108.

Schumann, J.H. 1979. The acquisition of English negation by speakers of Spanish: a review of the literature. In R.W. Andersen (ed.), *The Acquisition and Use of English and Spanish as First and Second Languages*. Washington, DC: TESOL.

Schumann, J.H. 1980. The acquisition of relative clauses by second language learners. In R. Scarcella and S. Krashen (eds.), *Research in Second Language Acquisition*. Rowley, MA: Newbury House.

Sherman, D. 1975. Stop and fricative subsystems: a discussion of paradigmatic gaps and the question of language sampling. *Papers and Reports on Language Universals 17*:4-31.

Trubetzkoy, N.S. 1969. *Principles of Phonology*. Translated by C.A.M. Baltaxe. Berkeley: University of California Press.

Ultan, R. 1978. Some general characteristics of interrogative systems. In J.H. Greenberg et al. (eds.), *Universals of Human Language*. Vol. 4. Stanford, CA: Stanford University Press.

Waugh, L. 1979. Remarks on markedness. In D.A. Dinnsen (ed.), *Current Approaches to Phonological Theory*. Bloomington, In: Indiana University Press.

Wode, H. 1981. *Learning a Second Language. Vol. 1. An Integrated View of Language Acquisition*. Tübingen: Gunter Narr.

INDEX TO REFERENCES

INDEX TO LANGUAGES
(excluding English)

n the TYPOLOGICAL STUDIES IN LANGUAGE (TSL) series the following volumes have been published thus far, and will be published during 1984:

1. HOPPER, Paul (ed.): *TENSE-ASPECT: BETWEEN SEMANTICS & PRAGMATICS.* Amsterdam, 1982.

2. HAIMAN, John & Pam MUNRO (eds.): *PROCEEDINGS OF A SYMPOSIUM ON SWITCH REFERENCE, Winnipeg, May 1981.* Amsterdam, 1983.

3. GIVÓN, T. (ed.): *TOPIC CONTINUITY IN DISCOURSE: A QUANTITATIVE CROSS-LANGUAGE STUDY.* Amsterdam, 1983.

4. CHISHOLM, William, Louis T. MILIC & John GREPPIN (eds.): *INTERROGATIVITY: A COLLOQUIUM ON THE GRAMMAR, TYPOLOGY AND PRAGMATICS OF QUESTIONS IN SEVEN DIVERSE LANGUAGE, Cleveland, Ohio, October 5th 1981 - May 3rd 1982.* Amsterdam, 1984.

5. RUTHERFORD, William E. (ed.): *LANGUAGE UNIVERSALS AND SECOND LANGUAGE ACQUISITION.* Amsterdam, 1984.

6. HAIMAN, John (ed.): *ICONICITY IN SYNTAX. Proceedings of a Symposium on Iconicity in Syntax, Stanford, June 24-6, 1983.* Amsterdam, 1984.

7. CRAIG, Colette (ed.): *NOUN CLASSES AND CATEGORIZATION. Proceedings of a Symposium on Categorization and Noun Classification, Eugene, Ore. October 1983.* Amsterdam, 1984.

8. SLOBIN, Dan I. (ed.): *ASPECTS OF SYNTAX, SEMANTICS, AND DISCOURSE STRUCTURE IN TURKISH* (working title). *Proceedings of a Conference on Turkish Linguistics, held at Berkeley, May 1982.* Amsterdam, 1984.